THE INSTANT
DREAM BOOK

TONY CRISP

The Instant
Dream Book

THE C. W. DANIEL COMPANY LIMITED
SAFFRON WALDEN

First published in Great Britain 1984
by Neville Spearman Publishers
(The C. W. Daniel Company Limited)
1 Church Path, Saffron Walden, Essex, England

This Edition published May 1989

ISBN 85435 125 6

Typeset in 10/12 Bembo by
Anne Buchan (Typesetters)
Surrey

Produced in Great Britain by
Ennisfield Print & Design, London

CONTENTS

Acknowledgments

I am deeply indebted to my first wife, Brenda, who shared the early years of dream investigation with me. She listened to so many of my dreams as I began to understand their language.

Next, a great depth of experience and new insight into the dream process arose during the '70's, because of the support, research and experiment shared with me by Sheilah Johns and Mike Tanner. The quality of their courage in entering new realms of experience with me and knocking through what had been boundary walls of thought and attitude, remain with me. Together we explored the rather shaking experience of allowing the dream process to break through into waking consciousness. This allowed me to observe the unconscious processes directly instead of through the symbols of dreams.

My friend, Prof. Graham Leonard helped me to find the strength to look at and feel at ease with the difficult areas of my own nature. By sharing his own search for health with me, he did me the wonderful service of showing how not to be afraid of the human unconscious, or of unorthodox techniques of approach to it.

I have never found a great resonance with the work of Freud, although we are all indebted to him. But the writings of Franz Mesmer, Carl Jung and Wilhelm Reich have been roots upon which my own experience grew. The approach I take in this book, however, is very much indebted to Richard Corriere, and J. Hart who wrote *The Dream Makers*. It showed a much more immediate approach to dreams than I had met with before. Patricia Garfield's work, *Creative Dreaming*, added to this concept also.

Personal friends who have worked with me on my own and their dreams, such as Lester and Jacqueline Shenton, Celia and Peter Hawe, Sarah Beanland, Brenda Clement, Kevin Kearney, Andy Hill, Robert Fielder, Anand Prabhat and Anna Ince, gave me the chance to learn from mistakes as well as success. In most cases, I have given fictious names where dreams have been used.

Gerald Rudge, editor of 'Femail' of *The Daily Mail*, opened the door to the nation's dreams for myself and Hyone. The stimulus provided by our column in the *Mail*, and now in *She*, has pressed us to define clearer and more immediate ways of understanding dreams. Certainly, without the column this book would not have been possible.

Although Hyone's name does not appear on the title page with mine, she has spent many days reading the manuscript, offering ideas and criticisms, and has helped carve the book out of unwieldy original ideas and the discarded first attempt.

Herbert Reed, editor of *Sundance*, the Community Dream Journal, sent me a mass of material which has helped to add depth to the book.

Thanks also to Bernard S. Siegal, M.D., and Barbara H. Siegal, H.S., for allowing me to quote from their writings on the connection between dreams and physical illness. Also to Ann Wiseman for allowing me to quote her article about children's dreams.

Without the help of M.M. the opportunity to deepen research and test ideas would have been more difficult to find. At times when I have been very uncertain about the value of my research, David Boadella, editor of *Energy And Character* and director of the Centre for Bio Synthesis, has always been a friend who helped me find enthusiasm again; and the opportunity to share my work with other people.

Lastly, again and again I give thanks to those of you who have sent us your dreams through *The Daily Mail* and *She*. Some of them appear in these pages. But with every new batch of dreams I feel humbled and grateful for your trust in sharing your inner life with us. It is because of this wide sharing and sampling that many principles explained in this book have become clear.

Chapter One

———————◆———————

Waking our Sleeping Genius

YOU can gain instant useful information and life changes from your dreams. The largely unused and unproductive activity and time of dreaming can become a source of enormous pleasure, creativity, new knowledge and positive personal growth. You can wake up to a world of new experience and possibilities to which you were literally asleep. By giving a few minutes each day to simple techniques, you can transform anxieties into confidence, passivity into productive action and old negative habits into new ways of satisfaction.

It does not matter that you do not presently remember dreams, because the process can be stimulated into awareness. But if you do remember any of your dreams you will realise what an amazing range of activities and experiences they cover. One night you may be running from an evil force and the next making passionate love to your favourite film star. From deep anxiety you may move in an instant to comic farce. In your dreams you can fly, swim under water without holding your breath, or change into a butterfly. But usually this is beyond your ability to influence or direct. Yet now, with techinques defined in recent research groups, you could learn to:

1. Through your dreams find a solution to problems facing you in everyday life.
2. Choose any partner and experience satisfying sexual pleasure with them.
3. In sleep release the enormous depths of insight into people, work problems, research projects, and everyday affairs, which

your unconscious mental processes and memory have in reserve.

4. Define your own philosophy of life out of your mass of experience in order to find a more positive and direct approach to life and relationships.
5. Face and transform the images of fear you usually run away from in your dreams, thus finding a new courage and self confidence in waking life.
6. Use techniques while awake, which allow faculties usually touched only in sleep, to emerge into waking use.

To begin this transformation of the unused area of your sleep into a pleasure ground, a place of love, a university, with a hospital for healing ills of mind and body, will not take hours of analysing dreams, or years of introversion and self searching. The pioneers of these techniques may have trod those paths of soul searching and heroic fear facing, to discover and open up the possibilities of the inner, sleeping mind. But from their findings have arisen ways of discovering change along easier routes. Like any new tract of unexplored country, the early travellers hack their way through difficulties. Later, roads are built. So your own changes could begin with as simple a start as recognising and giving a name to the overall action in your dream. In tests on many individuals, that small activity alone produced changes in the dream and waking life of the person participating. The only other qualifications needed are a motivation to explore and discover your own possibilities, and reasonable perseverance.

The following dreams illustrate some of these claims.

John and Liz are married with three young children. John has been made redundant from his work as a photographer. They wish to sell their house to move and start a small guest house in a seaside village. They have seen the house they want. It is almost pound for pound what they can ask for theirs. Can they sell without an agent? They advertise in a national newspaper and receive a few replies, mostly from estate agents offering to sell the house for them. But after paying an agent's commision they would not have enough money. The other replies do not continue interest. Then Liz dreams that she put a large 'House for Sale' sign in the front window, and one of the first people to pass by decides to purchase the house.

Liz is sceptical about her own dream, but John put up the notice.

That day a newly-wed young woman shows interest in the house, having seen the sign. She and her husband subsequently purchased the house. Certainly a useful dream. A very straightforward one, too, but it did need listening to and its information respected.

It is obvious here that the process of dreaming can respond to the real needs and problems of our everyday life. John and Liz were in the habit of noting their dreams as a possible source of creative ideas and insight, and this itself is a factor stimulating helpful response. This is not a dream symbolising something; it deals directly with a waking problem, the sale of the house. It is a creative dream and one in which direct action is taken. Later we will look more fully at what those factors mean. The important thing to be stressed here is that Liz experienced this dream not through chance but choice.

In our work as writers and interpreters of dreams, my wife Hyone and I have received dreams from people all over the world. Looking through these we find only very few which are as direct or helpful as Liz's dream. At the time of the house sale, Liz had two other dreams equally as direct and helpful. So the question arises what is Liz doing which is different from most other people? The obvious differences are that, first they are a couple who both have an interest in dreams, and they create a sympathetic environment which induces interest and acceptance of dreams. Second, they both expect helpful responses from their dreams and actively attempt to stimulate and look for it, and third, what seems helpful in their dreams they utilise in their waking life.

This next dream is unusual, but graphically illustrates the amazing way dreams can give direct insight into other peoples lives.

Susan and Bob were used to recording their dreams and considering their meaning. One night Susan dreamt about the baby of two friends. In the dream Susan looks at the baby. She realises it is ill and needs medical help. Then she understands it would depend upon a drug for the rest of its life.

On waking Bob and Susan attempted to understand the dream as representing some activity in Susan's life, but with little success. Then they wondered if it actually applied to their friends new baby, but were again uncertain. Rather than take a chance they decided to write to them.

Their friends, Jo and Bruce, had been worried about their baby because it was fretful and not feeding well. On receiving the letter their fears were crystalised and they immediately visited their doctor. He was concerned enough to hospitalise the baby for further checks. After many tests the baby was seen to be dying. Its body was unable to produce an enyzyme necessary to the digestion of calcium. This was righted by the administration of a drug, which the child would need to take for the rest of its life.[1]

How does our sleeping mind gather such detailed and relevant information? Bob and Susan lived two hundred miles away from Jo and Bruce, and had never seen their baby. But many dreams do reach out in this way to information of which we are not consciously aware.

Susan and Bob, like Liz and John, look to their dreams for information, and expect direct and useful insights. The expectancy which arises from the belief that dreams are as valid a source of information and insight as one's senses or thought, is an important first step. Without the expectancy we will not be bothered even to remember or look through our dreams each morning to check for usable information.

However, it is possible the expectancy is even more important. Experience suggests that our dreaming mind is in some ways like a lethargic genius. It needs some stimulus, something to awaken its enthusiasm to make it stir and stretch itself.

Liz was emotionally, mentally and financially involved in the proposed move of the house. This involvement, plus her habit of expecting a response from her dreams, provided the necessary stimulus to her own sleeping giant. In the case of Susan, she was herself already a mother of three, and Jo was the first of her close friends to have a baby. She, too, was involved in what was happening outwardly, in this case to Jo, and had the habit of looking to her dreams for help. The combination produced vital information of which she certainly had no conscious awareness.

Apart from creative information, dreams can be the area of our being in which we transform fears into strength, or defeatist habits into new confidence and productive tendencies. By approaching our dream life with not only expectancy of creative insight, but also positive life changes, we can lead our sleeping genius into becoming a talented psychotherapist.

Many of our life problems are caused by habits of emotional reaction or habits of expression. At some point in our life, these habits may have been useful, but now prove destructive. As a child, for instance, we may have learnt that if we feel ill we will get attention of even love. As seen in dreams and hypnosis, our unconscious mind can produce any imaginable feeling state, and we may begin to produce unconsciously symptoms of illness to gain our need for love. In adult life to feel ill much of the time is an economical and miserable way of gaining love. A much more satisfying habit could achieve the same end. A dreamer may have a habit of passivity and indecision which is unsatisfying. In facing this in their dreams they also face and change it in their waking life.

Our dream process is a part of the self-regulatory functions within us. Just as perspiring aids the self regulation of body temperature by losing heat. So dreams are a part of the process of keeping psychological equilibrium. Sometimes they do this by attempting to discharge painful or negative material from our memory and feelings. At such a time we have a disturbing dream. If we resist this dream, run from its images into waking, or fear it because we misunderstand it, the healing process cannot complete itself.

The dream following shows how a lifetime fear can be removed by understanding it.

'I had the same dream from early childhood right through to my forties. I always dreamt of the same place, a street I knew in childhood with railings in it. It terrified me and I invariably awoke full of fear and crying.

Then one day in my forties I told my sister about the dream. She told me that when I was five some older boys chased us down that street and were going to hit us. Then she told them our mother was dead and they left us alone. It was a lie but it worked. She said she could still remember the shocked look on my face when she said that.

Since we talked about it I have never had the dream again, and I am now over fifty.'

The dream is quoted to show how the dream process will persist year after year in an attempt to solve the problem, and how simple the solution can sometimes be.

The next dream shows how a solution can be sought, and found in the dream itself. The woman, May, had suffered years of emotional misery and alienation from her family. She says: 'Because of this, when I was down to absolutely rock bottom emotionally, I con-

13

sulted a hypnotherapist who explained that hypnosis was used only as a last resort. I went to her once a week for over a year. I was treated under psychotherapy, and I had to write down my dreams every day. Through this I recognised my areas of problem, and in time my problems lessened. However, with petrol becoming more expensive – I had to travel seventy miles altogether for each visit – I gave up the consultations. All the same, I felt I hadn't really reached the real root of the trouble. I delved into my known past, but not my *unknown* past. Consequently, after about six months I drifted back into my old depression and aggressive dreams and nightmares.

'I always seemed to be searching for the lost years. My real mother died when I was nineteen months old and my sister was one month. In the same week my Dad was called up for the War. Unable to get anyone to look after two young children Dad paid a woman to look after me, while my sister was adopted by an aunt and uncle.

'My father re-married when I was seven, and I have two half-brothers and one half sister. As I grew up none of my family would let me speak about the past, making it a taboo subject. Because of this I used to fall out with them on and off. Then, when my father died five years ago – I am now forty three – I got in such a rage, telling my family I was never one of them, and now that Dad was dead I had no family. The guilt and depression I felt about this was what led me to go to the hypnotherapist.

'This year, in January, forty one years from the day my own mother died, my stepmother died. This sent me into such agonising emotions I had to give up my job, and was near to a nervous breakdown. However, on the nineteenth of March I had this dream.

'My son had a spray which made him very small. He was able to speak to and see various small characters and Walt Disney people. He sprayed me so I could see the characters too. He found a minute friend, a girl of his own age. He was so small – insect size – that when he crossed a road with his friends he got trodden on. I had a terrible feeling of loss. Then my own son laughed and said, "We are all okay. We are too small for anyone to hurt us."

'My son sprayed other members of the family and I began to have the feeling I knew the answer to my years of depression and guilt.

'Then we were walking down a sunny promenade. I saw my father sitting on a bench. I hesitated, feeling I could not go to him. My son told me not to worry. He said, "If you can't love your father

14

I will love you both as son and Father. If you are too silly as grown ups to see it doesn't matter about all the past, I'll make up the love to you." The little girl with him went to my father and said the same thing. Then my father and I both laughed and went to each other, thinking how silly we had been all those years. We both got the feeling of forgiveness and saw how we had wasted all those years because we didn't have the simple love of a child.

'My father had then been sprayed and could see the characters, who all began to dance. On the beach nearby were my stepsister and stepbrother and wife, sun-bathing in the warmth. Instead of my usual *Pit* feeling I felt playful and kicked some sand over them. I had the wonderful feeling of happiness and floating. I told them the story, and said the answer was so simple – forgive each other, love and forget the past and look to the future. I felt it was a miracle, and knew it was the answer to finding peace with my family, living and deceased. And as the dream ended there was a crescendo of moving music, all the Disney characters were there, with pairs of birds in nests all around in trees. They had little comic notices hung outside such as "Goodnight", "God Bless", "Don't Snore."

'Since the dream, six months ago, I have become reconciled with most of my family – though I doubt if they can understand the reasoning behind it. I now have this wonderful feeling of well being, though life still has its difficulties.'

May's dream shows how one does not necessarily have to interpret the symbols to find healing or understanding. The dream itself is clear enough to understand directly. Also the dream actually gives May the direct experience of what it feels like to forgive, to feel the warmth of love, and to look forward instead of back.

She had developed the habit from a year of psychotherapy, of looking within herself for answers, and expecting help from her dreams. So once more this is seen as important, although this is not the only factor involved in finding help and creativity in our dreams. If we are to turn the unused time of our sleep into greater productivity we need to understand just why most people *do not* have problems solving dreams and their Genius remains asleep.

The following dreams are typical of hundreds we have received.

'Over the past five years I have had many traumatic, emotional experiences. I lost a baby, was divorced, lived in a flat with two other girls for four years, which I hated from the moment I moved in. I had

15

a long-standing relationship with a man that was not always satisfactory, and was taking tranquilisers from time to time. During this
period I had the same nightmare regularly, normally when I was
over tired and worried about something.

'After years of saving I was able to buy my own flat, which I
moved into a year ago. My life changed dramatically and I was, and
still am, extremely happy. I have a very good job which I like very
much. The nightmare stopped immediately I moved, and I thought
the only reason I had them was because I had many worries and they
were a way of releasing tension. Unfortunately, during the last
week, I have had the old nightmare twice, and hope you can explain
why I have started them again.

'The nightmare is nearly always the same. I am trapped in a
bricked up room with no way out and I shout for somebody to help
me. Then either a big bird or a creature with long arms tries to catch
me, and I scream. My flat mates used to wake me, since I would
wake the whole house with my screams. They described my screams
as "blood curdling". When I awoke I would be extremely upset,
heart pounding and sometimes crying. Twice I woke up sitting in
the windowsill trying to open the window. As I was three floors up
this was extremely dangerous.

'In the past I could explain the nightmare quite easily; I did feel
trapped in an unhappy situation that I wanted to be rescued from,
but as I am so happy now I wonder why I should start having this
nightmare again.'

We quote this letter at length to show the background to the
nightmares, their frequency, and their apparent disconnection from
an outer difficulty. Many people who have written to us have the
same disturbing dream as often as two or three times a week.

The next dream has far fewer comments with it. The dreamer says
it is a recurring dream, the only one she ever remembers.

'I am in a great barren space. The only thing to be seen is a flight of
stairs, made either of marble or basket work. These have no sides.
They lead right into the air. I, who am normally afraid of stairs and
heights, walk up these without fear. They grow smaller in size, until
reaching the top I am standing on a small platform only just big
enough for my feet, with a sheer drop ahead and on each side. I
decide to turn round and go down, but on turning round I find the
marble stairs have turned into a smooth slope, and the basket ones

are full of holes. In both cases they are swaying about, I cannot get anywhere and I am *terrified*! I wake feeling ill.'

The next is a man's dream, which he said has occurred many times.

'I drive up to an old house on top of a hill in a small white car. I am met at the door by a smartly dressed man in black, who leads me downstairs through a series of doors which are locked after us. We then come to a dimly-lit corridor which stretches into the distance, with doors on one side. The man tells me there is a story behind each door, except the first door, and he opens this door to prove it to me.

'Sometimes the man has narrated the stories behind doors two and three, but on many occasions I have been told the story behind door four. This story concerns a married man, deceiving his wife, who finally kills his male lover. I suddenly realise I am alone at this point and run for the exit, yanking open the doors, and feel such a sense of relief when I reach sunlight. However, I am always left with a terrible fear that one day I will not be able to open the doors to escape.'

The question we need to consider about these dreams is – what can hold a person in the same inner-dream condition year after year, and sometimes for a whole lifetime? If we understand this, it will be clearer what can produce the opposite, i.e. constructive change and pleasure, inwardly and outwardly.

Considering that in a dream we can do almost anything imaginable, such as fly, talk to an angel, meet our dead loved ones, look deeply into the workings of our body, find the solution to a problem, enjoy lovemaking with a degree of sensitivity usually not possible, define new ideas and insights from the process of our life experience – why should we remain in a lifetime of confused and non-productive dreams or constant nightmares?

The answer is very simple. It is habit. Each of us develop patterns of behaviour, conditioned or habitual responses to particular cues or situations. Some of these are obvious, such as our mouth watering when we smell delicious food. Our ability to walk, talk, ride a bicycle, are all habits we have built by repetition. If we had not developed habits we would not be able even to sit or read. Most of our habits are useful, but some are enormously destructive. Our positive and negative habits have usually developed because either the action, such as talking, was rewarding in that we could communicate; or the habit was a means of avoiding distress. Heavy drinking of alcohol is an example of this in helping to avoid anxiety.[2]

Some habits we develop out of our personal experience. A woman who was a child during World War 2 had to stay out of her house during the day because her mother went to work and locked the door. During school holidays she passed the day by frequently going for long walks with other local children in the same situation. As they often walked a long way from home, she usually felt afraid of not being able to find her own way back. To deal with this fear she subdued her own decisions and put her trust in whoever appeared most confident in the group. This became a habit, so that in adult life she still suppressed her own independent decisions and accepted the views of people who spoke confidently.

Dr. Thomas A. Harriss shows how some habits are passed on without reassessment, from parents to child. A woman with a teenage child, as part of her daily life, never put a hat on a table or bed. If her children failed to observe this rule, or if she herself forgot, her negative reaction seemed out of proportion to the act. After living most of her life with this rule, and realising she had learnt it from her mother, she eventually asked, 'Why do you never put a hat on a table or bed?'[3]

Her mother said that when she was herself small, her mother had told her this rule. At the time some neighbourhood children were 'infested', so it was important their hats were not put near the bed or table.

This particular habit had been passed on for three generations. However, there is reason to believe that such patterns of reaction are continued verbally or non-verbally, over long periods of time unless they are re-assessed and changed. National characteristics are frequently in this category, and are largely unconscious. A habit, in fact, is a pattern of psychological or physical behaviour which occurs in some degree unconsciously. When we have learnt to walk, ride a bike or drive a car, our actions are largely unconscious, and it is this fact which enables us to free our conscious mind for other activities; otherwise we would have to re-learn our skill again each day.

So a habit may be acquired ready made from our parents or social environment; we may develop it as a reaction to a situation; or we may consciously learn it as a skill or behaviour. The habit may be to avoid something, such as anxiety, loneliness, infestation; it may be a way of achieving something, such as pleasure, problem solving or reward; or it may be a means of doing something, such as work, walking or driving.

Dreams have a strong relationship with our habits, since the home of both of them is in the unconscious activities of our being. In looking at a dream we may in fact be looking at a pictorialised habit. This is extremely useful because some of our habits are quite unconscious. Perhaps they are obvious to others, but not to ourselves. If we become aware of a troublesome habit through a dream, we can use the awareness to begin a process of change. Likewise, if we become aware of a positive problem-solving pattern, awareness enables us to consciously use and enhance it.

The three recurring dreams quoted are typical of dreams arising from habitual attitudes, reactions, fears and tensions. Anything which recurs with little or no change from an unconscious source is, by definition, a habit.

Mrs. B.G., the woman who developed the habit from childhood of looking to others for certainty, recently told me two dreams. In the first dream she says:

'I am taking part in a horse race. I actually ride the horse and am doing very well. As we get to the winning post I come second. Even in the dream though, I realised I could have been first.'

The second dream is:

'A friend of mine, Sylvia, who in real life is divorced, has in the dream been to an "Over Thirties" club to find a new man. She meets me and has three men with her, and says to me that she has picked the best of the three to be her husband, but I and another friend can choose which of the other two we want for husbands. I look them over and see the two men have no real qualities, but I think I might as well go along with it.'

In both these dreams Mrs. B.G. is taking second place. In doing so she is accepting the fact that she deserves no more than second best in life. The second dream even suggests that if she goes along with this, she is falling into a trap.

When I pointed out that both dreams show her in second place, and asked her if she had a habit of feeling herself as second best she admitted that she did have such a habit. Seeing the habit so clearly, and realising how it was trapping her, she decided to begin a process of change.

An article by Dr. Wendell Johnson which appeared in the *Saturday Evening Post* on 5 January, 1957, told of his research into the problem of stuttering. Through observing case after case, Dr. Johnson saw that the problem in the child only developed into a negative habit 'after it had been diagnosed as stuttering by over-anxious persons unfamiliar with the facts of normal speech development.' By being told it was a 'stutterer' the child actually became one.[4]

Dr. Knight Dunlop made a twenty year study of habits, how they are formed and how they can be changed. He found that many destructive habits and emotional states had their roots in a similar situation to stuttering. Some part of the person's own nature stood in condemnation of himself with such statements as 'I am stupid', 'I'm ruined' or 'I am worthless'.[5]

Some time ago I had a dream which illustrates this inner situation. In the dream I stood facing myself. The second me stood above on something, and was condemning me for not being as good a father as I might have been. Meanwhile I stood begging forgiveness for all the wrong things I had done, and feeling terribly guilty and an awful failure. But gradually the funny side of the situation struck me, and I called out to the second me, 'Come down from there, you fool. You're only me condemning myself and making me a failure.'[6]

When I woke from the dream I could see how true the dream was, and what a destructive habit I had. If I projected the feeling of being a second-rate father, my children would feel it and believe they were second-rate children.

Many of us have such a voice, which stands superior and hurls destructive judgements at us. Unfortunately the voice is often not heard consciously. It penetrates us in the dark, so to speak, and creates lack of confidence, less creativity and depression. But the part of the wonder of dreams is that through them the unconscious activities in our being are made conscious. Our self-destructive habits are brought to light, the whisperings of our fears are heard.

William James, famous for his pioneering work in philosophy and psychology said that the main difference between the criminal and the creative genius, was their habits. The habits which create disturbing, confused or unsatisfying dreams, can gradually be changed to produce clear, satisfactory and creative ones. By changing the habits which create our dreams, we also transform the forces which create despair and dissatisfaction in our waking life.

Whether we wish to use our dreams as a way of restructuring our life, healing our sick body, as a creative source, or for the excitement of discovering who we are, dreams have the resources to help us.

Chapter Two

First Steps

THE very first step in making use of our unused dream world is to have a dream. For some people this is an easy matter, they remember their dreams every morning. Many others claim they never remember dreams at all.

On many occasions when Hyone and I have dream workshops or start working with someone on their dreams, people who have seldom or never remembered dreams before, begin to remember them as soon as their interest in them is roused. So the most stimulating thing we can do to aid rememberance is to become curious about what our own dreams are telling us.

A helpful procedure, prior to falling asleep, is to create a mental image of ourself waking with the memory of a dream. Our unconscious mental processes seem to respond more readily to images and feelings than verbal suggestions. So an earnest curiosity coupled with the mental picture of the event taking place is the most proficient memory stimulus we can have. But do not consider the mental picture of waking with a dream memory to be a command. Consider it as the giving of a clear image or definition of what you are seeking. When you try to remember a telephone number or address, a command to the process of memory avails little. One simply asks, and the memory is produced or not.

Herbert Reed and Dick Kohr, from their work with a dream project, list intention as the leading factor in dream recall. Intention means such things as having a specific purpose for a dream when going to bed; suggesting at bedtime that a dream will be remembered; being interested in the content of dreams; giving time to working on dreams, etc.[1] There is nothing mysterious in this, and yet it works. Not only does it help dream memory, but this type of intention stimulates the dream process to dig deep into the creative and therapeutic process.

Another aid is to have close at hand a small tape recorder. If this, or the microphone can be easily reached from the bed, the remembered dream can be recorded as soon as one wakes. Time and again a dream can seem to be well engraved in memory, only to be lost as soon as we properly awake, get out of bed, or a few minutes of the day have passed. Writing the dream down, recording it, or telling it to husband or wife in bed is the surest insurance against its early loss.

If you make the decision to ask, as soon as you wake, what you have dreamt, you will build a habit which will assure recall of many of your dreams, and be a foundation for what is to be built in the undeveloped area of your sleep. Also, because our body posture and psychological state are a unity, a dream will be more easily remembered if on waking we do not move our position in bed. Consider what you feel as soon as you wake. Dreams are expressions of feeling states, and awareness of what we feel leads to dream awareness.

Do not wait for a big or impressive dream before starting to record and work on your dreams. Each dream, each fragment, is intensely and intimately a part of your being, and throws light on how you function and what you perceive. Write it down in your notebook of dreams, no matter how unimportant it may seem.

After remembering the dream, recording it in some form, the next step is to start gaining insight into it, and working with it. Let us take one step at a time and work until we understand the step and see the results in our dreams and waking life.

FIRST STEP

The first step is to ask this question:

1. *Am I active or passive in my dream?*

The following dream will help to define the question.

'I was in a largish house in which I lived many years ago. How I got there I do not know, but I saw myself sitting on an ordinary chair just behind the closed door. It was very quiet and I was afraid, but did not make any effort to move.'

Without attempting to interpret the symbols of this dream, certain things are obvious. For instance, the dreamer is alone and afraid . . . 'but I did not make any affort to move'. Here the dreamer is certainly *passive*. Despite feeling ill at ease he is making no attempt to alter the situation or move toward satisfaction or pleasure.

Over the years I have come to see that a dream is created out of what we are, but it has in it the seeds of what we can become. For instance, if we could manage to put ten different people into the same dream situation of sitting in the chair behind the shut door, we would undoubtedly end up with ten very different dreams. One person might be so afraid that they become paralysed, or jump up in horror and hold the door closed. Another might dream of a friend knocking at the door, opening it and hugging the other warmly. Someone else might turn from the door disinterestedly and explore the house, discovering rooms they never knew existed before.

We are the creator of our own dreams. Every flourish, colour, person, event and feeling is created by our own attitudes, hopes, fears, secret ambitions, lusts, tenderness and deepest awareness. Nothing exists in the dream that is not ourself, woven out of our own repertoire of emotion, creativity and thought. The reason ten dreamers would create different dreams behind the door is because each would have different attitudes to life.

The dream also shows how much or how little we habitually use our creative problem-solving ability; it shows whether we allow ourselves to feel deeply, or remain always involved in our thinking. The dream shows whether we remain locked within our personal boundaries of experience and emotions, or whether we are willing to transcend these by reaching out to another person, another mind, or another dimension.

From this one dream we can tell an enormous amount about the dreamer. At the time of the dream they had closed their feelings and attitudes – the door – against contact with others. They thus felt alone and fearful. In fact they are a feeling person who needs contact with others very greatly, but are waiting for the move or sign to come from somebody else. They have not yet learnt how to step out of a set of attitudes and feelings when imprisoned by them. Thus they remain trapped by their immobility as well as their passivity.

The closed door dream may have been a one-off type for the

person who dreamt it. Maybe on that day they felt that life was pointless, and out of those feelings created these images in the dream. But the images of fear and loneliness do not form themselves if the dreamer has an inner attitude of actively reaching out for friendship. It is possible the dreamer habitually lives in the attitudes of passivity protrayed by the dream.

Here is another dream descriptive of a similar sort of passive relationship with events.

'I am on holiday, standing outside the hotel. It is warm and sunny. I turn and enter the hotel, but when I reach my room, my luggage has been removed and the room is occupied by strangers who seem unaware of the situation or of me. I then go to the dining room which is full of people eating and enjoying themselves. I know no one, and am left standing in the doorway, watching.'

The images here are happy, without fear, but nowhere in the dream does the dreamer, Mrs R.M, make any attempt to gain her rights or make friends. She remains in a passive, watching role.

Both these dreams suggest the dreamers are unconsciously passive in their life situations. Both also suggest this leaves the dreamers out of contact with other people, and trapped by fear and passivity in a non-satisfying life situation. The simple recognition of this fact – of passivity as a habitual attitude – and its connection with parts of our life which are unsatisfying or painful, is enough to start the process of change. Once we see the direct connection between our loneliness, non-achievement at work, or inner dissatisfaction, and an attitude we hold, it becomes easier to change our behaviour than if we were unclear and indecisive.

So the first step is to look for signs of passivity in our dreams and consider whether this relates to a similar attitude in our waking life. It is important also to observe if the dream we have woven has arisen from attitudes we habitually express during the day.

Joseph Adelson, writing in *Palmer Quarterly*, outlined research done on dreams with a group of girls attending a class on creative writing. He asked the girls to record their dreams. He assessed from their actual work in class which girls expressed themselves creatively, and which were non-creative. In looking at the dreams he found the non-creative girls had dreams in which they were sexually passive, and open to aggressive sexual approach from the males in their dreams. This group seldom had open sexual encounters in their

25

dreams, but usually alluded to it or symbolised it rather than directly experienced it. The creative girls dreamt openly of sexual experience, and were active and varied in their dream encounters.[2] This is another example of how our dreams emerge from habitual attitudes rather than being a meaningless fantasy of the night.

If we consider the two passive dreams quoted, there was no decisive move on the part of the dreamers to change the situation – being alone – or solve the problem – closed door and lost room and luggage – presented by the dream.

So the first step you can take in changing the quality of your dreams and everyday life is to look for signs of passivity in your dreams. Notice whether it occurs in many dreams, and is therefore habitual. If so, see if you can be aware of similar passivity in your everyday situations.

Robert, a man I recently talked to about his dreams, could see when using Step One, that frequently he took a role of never reaching his goal in his dreams. On considering this in connection with his waking life, he was aware of the same situation. Because he was unclear of what he wished to achieve, he missed opportunity both in waking and in dreams.

When Stewart began to record his dreams, his first showed him standing outdoors in the dark. He was in a park watching his daughter go down a slide. He took no part in the action, only watched.

Each dream Stewart recorded showed him in a similar situation – darkness, inactive, watching. They were obvious, passive dreams. He was in a difficult situation in his waking life being between a wife and a lover, without being able to make a decision in which direction to go. He felt torn and battered by others emotions. From his dreams he realised for the first time in his life that he was habitually a victim of other peoples decisions and emotions because of passivity. This led him to attempt, if only in his dreams, to be active and to move towards what he wanted, which was certainly not a dark, silent world.

After that decision his dreams suddenly changed. The first of such dreams was as follows:

'I am in a bungalow. It is daylight. The house is empty and I am re-decorating it, getting it ready to live in. There is a problem with the toilet, which I am working at to unblock.'

The dream shows a change from darkness to light, and from inactivity to creative activity in which he is solving problems. He is the central character of his own dream and making his own decisions. Stewart's everyday life began to change also. From indecisiveness he began to make decisions toward a positive future for himself. Things didn't suddenly have a rosy glow, but he nevertheless maintained his decisiveness, and has recently started his own business.

SECOND STEP

The second step is to have a more active and creative relationship with our dream. This applies whether the dream is already active or not. Also, this technique and those following are very real exercises in devoloping our creativity and potential in all areas of our life.

The next questions to ask then are:

2. *What am I feeling in the dream? . . . and . . .*

3. *How can I alter the dream to find greater satisfaction?*

To explain this step, here is a dream told to me by a man, Pete, during a dream seminar.

'I am taking part in a horse race. I am on my horse at the starting gate, but I am held up as the others get away and have to ride up the side to try to catch up. The others are ahead and go over the first jump, but when I get to it the size changes and it looms above me. It is now a massive steel structure and there is no way I can get past it to continue the race.'

In this dream Pete is certainly not passive, but an active participant with a group of people. However, he meets a problem which is not resolved in the dream. When I asked him what he felt in the dream, he said mostly a sense of frustration and failure. These, he said applied to his life situation. He was in his early thirties, and tried a number of jobs, but still felt uncertain about what he wanted to do. He had not maintained a relationship either, although he wanted to settle with a girl and have a family. 'So I feel I'm part of the human race; I'm participating, as in the dream, but I got left behind at the starting post. I muffed school and never trained for a career because I was uncertain of what I wanted to do. Now I look around and see my friends way ahead of me, settled into work and marriage while I'm still trying to get going.'

I then asked him the third question, how could he alter the dream

THE INSTANT DREAM BOOK

to find greater satisfaction? I pointed out that he had created the dream out of his own attitudes and emotions. Considering he created the dream, did he want to go on creating the feelings of frustration and failure? I suggested he imagine himself in the dream again and create a different plot.

Pete saw himself in the race again and arrived at the jump. No matter how he tried he couldn't reduce the size of it. But then he realised there were so many other options open to him. For instance, why had he created his dream as a race, with such a sense of competition? In the role of competitor, because of his beginnings, he couldn't help but meet feelings of failure. But what if it wasn't a race? Well, then he could simply enjoy riding the horse. Then the image of the racetrack disappeared and he saw himself riding through countryside, enjoying feelings of pleasure at his sense of freedom.

The experience of changing a feeling of failure into one of pleasure showed Pete the situation he had been creating in his own life. While he was feeling a failure due to the attitude that life is a great competition which you either win or lose, he gave up exploring the opportunities and pleasures which actually existed for him. In reality, although he had no regular job, he had involved himself deeply in learning psychotherapy and counselling. This interest was very real for him, but it seemed to be no part of the competitive world he felt around him. As soon as he dropped his unconscious order to compete, he allowed himself to be more seriously involved in counselling, and was offered a scholarship in the U.S.A. to further his studies. He is at present living in California.

Here is a dream from a woman, S.G., which can further illustrate this:

'I am in a big crowd of people when I see a large cockerel and a bright yellow canary, but the canary is the same size as the cockerel. The birds start to fight but almost immediately the cockerel overpowers the canary by forcing his head into the canary's, and tries to rip his tongue out. I become hysterical and start shouting, "It's humiliating – somebody stop it." My panic becomes worse because nobody seems concerned. At this point I wake up.'

The dreamer is in the passive role. She feels humiliated and helpless and wishes for somebody else to change the conflict she is experiencing. In this dream there are many options open to her as in Pete's dream. She could imagine herself stepping forward and parting the birds. She could imagine the canary fighting back. She could imagine the contest stopping, the canary being equal to the cockerel, and seeing the birds mate. She could have a cat come in and kill them both. But the question is – what would most satisfy her?

When one actually works on a dream in this way, satisfaction comes out of noticing the subtle feelings which arise as one works, or the resistances which occur. These feelings and resistances are enormously important and no attempt to manipulate them mechanically should be made. My ideal in dream work is for the conscious personality to learn how to co-operate and work with the unconscious life processes and drives, rather than attempt to master or subdue them.

To further illustrate how to work with questions two and three, and how to place oneself in the dream and consciously imagine it toward a satisfying end, I will quote the dream and remarks of Tom:

'I dreamt about being in a large removal van in a field. A woman sat on my lap as we were about to drive off, and I held her breasts with pleasure. It seemed the group of people I was involved with were in competition with another group, or fighting them. I think competing is the right word. Anyway, we were trying to move away fast.'

'In working on this dream I realise I feel two main things. One is sexual pleasure that the woman is sitting on my lap, and likes me holding her breasts. But I also notice I feel uncertain about where we are going. I am not in the driving seat, and if I were I wouldn't know where to drive.'

'When I realised how inactive I was in the dream by letting somebody else drive, I imagined being the driver. Sitting there I feel I would sooner be with the woman, and anyway, I didn't know where to drive. So, in seeking my satisfaction in the dream I go back to the woman and enjoy making love to her. I allow my body to feel the pleasure of the fantasy, and feel the need to experience touching her and entering her with shared pleasure. Feeling satisfied, I am then ready to sit in the driving seat, but again with the feeling of not knowing where to drive. This time though I can give my attention to it because I am satisfied in my feelings about the woman. I realise I want to find a building suitable for the dream people to work in to further my waking work. So I imagine driving around looking for the right building, and I feel complete in that.

'What I see now as I write it down is its relevance to my everyday life. It clearly shows me that when my sexual sharing is not satisfied, I become pre-occupied with that side of myself and lose the drive and clear direction I usually have about my work. I need to take time to care for my sexual needs. Then I am ready to be decisive in my work and planning.'

From what Tom says, it can be seen how relevant the subtler feelings are to everyday life. By realising their need and working with them Tom becomes more efficient in his work and in himself. Tom's restructuring of his dream shows how to work with those feelings, and how helpful it can be to write down a summary. It is Tom's summary which finally connects his dream work with his everyday life.

The simplicity of these first steps may tempt you to feel that they are not important, and to hurry to more powerful techniques. In fact, these methods have been stated first because they are the most important. If you use nothing else in this book, those three simple questions, plus the technique of visualising the dream on to satisfaction, if used on each dream, would produce profound life changes.

Take time to use these methods with your dreams. Each morning before you get out of bed, or soon after rising, consider whether you have actively satisfied yourself in your dream. Notice what feelings were experienced, and if they are connected with your everyday life. Then imagine yourself in the dream and create a satisfying situation, not only in events but with feelings. As you do this, notice any attitudes or feelings which block you from satisfaction. These are extremely important, and will be dealt with later in detail. Meanwhile, experiment boldly, as Tom did, until you find the right combination of events to bring satisfaction. In this way you are not only training yourself in positive self expression but are learning how to move out of attitudes and emotions which may have trapped you unconsciously all your life. With some dreams, if care is taken to work with the feelings, you may not achieve satisfaction. A negative feeling may prevent this. If subsequent dreams are worked with, however, the feelings which blocked them will gradually disappear, or a different approach to them will be developed. Therefore do not feel you have failed if some dreams cannot be taken to a satisfying conclusion.

Thus you will be creating a new world for yourself. You will learn to be expressive, honest about what is required to satisfy you, active in getting it, deeply feeling and creative. You will slowly break through the boundaries of habit, lack of imagination and of daring which have imprisoned you. As you will see, the new world is not just inside yourself; it is also the world of hard facts.

Chapter Three

The Dream World Revolution

IN her book, *Creative Dreaming*, Patricia Garfield quotes the story of Margherita, wife of the Italian writer Giovanni Guareschi. Margherita suffered a period of deep depression during which Giovanni discovered a simple way of helping her. Margherita told him of her disturbed dreams in which she wandered endlessly alone through streets, and felt imprisoned by feelings of unhappiness, desire and fear.

In response to this Giovanni suggested, much to her annoyance, that in her dream she get herself a bicycle – she did not know how to drive a car.

After only a few days Margherita actually began to dream of using a bicycle and told Giovanni that her dreams were in fact made easier by it, and she awoke less tired. However, after only a week of success she fell once more into her deep depression because she had a puncture, and had again to walk. Giovanni, in his urgent attempt to help her, told her to mend the puncture in some way. Margherita said this was not possible as she was completely alone in her dreams and did not know how to mend a puncture. So Giovanni took her into their garage and taught her how to remove the tyre and mend the puncture. He helped her to practice this until she could literally do it blindfold. In this way it had become a new habit.

It took three nights of dreaming before Margherita excitedly woke to tell she had successfully mended her puncture. Her new happiness and sense of independence, real in her waking life as well

32

as in her dream life, lasted for several months. So much dependance had grown out of her dream success, that when her next problem arose she was cast down not only in her dream but also in her waking life. While riding a mountain road in her dream, she had slipped and fallen into a steep gulley, where she lay injured. Giovanni tried once more to help her, studying books on rock climbing. Margherita felt, after attempting to use these techniques, that she was too weak and injured. So Giovanni pressed her to call him in her dreams . . . call him again and again to come and help her. 'Don't stop calling me' he pleaded, 'who knows, I may hear you.'

That very night while away from home he felt sure he could feel Margherita calling him. Hurrying home he found her calmly getting a meal ready. On asking her what had happened she told him she had slept and dreamt again of being in the ravine. This time she had called him continually, and at last he had appeared, thrown a rope to her and pulled her out of the ravine. Margherita's summary was, 'I am not worried any more. I now know that if I am ever in danger and I call to you, you will hear me and come.'[1]

Just as a dream can deeply influence our waking life by its fear or pleasure, so our waking activities and imaginations deeply influence our dream life. For instance, when counselling people who find it difficult to make friends or show affection, there is a way of helping them to examine and disperse their fears. They can practice, in the counselling situation, the process of making friends and actually physically reaching out to hold hands, hug and express their feelings. For them, the act of reaching their arm out to somebody else is usually like breaking through a powerful barrier. The barrier is actually made not of bricks or wood, but of anxiety, feelings of not being likeable or being different to other people. So strong are these walls of feeling that some people remain imprisoned in them for a lifetime. Breaking through them requires new action, a revolutionary new relationship with oneself and the world.

Bill, a man Hyone and I worked with, had felt since childhood that he was physically unattractive. He had developed this feeling about himself because his mother had never shown any pleasure in handling his body as a baby. All his childhood messes and dribbles had been treated as repulsive and dirty and these feelings surrounded him in his personal prison. We asked him to feel his need for making contact with us, and when he was ready, reach out for us, but not to

33

do so as a mechanical action. For ten or fifteen minutes he could not move, his walls of negative feeling were so strong, but gradually and with deep emotion, he came to us and held us, feeling our pleasure in response to him.

Margherita and Bill were prisoners of their own feelings. Margherita managed to break out of her prison by first learning to feel more independent and capable through the bicycle; and secondly by learning to reach out for contact and help when she needed it. Her calling in her dream was as difficult for her to achieve as it was for Bill to physically reach out to share contact. In both cases a pressure of negative feelings, almost like a resisting gravitational force, held them back. And the important point is that although not everyone has the opportunity or cash to visit a psychotherapist to help them work their way through the wall of feelings and habits which imprison them, almost everyone has the chance to do it in their dreams.

Whether we learn to meet our problems and transform our life in waking or in dreams, the results are the same. Wherever we do it, we have met the negative feeling and passed through and beyond into a new area of expression. In fact, our dreams and fantasies give us a much more varied sphere of experience in which to practice meeting our fears, making love or exploring new areas of ourself. However we practice, we gain confidence for real-life situations. After practicing making contact with us, Bill actually met and developed a relationship with a young woman that same day. The relationship lasted several months and enriched them both.

Patricia Garfield gives examples of several people with a naturally retiring disposition who, after meeting a dream attacker with real aggression, were able to directly ask for what they wanted in waking life. One woman asked a man smoking in a non-smoking area of an aeroplane to stop, which he did. This followed successful positive action in a dream. Beforehand she would not have dared ask for such a simple request, but would have remained angry and unsatisfied.

It might help to understand how this action of changing a few images in a dream can change our life, if we realise something about a dream symbol.

The nearest everyday thing which can help us understand a dream image is a word. If I write the word SAUCEPAN, you will find it almost impossible to have any other view of it than as a cooking implement. If this is changed a little by writing – red-hot saucepan – something different is communicated.

If you are not used to dealing with dreams, you may believe a dream image can never be likened to a word. A word has a fairly precise and commonly agreed meaning. A dream image, you might believe, is a rather random thing. But if you had not developed words for communication but had to use mime, posture, environment, to express meanings, would you use the image of someone slouched in a chair smoking to depict happiness and creativity? Our sense of body language, scenery, situation, is so acute, thousands of people can watch the same communal dream – a T.V. film – and feel similar responses. So, without realising it, we have commonly accepted and fairly precise meanings attached to particular images, body postures, clothing and so on.

When we go to sleep we do not lose that acute sense of dramatic meaning of images. It is, in fact heightened. Our unconscious mind is a heritage from our distant evolutionary past, when language as we know it did not exist. In the past, body language, tones of sound and emotional presence were everything. The posture and the feeling tone of aggression or friendship were one and the same thing. To understand the language meant survival.

A dream image is an expression of a feeling, a body process, or subliminal impressions. An unconscious body process cannot arise directly into consciousness as a clear and definite thought. One of the stages it passes through to emerge from deep unconsciousness to conscious verbalisation, is dream or fantasy imagery.

In our dream we drop back to this pre-verbal level of thought. But it is also largely a pre-sense of identity level too, for few people can maintain an intense sense of self in dreams. The life processes of our being are in fuller expression than our personality. Or, at least, it is a point of meeting and communication between the two.

This next dream illustrates this.

'I am forty-eight, have two children in their late teens and definitely do not want another baby. Nevertheless, I have a recurring dream in which I am always in labour but experiencing no pain. Although there are nursing staff I am in some sort of laboratory, but everything is very pleasant. I never actually give birth and when I wake I always have a vague feeling of disappointment.'

The main feelings here are of the physical drive to produce a baby and the disappointment because this had not been achieved. This is an expression of the biological urges in the woman to reproduce. But her conscious personality has made a firm decision not to have further children. The dream is an expression of these two facets of her total self meeting and experimenting with – the laboratory – a direction satisfying to both aspects. In the dream this was not reached and she wakes dissatisfied.

Considering that the image of herself having a baby is possibly a direct expression and link with her deeply-rooted biological urge to reproduce like any other mammal, if she carefully took hold of the image, mentally she would be in touch with the urge behind it. She could of course, mechanically – i.e. without sensitivity – manipulate the image. In social situations many of us have trained ourselves to express a mechanical smile in order to impress a superior, or others. Beneath our warm handshake a feeling of hidden boredom or even repulsion may exist. If we approached work on our dreams with the same dishonesty and absence of sensitivity we would miss, or even irritate, the contact we could make with our deeper feelings. In my experience it is enormously important that we do not mechanically remove or suppress our negative feelings and dream images. We must learn to respect them as living, feeling parts of our total being and lead them into a transformative expression rather than repression.

I am suggesting that the image in a dream is a direct link with the psychological or physiological state which gave rise to it. If we work with the image, we are also directly influencing the inner condition. This is an enormously important but often overlooked fact of our mind and body. If we respect the dream image as a living, feeling part of our being, we can work with it consciously.

Working with dreams does not hold out a carrot of temptation promising freedom from all human problems. Writing about the results of penetrating inner work on oneself, W.V. Caldwell says, 'They (the people who have worked), are not omnipotent, nor are they helpless – but something in between; they are participators in life. To a certain extent they can direct their own minds, their actions, and the world about them – but only if they recognise and work through the laws of reality, that complicated web of relations they only dimly understand. Neither gods who control the universe, nor passive beasts who must suffer dumbly, they are men and women. And in that acceptance they find contentment.'[2]

To move toward this greater direction of our own being we can learn how to deal with certain dream situations. The laws of reality Caldwell mentions are the functions of our own body and mind. Working with our dream images is a recognition of the place the symbol occupies in the functioning of our being. Where a dream suggests we are being directed by a negative habit, we need to find not only a more satisfying direction for our dream, as in the last step, but also to practice and reinforce the new step.

THIRD STEP

4. *Is there something I need to practice?*

To understand this question clearly, we must look at a series of dreams from one individual. This man, Roger T., had been given a new work situation in which, although not completely self-employed, he had the opportunity to explore a number of alternative areas for his work. Some of these, in different countries, were outside his experience.

This is Roger's first dream:

'I was standing in the main road of a town in which I once lived, talking to and working with various people. A man came up to me and placed a small piece of electronic equipment on top of my head. I understood it tested one's quality by giving out sounds. With me it gave a base rhythm, like a signal of brain activity or bio-electrical pulses. But above the base sound was a lovely higher theme which was most unusual. The man said this was so far the best response in the area. I knew it gave me the opportunity to have training of some sort, to open the doors of opportunity for me.

But the man was also going to test others, so perhaps somebody else would be chosen. I felt my younger son would register slightly lower, but that my other son would be higher. Then I was standing looking along a road edged each side with jungle. It stretched far into the distance. I knew that lions sometimes lay in wait to catch unwary travellers, and I stood there trying to decide whether I would dare take the road.'

Roger is not particularly passive in the dream. He is working with people, relating to them. His feelings are that he is being assessed, and he proves to be of high quality. He also feels opportunity lies ahead. But the end of the dream shows him trying to decide whether to take a new direction; the hesitation, if we discount the symbol and simply ask what he is feeling, is anxiety about the unknown.

So, by asking the questions given in the first steps of dream work, Roger saw that his dream was about his own assessment of himself. It is a positive one. The dream concerns the opportunities which are presented in his work. It shows him that, in fact, he hesitates from exploring the opportunities because of anxieties about what *might* happen.

Roger's comments were, 'My family has a history of being cautious about initiating new ventures. Also, I have always felt uncertain of succeeding in anything except what I had already tried. The dream shows me how this is stopping me from going ahead with complete enthusiasm.'

Working on the dream, Roger imagined himself walking along the threatening road. 'I don't want to be forever held back by my unrealistic fears. Obviously there will be problems in any new undertaking, but I accept them, so I decided to walk along the road, and did so in imagination, therein meeting my fear of the lions.'

Roger's next 'Work' dream is as follows:

'A group of us were walking near the Aldwych in London. We were all young adults just leaving school. A girl and I were to start a completely new experience at University. As I dreamt it I really felt I was leaving one life situation and about to enter another. I felt it as a powerful change in my life toward a much wider experience. The girl was coming with me.'

About the dream he says; 'In the dream my feelings are of moving toward great achievement. Although I am only walking, I feel I am positively active in the dream, and this has come about because I decided to face my fears and walk along that road. In the first dream I had the opportunity for training. In this dream I am going to the best of training schools. This gives me a wonderful sense of growth and movement and is very strengthening. I don't feel I want to do anything with this dream to make it more satisfying.'

Here is Roger's third dream:

'I am at a large school, looking around, and come to a huge gymnasium. Near the end where I am standing is a diving board, about twenty feet off the ground. Girls are learning to dive off the board and land flat on their backs on the bare floor. If they fall flat they do not hurt themselves. I am then walking in the gym and it is filling with water, a pleasant milky green colour. I feel the divers are safe now.'

Roger is now in his new place of opportunity, the school, but is rather passive. His comments are: 'My main feeling in the dream is the anxiety that the divers would hurt themselves; this fear lessens when the water appears. In wondering how I can find greater satisfaction in the dream, I realise, like the divers, I am afraid of falling flat on my back in my business ventures. Yet in this dream people are actually practicing as if it were an exciting sport. So instead of avoiding the image of diving and trying to make it safe, I imagined myself diving with the girls. Sure enough, I feel the uncertainty I do in business. But as I dived again and again, the anxiety lessened until it finally disappeared. So I realise I have a habitually anxious response to new life situations and I need to practice taking the high jump, taking the risk and coming through those feelings.

'Once more I am intrigued by my dreams which are actually developmental, and I am now at the place of training. It seems that my new training is to do with taking risks, which opens a whole new realm of possibilities.'

Roger practiced his diving in imagination for several days. His next dream was this:

'I am up a ladder working on the roof of a rather nice house. The ladder was wedged against the base of the wall, leaning away from the roof to rest on another outcrop of the building. Wanting to climb higher up the ladder I held onto the roof, rested one foot on the outcrop, and moved the ladder to a steeper angle with my free foot. Unfortunately, it fell. I was perfectly safe and called for my father, who was below, to put the ladder up. He tried, but could find nowhere to make it stable.

'Then I was on the ground, but it was in the shop my father owned. I was trying to find some place the foot of the ladder would be secure. Everywhere I placed it, it slipped.'

The whole essence of this dream was on the *foot* of the ladder, i.e. his basic experience. This is the most active and creative of all the dreams in this series.

Roger says: 'My main feeling in the dream is happiness that I am improving the house, and my determination to secure the ladder. I can see that it is only unstable when I wish to climb the next rung on the ladder – I presume – of success. As I have already said, I did not

39

inherit the confidence from my father to initiate the new. So the slippery condition in the shop is no news to me.

In considering what I can do to make the dream more satisfying, a solution immediately jumped to mind. I imagined myself nailing a block of wood to the floor of the shop. Against this the ladder rests without any hint of slipping. I have no problem in maintaining the image of the block of wood which is a clue to the lack of negative feelings working against my new resolve.

So, what do I need to practice? Well, my wife and I have been talking about buying another house as an investment. This is something neither of us have ever done before, or dared to consider – the anxiety of looking after one house used to be enough for me. Now I seem to have no qualms about further responsibilities. So I see the house in the dream as this new courage in my life. Therefore I need to practice going up that ladder until I feel easy on the higher rungs, and have completed the work on the house.'

Practice is fundamental to the development of any new skill. We practice walking, talking, social interractions, work skills, sometimes for years before we become relaxed and proficient in them. The dreams quoted and the work Roger did on them took place over a period of five months. This is a comparatively short time to transform a history of anxiety into the pleasure of exploring the new. The last dream of this series is as follows: 'Last night I had a lovely dream. I was reading a typewritten list of computer programs. They were about potentials. The only one I can clearly remember on waking is designing. I realised while still dreaming that these were my own abilities and I could call them out of myself. I am in fact doing just this through my love for human beings.'

This dream is not only pleasurable and the obvious result of the previous dreams; it also has a completely new and important feature. Roger says; 'I realised while still dreaming that these were my own abilities.' Even while asleep, he penetrated the symbols and has direct insight into what is occurring within him. Roger's work on his dreams has led him to emerge through anxieties to the discovery of new abilities. Each new step of practice speeds up the process of impressing the new habit into one's unconscious. Since these dreams, Roger's new confidence has helped him attain a completely new and more satisfying work situation. Because it involves free-lancing his skill, it offers little security, which in the past he would not have been able to cope with. But being able to cope with the stress of taking chances opened the doors to wider opportunity.

Here are a few more dreams from various people, indicating how dreams reveal areas of self which could be helped by practicing a new approach.

This first one is from a man, B.Y., who writes: 'I am at a wedding. We are being served a celebratory chicken lunch. While my back is turned a female guest removes my plate and substitutes one without chicken. At this I rather petulantly decide to leave, without saying anything to the bride and groom. I go into a cloakroom, wash my hands, and while looking at my moustache in the mirror, realise the face is that of Adolf Hitler.'

Mr. B.Y. is a victim twice over in his dreams. First he *feels* victimised because he doesn't get his fair share; he then victimises himself by responding petulantly. At the end he sees himself as perhaps an unsavoury character. The non-satisfaction at the end of the dream suggests a need for change. To achieve this he could be more active in his dream by demanding his rights. He could imagine himself getting his plate of chicken back again, and having more enjoyment with the other guests. His habit is perhaps one of not directly seeking his needs in a social situation, but reacting 'petulantly' and so missing any satisfaction.

A lady of 'sixty plus' reports the following dream; 'It has' she says, 'been occurring for years.' This statement alone tells us that a part of her personality is habitually producing these feelings.

'In it I am seeking a "penny house" (toilet) and can't find one that is decent. They are all in an appalling condition and some have no doors. Finally I have to use one in full view of everybody.'

It is difficult to know what would satisfy this lady. She is clearly stuck in a feeling habit and needs a new direction. She could try practicing going to the toilet in 'full view of everybody' in her dream until the difficult feelings disappear and she relaxes. She could imagine cleaning the toilets and fixing the doors, or telling people to clear off while she needed privacy.

When seeking what will satisfy us we must remember that fantasy and dreaming are *safe* areas in which we can explore freely without coming to harm. So feel free to try even the funniest solutions. Explore until you feel satisfaction. When Roger imagined nailing the block of wood to the floor, not only did he feel satisfied but he also felt confident of success because no negative feelings robbed him of his positive image. Any negative feelings or inability to hold the positive image must be given attention as described. With practice you can gain real skill in creating satisfying situations out of even the most distressing and negative dreams.

Practice is the key note of this step, and it must be a pleasure rather than a task. Negative habits may not be concerned simply with fear or shyness, they can occur in any area of our life. Through practice we transform one pattern of reaction to another. Learning how, opens up enormous new possibilities for human life. Also, since it can be tried in almost any situation where you can close your eyes for a few moments, it requires no great discipline.

Chapter Four

Changing Nightmares into Pleasures

Not every human problem or misery is curable. Over the centuries, however, human ingenuity and experiment have found ways of alleviating many ills, wiping some completely off the face of the earth, and making hopeful inroads against others.

Pleasure is not the absolute goal in human life. Wisdom, ability, love and self responsibility are also greatly sought after qualities. Pleasure without wisdom can defeat its own end, and have a hollow centre. But wisdom without pleasure is a contradiction. With sufficient wisdom we should be able to find a relationship with ourself and the world around us which has some pleasure for us and others.

Amongst our huge collection of dreams sent to us from people in all walks of life, and all age groups, there is a very high percentage of nightmares and anxiety dreams. In a certain sense this is not surprising since the dreams you are most likely to remember in the morning are the ones which stir you deeply. As nightmares also frequently leave us worried about meaning, we are more likely to report them to somebody else, or seek assurance about them, than other types of dream. However, among the nightmares reported to us, a high proportion are recurring. Frequently the nightmare has haunted the dreamer throughout life, sometimes occuring several times a week.

Here is an example, from a Mr K.T. He says : 'For some time I have been troubled by a nightmarish dream which is so realistic I sometimes think I am going to die. In my dream, which sometimes comes within forty-five minutes of going to sleep, I have swallowed something which is literally choking me or is going to poison me. I wake up and rush down the stairs to the kitchen, spitting and choking, holding my throat, and making all sorts of disturbing noises which you can imagine frighten my wife out of her wits. I have had this dream as many as five or six times a night, in the space of maybe five or six hours. My doctor says it could be to do with the last war, because I was a child then, and my dad had to constantly wake me up to take us down to the shelter.'

Our dream process is in part also a healing process. Charles Rycroft describes the observed results on people of unexpected disasters such as earthquakes and train accidents. Among other things they have a tendency to 'waking actions and dreams in which the traumatic experience is repeated.' He goes on to say that these repetitions in dreams or actions can be 'thought of as manifestations of the healing process. By repeating the trauma the traumatised person is, as it were, trying to get it in front of himself again so that he can anticipate it, react anxiously to it and then assimilate or 'get over' it in the way he would any other distressing experience.'[1]

Dr Rycroft holds the theory that much anxiety is caused by sudden traumatic events which are unexpected. For instance, a child suddenly losing it's mother. While this sometimes is the case, in my own experience much anxiety is in reaction to situations or emotions over which we feel we have no control and which may threaten to overwhelm or destroy us. Nightmares also frequently deal with new experience, such as work or old age, which we are anxious about.

Nevertheless, Dr. Rycroft's experience in the field of psychiatry is very helpful in understanding the realm of our inner anxieties. He says there are four basic ways we respond to anxiety or over-whelming emotions such as grief and anger. They are defence, submission, flight and attack.

These reactions to anxiety are usually defined in our dreams. We have, in fact, begun to clarify this for ourselves in the first Step, where we ask if we have a passive or active role in our dream. But here is a dream clearly illustrating flight.

'This dream has occurred for years. I am in the large mansion house that I lived in from two years old until I was eight. I am going up the staircase of the West Wing. But as I go up I see the stairs lead into the ceiling and end there. I have to keep walking though, as

44

there is something I am afraid of behind me. I put my hands on the ceiling, and my legs are nearly as high as they can get. When I am pressed up against the ceiling I look down and the stairs and bannister rail are swarming with wave upon wave of crawling things, like awful insects. In the hallway below is a swamp with crocodiles and other hideous things. My terror is terrible and I cry out to stop dreaming this horrible nightmare.'

The next dream, from Mrs G.L., who says she is in her mid-fifties, is an example of anxiety about what may come into our life beyond our control; in this case death. This is also a recurring dream.

'I have been so busy pressing and sorting out suitable clothing for my husband and two children to wear to a funeral. I then rush to prepare the funeral breakfast – cutting endless sandwiches, folding serviettes, setting out cups etc. When I finally rush upstairs to get myself ready I see the hearse and coffin have already arrived, and my husband and children in the clothes I ironed, are going down the path weeping. I think, "Cheek; they're going without me." Then I realise the funeral is mine.'

Because many people have worked on the investigation of their nightmares, it can safely be said the cause of them is known. They are brought about by a fear, problem or painful experience which was not fully felt or integrated at the time.

Or the nightmare is an attempt to meet and integrate into our personality things which are new and as yet unknown. The thing approaching may be outside of us, such as leaving school, seeking work and independence. Or it may be changes within us, such as emerging sexuality at adolescence.

To protect ourselves from the emotional shock of a tragic event or of an approaching 'unknown', we often dissociate ourselves from it.

Alexander N. Hood, telling of his personal experiences in the Great Earthquake at Messina in 1909, says:

'Men recounted how they lost wife, mother, brothers, sisters, children and all their possessions, with no apparent concern. They told their tales of woe as if they themselves had been disinterested spectators of another's loss.'[2]

It is so easy, in such circumstances, to believe that human beings, as babies, children or adults, can survive the most horrendous physical or psychological battering without being moved emotionally. The more I hear of people's dreams, however, the more I see how deeply sensitive human beings are, not just to injury, but even to such non actions as not being spoken to or being ignored as a child. The apparent non effect of widespread trauma after wars, and general mishandling of babies, is because of this defence mechanism of disassociation.

There are most likely areas of everybody's experience which they do not consciously wish to be aware of. These hidden fears lock up, or build walls around, areas of our ability, and break up our wholeness. Maybe without realising it we live in a restricted part of ourself. We build our life within such restrictions, avoiding relationships, turning down opportunities, drawing less on our creativity. In the sense of the way dreams portray the situation, we have at some time a ghost in the library, a tiger in the corridor leading to the roof garden, and a gangster in the bedroom. So we do not use our full mental ability; we avoid any sense of a religious feeling about the cosmos, and our sexual pleasure is erratic instead of erotic.

The dream literally portrays in images what we have done with our fears. The tendency, as described by Alexander Hood, is to disassociate ourselves from our feelings. 'They told their tales of woe as if they had been disinterested spectators of another's loss.'

But later come the nightmares, because the healing action of our being prefers not to have artificial barriers erected between full creativity, sexuality, and everyday life. The situation and feelings we avoid experiencing are portrayed by the dream process, literally as another person, or the Thing, trying to open the door. Assuming that we can work with or against this healing process which attempts to bring wholeness and meet our nightmares by flight, submission, defence or attack, which shall we choose?

From long experience in helping people deal with anxiety and nightmares, the most creative approach, if we can manage it, is to seek awareness, and through that, understanding of the things we are frightened of in our dreams. This removes the imprisoning walls built by our anxieties, is healing, and also expands our self confidence to respond creatively and satisfyingly in life.

THE FOURTH STEP

The fourth step, then, is to work with this question:

5. *Am I meeting the things I am afraid of in my dream?*

When I first started working on my own dreams, I felt certain after a few months that I had dealt with all my personal inner fears. As if in response to this attitude I had this nightmare.

In my dream my wife told me she thought the bungalow we were living in was haunted. I told her that I didn't believe it was, and even if it was I wasn't afraid of ghosts. On going to bed that night – still in the dream – I sat in bed as my wife went to sleep, and issued a challenge for any ghosts to show themselves. Nothing happened and I rather smugly prepared to go to sleep. At that moment the door to the room creaked open and two terrible figures entered. They were black men who looked as if they had been dead for some weeks. Slime was coming out of their rotten mouths, yet they were walking, looking for me.

In great terror I made the sign of the cross and said a fervent prayer for help. This dispelled the men, and I began to feel smug again and to congratulate myself on knowing how to deal with them. But again the door opened and the living dead men came in. This time all my signs and prayers did nothing to stop them. I became paralysed with terror as they came forward with hands reaching for my neck. They grasped my throat and I woke screaming and very frightened. I had to put the light on for a while in the bedroom.

Obviously I had been smugly overconfident in my self assessment. I still had things I was very afraid of. So much so I went beyond the stage of passivity or flight into paralysis. The dream also suggested I had used my religious beliefs to hold back my inner fears, but these were no longer working. At that time I had not defined the techniques of visualisation already described, but had found in other people's writings, and then clarified for myself, an enormously important realisation which enabled me gradually to meet the fears shown in my nightmare.

This forms the basis of the next question, which is:
6. *What have I mistakenly introverted?*
Without an understanding of this question we may remain lost and anxious explorers of our inner world. With it, the inner world of dream and fantasy takes on an enriched meaning, and the terror is removed from our nightmares.

There is a riddle which illustrates the meaning of the question. The riddle says: If you had a very large bottle with a neck wide enough to put a goose's egg in, and you kept the egg warm until it hatched in the bottle; then you fed the goose till it matured, how could you get the goose out without breaking the bottle?

When the question is eventually asked – How do you get the goose out of the bottle, the reply is;

I don't know, you thought it all up!

Literally the bottle, egg, goose and problem are all in one's own mind.

In the world of dreams such truths are even more important to understand. In the first place, everything in our dream is, like the bottle and goose, a creation of our own imagination. To react to them as if they were physically real is not only ridiculous but causes incalculable misery. Imagine an artist painting a picture of a tiger. The tiger is so real it moves and roars. At this the artist is so frightened he runs away.

If I cross a road and a fast car comes along, I am sensible to get out of the way quickly. But if I *dream* a fast car zooms toward me, it wouldn't matter if it hit me. All I am facing are my own feelings and thinking processes. What my feelings and thoughts create in a dream, and how I react, is interesting because it says a great deal about who I am as a person, but I must never make the mistake of believing the dream is external reality. The two zombies in my nightmare are parts of my own thoughts and emotions of which I was terrified.

The important point is that while it is wise to avoid danger in the physical world, avoiding it within ourselves only means we are frightened of our own emotions – literally of ourself. In fact, if this process of self avoidance is not checked, we gradually refrain from using any of our faculties because they threaten us. We thereby become prisoners of our own mind. But if we reverse this process, and despite any anxiety or guilt play with the images and feelings of our own mind, we become freer and more creative. For instance, feeling that sexual fantasies or dreams are wrong, could be likened to a pianist having the same feelings about the high notes. If he also felt frightened of certain notes, his ability to play would be curtailed. In a similar way, not being able easily to express or play upon the full keyboard of our mental, emotional and sexual range, is destructive to our pleasure and creativity.

But fear is not the only thing we introvert into our dreams. In exterior life there may be certain values of right or wrong we can usefully attach to sex. For instance, it is a deeply felt taboo to have sexual intercourse with a member of one's own family; or it may be wise to be careful about promiscuity to avoid disease. In our dreams, however, to introvert these codes serves no useful purpose whatsoever. In fact they are detrimental. They create fear where there should be freedom. If we cannot freely manipulate or be mobile in our emotions and thoughts, then we are prisoners of our own mind, frightened of shadows and images.

Also, to avoid physical violence is usually a wise precaution in our exterior world, but to run from an attacker in our dream shows we have become afraid of ourselves, and that is a terrible situation, for where is there then to go to be safe?

If a dream shows us a road, and a bomb hidden in a suitcase, it is only a cause for avoidance if the dream is warning us about a real bomb in the actual road. If it is referring to some explosive situation in ourselves, then *running away* is the *dangerous* course to take. Because if we fail to understand what the situation is, it can happen and disrupt our life. If we understand it we can avoid or alter it.

Recognising my two nightmare zombies as creations of my own emotions, which could only harm me through fear, led me to have this dream.

I was on an underground train, standing at one end of the carriage where there were no doors. I wanted to get off but the gangway was blocked by two black men. They were quite well dressed, and one of them readily allowed me to pass, but the other belligerantly ignored my request for him to move. After asking several times I pushed past him. He then came at me while I stood at the doors. His hands went for my throat, but this time I was not afraid, and I caught his hands in mine and wrestled them down. I then got off the train.

Here we can see that something which had previously aroused terror in me is now met, simply by changing my attitude to it. While I am frightened of the self-created figure in my own dream, it has power over me. But when I approach it confidently, I gain something, because it now becomes an accessible and usable part of my own nature.

While L.S.D. was being used in this country as an aid to psychotherapy, selected patients were helped to face their own images of confusion and fear using the drug. Drs. Ling and Buckman, working at the Marlborough Day Hospital, describe the case of a thirty-year-old writer who could not finish his manuscripts. The writer was Jewish by birth, had escaped the Nazis by acting the part of a Dutchman, and had worked in Holland until the end of the war. During L.S.D. psychotherapy the patient was helped to experience his own fantasies and fears, and to recognise these as wrongly introverted parts of everyday life. During his youth he had lived under the constant and real threat of death, and this is what he had negatively introverted. He says: 'This came to me one afternoon in treatment. I felt I was dead. I now recall very vividly how I called you (the doctor) and said, "I'm dying" and you said, "Don't worry, you are not really dying, but reliving a childhood experience." I then said "I feel I am dying. This is the end".'

After having experienced the feeling of dying he goes on to say, 'With this horror of death realised, I started to experience a most fantastic happiness with the realisation I do not have to die now. I felt I was no longer with my neck under the guillotine. Prior to this treatment my mind had always shied away from experiences as a writer about other peoples lives. I think the cure, from someone who did not write successfully, to someone who does write successfully, came this very moment when I felt that this mind of mine was part of me. It has become harmonised with the rest of my feelings.'

In fact he has become a writer with international acclaim, although his name is witheld for personal reasons.

This is a graphic example of how, by meeting his images of fear, a very terrible fear in his case, he was no longer the prisoner of his own mind, and his potential was released. Methods of transforming our nightmares can be seen if we now summarise this information.

First of all there is the type of nightmare which Mr. K.T. has, already quoted in this chapter, in which he has actual physical movements as well as his fear. His nightmare carries on into his waking life, causing him spontaneously to choke and spit. He feels there might be a connection between his dream and his childhood experiences during the bombing raids of the war.

This type of dream is almost certainly an example of the traumatic experiences being repeated in an attempt to relive and thereby integrate past shocks. We see the completion of this in the example of the Jewish writer re-experiencing his fear of death.

So the most helpful course of action is to allow the physical movements to continue and the fears to be fully felt, and thus healed.

During the past eleven years I have worked very deeply with this approach, on myself, with other individuals and with groups.

It is effective if one can find some trust in the healing functions of one's own dream process. However, unless one has already experienced this process of meeting these deep fears several times, it is difficult to do so alone. A therapist skilled in helping people allow the spontaneous catharsis or abreaction, as it is called, is then helpful. As there are a growing number of such psychotherapists and hypnotherapists they should not be too difficult to find.

In my own nightmares of the two coloured men, this was my own eventual solution. Each time the attack had been on my throat. I noticed, prior to the eventual resolution, that as I relaxed to sleep, my head was slowly pulled back by a powerful tension in the back of my neck. It was the same sort of movement I had made in the first dream where I woke up screaming as I was being strangled. I noticed also my head pulled back if I relaxed and allowed the body to move as it wished. Having studied the phenomena of the dream process breaking through into consciousness as spontaneous movement I felt confident about exploring the process. So, with the support of two fellow researchers – Mike Tanner and Sheilah Johns – I allowed the movements and feelings to continue and express in any way. In other words I became a passive, non-interfering, yet involved observer, as in a dream. I held the attitude that I would allow my body, emotions, thoughts and voice, as free and spontaneous expression as occurs in dreams. In fact I would allow more expression than in my dreams, because in my nightmare, I ran away into waking instead of actually experiencing and arriving at understanding of my fear and symbols. Now I would allow even my fear.

As I relaxed, my head began to pull backwards. Slowly the rest of my body began to enter into what was happening, by expressing movements of struggle, fighting against restraint. My mouth opened and locked wide, and spontaneous cries emerged. I sounded like a child calling for my mother. Then, with enormous physical movement, cries and tears, I re-experienced having my tonsils removed in hospital as a six-year old.

That was the 'attack' on my throat. My dream movement and neck tension exactly reproduced the movement I made in my terror, mouth clamped open, to pull my head backwards from the surgeon. The physical scars were nothing at all, but the psychological ones

51

were quite crippling. A nurse had held my head while the surgeon attacked my throat. I could feel the comfort of a woman's body, but it was indelibly linked to the terror of attack and pain. Not a very good combination for lovemaking or trust of women. Also I felt my mother had left me forever, and the experience haunted me in adult years with a feeling of being alone. After reliving the event and having insight into how it had influenced my adult life, the neck tension, loneliness, and fear of pain in connection with a woman's embrace, disappeared.

Many nightmares, perhaps most, have as their source, some such traumatic event, either in childhood or adult life. Many people still have nightmares from their adult experiences during the war. Very often, like Mr. K.T., the nightmare recurs, simply because the inner feelings it is an expression of, are not met. If, like Mr. K.T., the dream movements break through strongly into waking, it suggests the trauma they express is not deeply buried under enormous resistances, and could be fairly easily allowed into consciousness.

Another important point is that the movements or posture expressed in the nightmare are almost certainly a direct expression of the positions, tensions, and movements which arose at the time of the original shock. If one actually reproduces these tensions or movements while awake and leaves the body and emotions free to express spontaneously, the healing process behind the dream is given an opportunity to complete itself.

Secondly, by using questions five and six, one can gradually transform nightmares and their causative fears, even if one does not wish to go to the point of re-living the past trauma. In any case, some nightmares are not caused by past shocks, but by current relationship with oneself. If examples of using the questions are looked at in more detail, these points will become clear.

Here is a typical recurring nightmare, sent by Mrs. C.M.

'I am driving round a bend when the car goes off the road to a long drop below. We glide through the air for a while before dropping. The fear is absolutely horrific, but I always wake up before hitting the bottom.'

If questions five and six are applied to this dream, Mrs. C.M. is not meeting the thing she is afraid of in her dream. Instead she wakes up. Therapists sometimes call this escaping or running away into waking. We wake up because in that state we have a stronger ability to suppress our feelings. Also she mistakenly introverts the conviction that if her car crashes she will be injured or killed. Perhaps that is her fear.

What can she do with this dream?

First, it is a recurring dream, and with this, or any other dream, she must be aware of what feelings she has immediately on waking. The dream is most likely an expression of these feelings. Before any wise move can be made, these feelings need to be heard out, just as a judge hears out all the witnesses before any decision is made. Question two, 'What am I feeling in the dream?,' is important in dealing with a nightmare.

Since the most transformative single thing we can do with our fears or negative feelings is to hear them out, the technique will be dealt with fully as we go along.

Second she has introverted the conviction that to crash in her dream would mean death. This is completely untrue. I know there is the belief that if one falls and hits the bottom in a dream one actually dies, but that is pure superstition without any basis in fact. We have received a number of dreams where people *have* hit the bottom and continued the dream. In one such case the woman then explored, in her dream, what it was like to be dead. In other cases, the person experiences and goes beyond the feelings they feared and previously woke up to avoid.

So even if Mrs. C.M. is anxious about a car injury and death, if she understood that she can safely explore these situations in a dream, and thereby come to terms with them, her nightmare could become a means to greater relaxation.

Therefore she needs to say to herself, 'It is perfectly harmless, even helpful, to crash *in my dream*; but obviously not *in waking*.' Then she needs to visualise herself driving the car and actually completing the crash again and again until she feels easy with it. After that, and only after that, she can experiment with driving the car off the road and making it fly, land safely, fly back onto the road, or anything else which takes her fancy.

What is being done here is consciously to live the dream over and over, and gradually create a new habit of feeling and thereby develop new confidences in meeting that particular fear. If this is done the nightmare will begin to alter. The habit pattern which produced it will be transformed. When that happens Mrs. C.M. will know she is

53

healing a part of herself, and her further work will be more assured and exciting. A sign of success will be that her recurring dream no longer occurs.

As human beings we have learnt to manipulate and be extremely mobile in the physical world. But inwardly, as a species, we are paralysed, stumbling, clumsy creatures. We are virtually prisoners of our own thoughts and fears. Often we hide these from ourselves, as we strut like convicts with a ball and chain around our ankle, playing at freedom. Yet survival seems to depend more certainly upon the ability to direct and be at peace with ourselves than ever it does on making a better car, reaching the stars, or building more deadly weapons of war. This work on our inner nature is more surely a peace work than an anti bomb march.

The next dream is less directly a nightmare. It is sent by Mrs. J.W. She says, 'I would be grateful if you could help my son. He only recently told me his problem as I have pulled his leg after hearing him call out in his sleep. He is eighteen and his father died when he was twelve. He dreams that a heavy weight of bricks is being piled on his back and he cannot move.'

If all the questions are applied to this dream, an idea can be gained by using the whole spectrum of approaches to the dream outlined so far.

1. *Am I active or passive in my dream?*
   The dreamer is passive to the point of not being able to move.
2. *What am I feeling in my dream?*
   The dreamer is feeling weighed down, immobilised and perhaps incapable.
3. *How can I alter the dream to find greater satisfaction?*
   One possible way is to imagine reaching behind and taking the bricks off his back and even building something with them. Using the symbols, he would thus take his own emotional energy by which he felt depressed, and start using it creatively.
4. *Is there something I need to practice?*
   The indication here is to practice moving from the passive, immobilised feeling situation to one in which he frees himself by being active and creative.
5. *Am I meeting the things I am afraid of in my dream?*
   There is a 'life is getting on top of me' feeling in this dream. So there is the possibility the dreamer fears he is incapable in life,

or does not have the qualities to meet everyday life. Whatever the fear is, he needs to put into words what the actual feeling is. Only then can he honestly say, either, 'That's right, I am absolutely helpless in my present life situation. I have no way of dealing with it.' Or, 'No, I only feel helpless, and when I look honestly at the situation I can see there are things I can do.'

If the answer is the 'or' one, then he can get on and do it if he wishes. If he doesn't want to, at least he can see non activity is his choice.

If the answer is the 'either' one, then the admittance of his own helplessness opens up the option of asking someone else for help. Again, non activity would be his own choosing.

Certainly the idea that 'bricks', or, in fact any other form of restriction in a dream, can actually imprison one. In a dream one can pass through walls, do magic simply by thinking about it, levitate, withstand explosions – anything. In dreams we are pure consciousness. Our potential is infinite. It is restricted only by our own poverty of conception. We are prisoners only of our own emotions and fears. We are trapped in one environment only if we cannot envisage another.

The following dream is an example of a nightmare which was transformed into a problem solving dream. The dreamer, A.T., had been working on his dreams in the way described, and had begun to change the negative introversions.

'I had been accused of something by an inspector. Two toughs held me and he was going to drill my teeth out with a hand drill and beat me up. I was terrified but fought back, kicking one on them in the testicles, but I could not break away.

'Then I feigned madness and regression to childhood to avoid further torture. Seeing this one of them led me away to be shot. I knocked him out, took his gun, thought of killing him but did not.

'Being free I wondered what to do. Whether to go away, or return with the gun. Suddenly I thought I would go back and hand myself over again. As soon as this was decided I saw through the whole set up. The thugs thought they were part of a huge crime organisation, worldwide. But in fact their leader had no higher authority than himself. So I went back and gave them the gun. They rushed me but I made no effort to struggle. This shocked them far more deeply than any attempt to escape. I then explained that I was no longer afraid,

55

because I saw how petty and futile they were. This literally shattered them and the dream ended.'

What is shown here is that A.T. was no longer afraid of fear. When we recognise it simply as another of our useful feeling reactions, we are no longer imprisoned and tortured by it. As A.T. introverted this new attitude, his dream world changed. He had worked particularly with questions two, three, five and six to bring about this change in himself. In his waking life he found himself capable of a much wider range of contacts with people because of the new attitude shown in his dream.

It is also worth pointing out that A.T. did not 'run away into waking' while feeling terrified, but stayed in the dream and fought back. By doing this, and by recognising his dream tormentors as without influence, he solved his problem while asleep. This came about because, even though he was dreaming, as he says, 'I was no longer afraid.'

The next dream, and the comments by the dreamer, are quoted at length because of the great interest. The dreamer, Paul, had worked intensely on his dreams prior to this one and had developed the ability to allow a wide range of feelings from within. He had found a great deal of mobility in himself before this dream. What Paul's dream and comments begin to show is how, by listening to the negatives in the dream, a great deal of personal change and understanding can be arrived at.

'I was looking for a particular underground station which I felt I had been to before – in other dreams. I came across a branch line to it above ground. The tracks had been removed and the underground passage blocked with earth. I walked and arrived at a large boggy lake. It was on a site where much digging or building excavation had taken place. Water had filled the diggings. In the lake were prehistoric animals. I felt it was like a 'Lost World', where these creatures still lived on. One rose from the water and I felt afraid. I hurried away but the creature followed me. I ran, and the creature spoke in a human voice, but I don't know what it said.

'I worked on the dream by imagining myself as the creature, to see if I could find what feelings in myself I was running away from. As I did so I began to experience myself as the mystery of life which has become a beast, an ape/man. I felt the extraordinary agony and wonder of growing from being an animal, as we are when we are a baby, to becoming a human. I understood then, in a flash, the creatures in the swamp. I *am* life, ancient, prehistoric life, meeting the demands of today's human world, the social scene, and the need to make conscious decisions. It is this ancient self, these basic life processes or drives in me, which my work on dreams, my digging into self, has uncovered, yet I have been running away from them – from me!

'I understood as I allowed these feelings, that the beast in me has a healthy fear of much that goes on in today's world. In the dream I run in fear, and I realised now that fear is a guardian which protected ancient beast from uncountable dangers for millions of years. There were so many real dangers which fear gave us the strength to run from. The healthy beast still feels fear when it looks out of the eyes of modern man. Often the beast in us is crushed or repressed because people are frightened of fear, so drown it with alcohol, drugs, or nicotine. But it should never be crushed like that. Like any wild animal, or a new-born foal in a field near a railway, at first it is frightened. But if it feels its fear freely, it gradually gets used to the train. If the fear is never felt, the feeling part of us is never given the chance to grow.

'Also I saw that if we cannot allow this animal part of ourself to grow into everyday life with us, we actually have no contact with some of the most important instinctive urges and emotions, such as a mother feeling instinctive tenderness and desire to breast feed her baby. If she had repressed her animal she would care for her baby from being shown how to do it rather than from powerful inner feelings. Also, she would not understand intuitively the body signals and needs of this tiny animal form which is her baby. She would not be able to guide it to becoming a full, whole, human being, because she had not achieved that herself.

'In exploring the feelings of the dinosaur I felt anger. It connected with feelings of anger I had towards the children of my wife from her first marriage. I realised I was angry deep inside because I was a beast/man, originally a wild animal before socialisation, who had not only been broken in, as it were, by society, but I was now disciplining my own urges toward going to work everyday, to a job that did not interest me – the deep me. I had restrained my desire for rest and pleasure to be able to do that. I felt enormous resentment I was doing this while the children were never disciplined by their

57

mother, or gave from themselves a token of help as I worked to provide for them and build a home (we were renovating a house to live in, and the teenage children gave no help).

'Then I felt the anger as tremendous, like a great creature which has burst out of the bonds restraining it. I felt I had the strength to tear the children apart with my bare hands if I wanted to. Once released, however, the feelings softened into wanting to build an area of protection for the children, but I did want some help from them.

'I felt the job in hand, arising from my inner life through the dream, was to allow this animal me to be released and find orientation in the present world. I could feel from the anger, that much of my enthusiasm to work, be a caring parent, and a useful social being, was bound up with the animal me. If it wasn't dealt with wisely it could rebel into destructive anger, anti social criminal acts, and hate toward social pressure. If it could be allowed to find its orientation in the present though, it could go on to a further level of growth. We need to be gradually introduced as children to social training. If we lose this animal, I feel we lose something very precious. The deep streaming pleasure of loving, of parenthood, of work, and of intuitive insight into others via their body signals is missing. We have been brought up to believe that the animal man is an uncouth brute. Nothing is further from the truth. The animal I am beginning to discover within myself is only violent when made ill by ridiculous social pressures. In its acceptance it is a deeply sensitive, creative and loving part of us. It has the most intense social sense I have ever met. It is not uncaring, but super caring. It feels society is to do with caring for each other, and particularly children. I wish everyone could share this discovery with me.'

Paul's fearful dream was not about a shocking past experience, but about how he related to himself today. He had been brought up to believe that good behaviour was something which you had to impress upon yourself from outside. In a culture which has a long history of believing humans are innately sinful and brutish, it is no wonder Paul had repressed his animal. Dreams are here shown to be a vital link between our evolving conscious self, and our long evolutionary history embodied in our biological functions.

So many people in our present society in the West feel divorced from any experience of flowing and natural social morals, parental caring, and love, that it has become a disease. We are so unaware of being a part of a natural order, we suffer a sense of life's pointlessness, of its meaninglessness. In our file of dreams, the number showing a bad relationship with the animal self is extraordinarily high.

Paul's further discoveries in this area of his work on himself are also important in discovering a way in which we can usefully relate to the fears in our dream and waking life.

He says, 'While I worked on the dream of the dinosaur I became aware of my animal anxiety. Later, because of the dream work, I was able to recognise those feelings and their source when they emerged into my everyday life. One of the most striking examples of this is as follows.

'I had been going through the terrible conflict of separation from my first wife and children; and had for six months lived with my new wife in a country cottage. Because of the misery of being distant from my children, plus the guilt and conflict over the divorce, the cottage was not a happy place for me, and we moved to a house nearer to my children.

'Some months later my new wife and I drove over to the cottage to collect a beehive we had left there. On the way I developed grinding pains in my abdomen, which I recognised as intense anxiety. Because of the work on the dream I was able to take an objective view of this fear instead of being devastated as I usually was. I thought of it as an actual animal, with all its instinctive fears and sensitivity. So I took time, there in the car, to give attention to the pain and subtle feelings arising with it. I put into words what I felt.

'What happened then really amazed me. I understood that my dinosaur, or animal self can be conditioned just like Pavlov's dogs. The feelings showed me that because the cottage had been a place of such emotional pain, the animal in me couldn't help associate pain and place together. If a horse or a dog has been badly hurt in a place or building, it will struggle madly if we try to take it there again. Yet here I was, taking my body back to a place it had been tortured in. No wonder it was complaining in the only way it could communicate with me.

'Then, clearly realising what the problem was, I literally talked to myself like talking to a frightened horse. I said something like . . . "Steady . . . Steady! I didn't realise you were so frightened. I see

59

now how much that place hurt you, but I'm not taking you back to that sort of hurt. We are only visiting for a short time, then going home again near the children. So it's only memories now, and we can manage to meet those."

'As I said those things the fear and pain melted away. Within a minute it had gone, and the rest of the journey was accomplished without difficulty.'

What can be learnt from Paul's experience is how important and useful it is to listen to or face what we are afraid of in our dream. Paul did not 'grin and bear it' for the sake of facing fear or being brave. He met and experienced what he feared, in order to arrive at insight which enabled him not only to understand much of his everyday actions and anxieties, which were previously troublesome and confused, but also to discover a very richly endowed part of himself and change his life. He did this by

a) Using question five and deciding to meet what he feared in his dream.

b) Imagining himself as the dinosaur and allowing his feelings to arise freely in association with the image. In this way he experienced an aspect of himself which he had previously been avoiding. The dream itself shows it talking to him, but him running away.

c) He put his feelings into words and thus defined a part of himself which had never integrated with his thinking, verbal self before. His thinking faculty now had tools with which to meet and help the non-verbal area of instinctive reaction. In fact the dream, and Paul's work, shows how much of our nature remains unconscious; our body processes for instance. A dream is a link between our aware sense of identity, and our natural functions. The two can, through the dream, meet and relate.

Chapter Five

Creating a Happier You

DREAMS describe the human situation very graphically. In our dreams we are the main character around whom the people, animals, events and experiences of our dreams revolve. If we hold the view that all these parts of our dreams are parts of ourself, then the various experiences and people we meet in our dreams are contacts with the diverse aspects of our own nature.

If we look at a few dreams this will become obvious.

'I watched a small boy climb all over a bull. It had been chained too long without attention, and tore away to seek the cows. The gates were closed but the bull smashed through the enclosing fence. I had sat on the fence, but now looked for somewhere safe. Meanwhile the bull charged to the first cow to mount it, but so terrible was its energy and emotion they could not express as sex. It smashed the cow aside like the fence, and rushed toward the next cow.'

This dream is obviously about long witheld sexual desire, so is concerned with the man's sexual drive. The bull is an objectification of his own sexuality.

The next dream is from a woman, Mrs. P.P., and shows her meeting her feeling and thoughts about religion.

'The sky opened just enough to let Our Lord through. I felt calm, thinking this must be the end of the world. The Bible says Our Lord will appear in the sky, and those not already dead will die of fright. He floated down by the dining room window. I thought, "I'm still alive!" Two nuns followed him dressed in white. One said to the other, "She gave me the sack!" I thought to myself, "This certainly was not in the Bible and it can't be the end of the world." '

The following dream is not only a confrontation with death, but also looks at what the dreamer, Mrs. J.M., most wishes to do with her life before she dies.

'I dream I have a weak heart which may be fatal. The doctor administers a tablet which on the day it is taken will cause me to painlessly "go to sleep". I and an elderly lady each take a tablet. She dies very quickly and disappears. I am completely calm and accepting my fate, but suddenly realise I must leave notes for my parents and children. I must let them know how much I love them before my time runs out. My husband, busily running our shop, says he hasn't got time to find me pencil and paper.'

Each of the characters in the dream is an objectification of a part of the woman's nature. The old woman is most likely her own ageing process, her own feelings about growing old. The husband is her business, working attitudes, which may have been the cause for her not showing as much love to her family as she would have wished. The doctor is usually a healing or helpful attitude, information, or the self regulatory forces in the body. If Mrs. P.P. explored the feelings underlying each of these figures, she would experience them directly as her own feelings, attitudes or internal processes.

The next dream is a clear look at the love between a man and a woman. It also shows how the dream process can sum up a situation and solve its problems, Often these are ways we may not consciously like.

'For the last year I have had an affair with a married man. In my dream I visit his home and float up to the front door. I can see him in the hall. One of his sons is shouting down the stairs and he is answering back. He seems agitated and harrassed. My man sees me, comes out, and indicates he cannot leave his family and home for me.

'Sadly I turn to go, and see a scraggy Irish Wolfhound, which has come out of the back door. I look into its brown eyes and see love and devotion, which warms me. As I walk away the dog stays close. I know I have a devoted friend who will never leave me.'

Lastly, here is a 'body' dream, where the dream examines what is occurring in the dreamer's lungs.

'I was in hospital. Doctors and nurses were about. I was led to realise my lungs were filling up with mucus and phlegm. The doctor said to me it wouldn't affect me in the short term, but if I kept on smoking I would feel the effects badly in later life. The dream was so vivid I decided there and then to give up smoking.'

In this particular dream the person and their body are one and the same, but frequently people examine their body in dreams by seeing it as the body of someone else. In that way, dreams portray our personality, our sense of identity, as existing amidst and having to find a relationship with many different forces or influences. If, for instance, a person is on a small sailing vessel, crossing the Atlantic alone, it is obvious that unless they find a way of coming to terms with, and working with the craft and the elements, they will not survive. If they set themselves in foolish conflict with their environment, they have little hope of dealing with the incredible forces surrounding them. Yet with courage and a willingness to learn, humans have survived and even exulted in the most terrible forces of nature.

The unconscious mind, with its ability to summarise a mass of experience, barely tangible internal biological processes and gathered information, presents a picture of human identity as being in a similar situation as the lone sailor. Identity, amidst the forces of the body, social pressure, the physical environment, is as frail as the tiny craft crossing the Atlantic. If it is in conflict with these forces, identity can be lashed by the sex drive, battered by social demands and inundated by waves of emotions, such as a sense of failure, inadequacy and violent hatred. Undirected and disordered memories can threaten to dismember the frail craft of identity in madness.

Let us be honest. Each of us is a lone sailor crossing his own personal Atlantic of experience. Many fail to survive. Even in some of the most economically sound countries in the world, suicide rates are high, mental illness claims many, and thousands retreat into alcoholic somnambulance, emotional deadness, or the escape into non-involvement with life.

Yet the very forces which crush some carry others swiftly forward into a creative life. This dream, from a sixty-four year old lady, who never married, shows something of the first situation.

'I am in the dining room of our old London house holding my cat. A conservatory opens off this room through double doors. There is a black and white cat in the conservatory, but I said to Nan, my cat,

"It's quite safe, the doors are locked." Then I realise the conservatory is full of ferocious looking monkeys. One large grey one started opening the doors. I ran holding Nan, and woke in panic.'

The dreamer has locked herself away in the attitudes and feelings of her past – the old house. She holds onto her own love and sexuality, her cat, and will not let it meet/mate with those it has a natural attraction to. The monkeys are her own living biological energies she is frightened of, so runs to wakefulness in panic.

Here is a dream in which the man is learning to relate to the elemental forces of his being in quite a different way.

'I was out of the village near the edge of a cliff. There did not seem to be anything such as sea or landscape beyond the cliff. I could not see this, only had the impression of a vast emptiness. But a strong wind blew, and curving my arms backwards the wind lifted me like a kite. An old man and boy watched me from below as I flew. I could manouvre the uplift by moving my arms. But sometimes the wind was so strong I could not go where I wanted.'

This reminds us of the sea and the sailor again. The dreamer is in a learning relationship with the elemental forces within and around him. By altering himself in relationship to them – arm movements – he can bring about a change in the way they relate to him. This is fundamental to the way we connect with the outer forces of nature, and how we relate to our own internal nature and its vastness.

The original boats humans used were probably floating logs. These went wherever current, wind and tide took them. But soon paddles, rudders and primitive sails were added. Still the forces of wind, tide and current existed, but now one energy, the wind, can be more fully utilised to move against another energy, the current. Today's sailing craft are incredibly ingenious. From a position of being pushed wherever the forces of nature took them, humans have found ways of directing their own course in the vastness of ocean, not by conflict, but by using the energies surrounding them. Similarly, the boundary of our sky had been breached, and our exploration of the cosmos begun.

Primitive human beings were certainly almost entirely moved by instinct. As a species we have gradually developed our ability to decide which of the energies of our being we will sail by. Will it be fear, sexual impulse, ambition, love, which moves us into action? But as individuals there are many boundaries we have not yet broached, many tides we have not used and many unexplored areas of self.

In our dreams everything is alive and everything is intelligent, because every part of the dream, even empty space, is created out of our own living process. As such it is deeply feeling because our own being is sensitive and capable of response. Intelligent because it is made of our own mind stuff and our own spontaneous creativity. Life itself is intelligent. Our intelligence arises out of the co-operative and harmonious functioning of the life processes of our being. Thus every tree, every object, every animal and person in our dream is an expression of livingness.

Does it then sound far fetched to say that we exist in our dreams within a community of living, feeling, intelligent beings? And our happiness depends upon whether or not we live in conflict or harmony with this community? Whether we murder or run from, whether we create with, make love to, learn the wisdom of and satisfy ourself with them?

For instance, consider the difference in these two dreams.

'I dream I am given a small animal to look after. I then completely forget it, go away, and when I return the animal is either dead or dried up, or has been got at by another animal and is dying. I wake up from this dream feeling dreadful.'

The second dream is, 'I was sitting on a bank between two fields. One field was two thirds bigger than the other. Someone was sitting with me. I couldn't see who it was, but there was a loving feeling between us. Suddenly a little red fox appeared in front of us, desperation in its eyes, tongue hanging out, exhausted. The person with me lifted it over the bank into the smaller field where it ran off happily.'

The second dream is problem solving. The dreamer does not wake with a dreadful feeling. There is mutual respect between the three living beings in the dream, an actual change being brought about to aid one of the beings. This leads to mutual satisfaction. In the first dream no such mutual caring occurred, and, as a result, the dreamer experiences disturbed feelings.

Dreams show our nature as many sided. Their themes suggest human identity exists within this variety of influences, and relates to them as living, feeling, intelligent beings, capable of response. If we repress and torture our sexual drive, for instance, it responds very powerfully. This can be rephrased, and we can say instead – if I

65

repress and torture my sexual feelings, I notice changes in myself. Whichever way we explain it, however, the experience is similar, the inability to relate warmly to others sexually, with possible irritability and rage. And we are talking here in the language of dreams, the language which, in the 'bull' dream quoted earlier in this chapter, shows an outrageous sexual response to being chained. Dreams, through analysis by comparison – that is comparing the two animal dreams above – show happiness being achieved by mutual respect and the giving of aid, and by not rejecting or actively harming parts of our nature.

Without giving dream examples for each of the following statements, my experience is that important life enhancing factors are:

1. Giving attention or awareness to the community of factors that is ones being.
2. Actively attending to any of the needs of this community as they become evident through given awareness, e.g. a health problem may be shown which needs more physical exercise, or less stressful striving. Or feelings of aggression may be shown to be damaging parts of the body, or destroying creativity.
3. An attempt to define a direction in our work and social life, which allows the greatest involvement from one's inner community. Then positive attempts to create this in waking and sleeping. This avoids inner conflicts which waste energy and are non-productive of satisfaction, and are detrimental to health.
4. Self-acceptance and forgiveness. Again and again, dreams dramatise the enormous life changes brought by these. The dream in the first chapter, in which the woman forgave her father, is an example. Acceptance or admittance of our weakness and fears as well as abilities and strengths, is not a retreat from life or a running into submission. It is actually one of the most courageous things we can do. It forms the basis for real honest assessment, from which effective planning and action can grow. It also frees us from the restraints imposed by hiding who we really are. Even the non-admittance of our strengths is a cop out, because by denying them we may avoid their use in a world which needs them. We may thus be avoiding fear of responsibility. Similarly, forgiveness frees us from the crush-

ing guilt and self-condemnation we shackle ourselves with. For even if it is someone else we feel is guilty of a crime against us, we unfortunately judge ourselves by the same standards we impose on others.

5. We are not at peace with ourself until we find a relationship with the world about us – its animals, its people, its religions, politics, science, and art – which satisfies us. It may be our own satisfaction is that of agitator. But our action needs to flow out of what is described in No. 2.

6. The ability to respond and bring about responses from the outer and inner world. If we cannot do this we feel trapped pawns in a game played by nature and other people. Despite the argument of behaviourists such as Skinner that we simply react to stimuli and can be manipulated, present research and dream themes show that as humans, we can grow toward greater self responsibility, and have a capacity to learn to direct our own being, and sail our own craft on a chosen voyage.

7. To partake in the adventure of life.

Without some challenge, without boundaries we have not yet crossed, life is not only boring, it actually produces an illness of our soul such as we see in affluent societies that have everything except a place to go and a reason for going there.

What is left after total commodity availability, easy sexual exploration and movement? Dreams show whole areas of our being, new faculties, yet untouched. They show human identity existing amidst eternity, the wilderness spoken of in the Bible. There is no beginning, no end, no path in that wilderness. Can human beings, or have some already, broken through the barriers of mind and body imposed by sleep and death? Can humans uncover resources in themselves to meet the needs of change in the world today?

Here is a challenge which faces us now. Can we break through the limitations of our own attitudes, habits, and ready formed ideas to create a world we want and can live in? For many of us, the adventure starts here, with our own mind and body, and its potential.

STEP FIVE
This step is to work at removing areas of conflict, irritation and non-creativity rather than dealing with trauma and fear. The steps already given are sufficient to deal with most dreams, but these

further steps add depth, precision and greater craftmanship to one's dream work. So the next question is:

7. *Is Conflict or Co-operation Shown in the Dream?*

In some ways this is a difficult question because a certain amount of conflict is inevitable and healthy in life. Out of its stress new ideas and progressive changes occur. Nevertheless, conflict often robs us of our ability to be decisive and enthusiastic.

When we can find a good degree of agreement between the various parts of our nature, we have a lot more energy and can usually achieve more in whatever direction we are going. Indecision is the child of conflict, and the thief of our achievement.

Here is a dream about a fairly gentle but important area of conflict.

'I am an 18 year old Dutch girl living in England as an au pair.

I dreamt my boyfriend and I were in a peace demonstration. My ex-boyfriend was there too. On a bookstall I saw books he had written. He then took me to his house where he showed me a shelf filled with books written by him. Unexpectedly he asked me if I wanted to go back to him. I was still looking for an answer when I woke up.'

M.A., who sent the dream, has a conflict over which type of boyfriend she wants, or perhaps which direction in life she wishes to go. If she answered question seven she might say she has a conflict over who to co-operate with. She has feelings for both boyfriends, so which set of feelings, or what part of herself shall she allow to dominate, or shall she co-operate with? The question on her mind might be — in which direction will I find the greatest satisfaction?

Using the already listed questions, M.A. could explore each direction in imagination to see where or with whom she felt most satisfied.

To deal with conflicts it is an enormous help to be able to see clearly what the conflict is about. Strangely enough, even very powerful internal discord may be raging without our being able to define what is making us ill at ease. This is why dreams are so helpful. In the dream the internal feelings are embodied as people and objects, and through the drama enacted we can begin to understand the conflict. M.A.'s dream defines the conflict as occurring over choice between two men, or two ways of life. Knowing this, she can take time to consider what she does want. Even if she cannot immediately decide, her efforts will stimulate her dream process to further explore the subject.

Some dreams dealing with conflict need to be dealt with in a similar way to nightmares. This dream of Mrs. D.W. is an example of such. She says:

'I am eating a bowl of creamy porridge and I notice thin strands floating in the milk. As I put the spoon into the porridge I see a black lump that keeps bobbing to the surface. I fish this out and am horrified to see a big black cockroach spreadeagled on the spoon, its legs clawing and scraping against the metal. I am filled with nausea and crying, fling the creature onto the tiled kitchen floor. I shout for my husband to do something and see there are now two of them copulating. I start retching and wake up.'

Mrs. D.W. is sick of sex. The cockroach and the copulating tell her what her aversion and conflict is. She can deal with this by imagining herself in the dream and attempting to find a satisfying solution instead of escaping into waking. It might be that she steps on and crushes the cockroaches. That might satisfy her, and maybe that's what she needs. Instead of being passive in the sense of calling for someone else to solve her problem, she needs to affirm her own feelings by acting on them herself. The importance of Question 7 is, however, brought out here because crushing the cockroaches still leaves her in conflict with what is a part of her nature – sex.

In their book, *Self Watching*, Drs Hodgson and Miller describe a process of desensitisation which is helpful here. The technique requires the person either to gradually get closer to the object, such as a lift which frightens them; or witness or imagine slowly intensifying scenes of the thing such as sex, which they are anxious about.

With dreams showing conflict, this technique can be used by imagining oneself in the dream and then slowly approaching the object or person which caused repulsion, etc. There need be no hurry, but the aim is to approach and eventually imagine oneself *as* the object. So Mrs. D.W. needs to approach and become the cockroach.

Because the dream image is an objectification of an actual living urge or emotion within ourselves, to become the object is to contact and integrate the part of ourself it expresses.

Here is a dream worked on in this way, described by Tom:

'In my dream I am hiding from a large leopard. It is standing in an

69

open doorway growling and menacing passers by. I have the door pulled back so I am sandwiched between it and the wall. I'm scared!

'On thinking about the dream, I see that the cat and I aren't getting on well. I wonder what part of me the cat is, and imagine walking toward it. It immediately leaps out at me and swallows me. I am now the cat, feeling what it feels, and I am angry – spitting mad. As I allow myself to feel the anger I remembered how an older cousin used to tease me, then hold me at arms length while I tried to hit and kick him. I never did get satisfaction, and as I feel the anger in me, I realise I have hidden my real feelings from people for years. That was why I stood behind the door. Contacting the cat has put me in touch with my real feelings again.'

Tom had unconsciously decided as a child that he would not express his anger or honest feelings because adults could manipulate him. This decision had interiorised so that even in his dreams he couldn't easily express anger. Without such interiorised restraints, which come in the form of fear, guilt or decision, the dream process would usually resolve conflicts and tensions while we sleep. When we begin to remove such restraints by working on our dreams to express what we feel and find satisfaction in, our dream process is gradually helped to function more efficiently again. As this occurs we have dreams in which we solve our own problems. Below is an interesting example of this, sent to us by Maria.

'I'm a nurse involved with a married doctor. He is a keen sportsman, has two daughters, dearly wants a son, but his wife wants no more children.

'I dreamt I was in the labour ward, and was helping him deliver his wife's third child. I was in agony feeling I should be giving him a son, but kept on smiling encouragement.

'It was a boy. I felt my heart was breaking. Suddenly our local "tough guy" was with me. He led me away saying he knew how much it hurt. We lay on a bed together. He said "You can't do everything. You love him, he loves you, but his wife must give him a son." I felt an enormous peace descend on me.'

The conflict here is whether Maria can allow her love to continue for this man, and at the same time allow him to have a life of his own quite distinct from her. Could she love him without having his child?

She resolves this conflict by living without grasping or manipulating. A painful process of growth for Maria, but the dream, looking at the hard realities of life – the tough guy – found a direction which gave peace.

My experience of dream work shows that Maria's problem, even though solved in her dream, will not necessarily be solved immediately in waking life. Dreams are a bit like the genetic patterning held in the cells of a seed. The form only becomes externally real as growth occurs. Sometimes it takes weeks before what is achieved internally in a dream, becomes real in everyday life. Such changes are helped by remembering the dream solution, and practicing it as suggested in Step Three.

This brings us to the next question. While we simply watch our dreams we are still to some extent in a passive role. Dreams do respond to our attention as seen in Roger's series of work dreams, but they will also respond to a direct question.

Whenever there are things you wish to know more about, consult your dreams, just as you would a friend whose wisdom and insight you deeply respected.

8. *Do I Need to Ask for Help?*
This is the first question whereby we seek a response from our dreams about a particular subject. All dreams are in fact a response to what is going on in our life. So asking a question is simply a way of using that process consciously. Thousands of individuals and many groups throughout the world use this technique to help them with their everyday problems, business decisions and creativity. It is called dream incubation. It is very easy to use, and most people can have dreams which are direct comments on what they are seeking to understand. Because the dream process has a readier access not only to our complete memory, our unconscious insights into people and events and our own overall view of ourself, but also to a predictive and ESP ability,[1] such dream responses frequently answer our question in a way we could not manage consciously.

STIMULATING A HELPFUL DREAM
To ellicit this response we need first to define the question we wish to ask. Make it a clear, one-line query. Next, think about it several times during the day. Then, before going to sleep, repeat the question several times. It is helpful to imagine the question in the form of a letter which is being posted to the unconscious dream process.

71

Once posted, one relaxes and awaits the response. Another technique is to imagine phoning the Dream Maker and asking them to give a helpful dream regarding the question.

Some examples of this in action will make it plain. The first example is from a man, Allan, who is in his early thirties and although having begun relationships with women in the past, had pulled back each time because of difficulty in becoming involved emotionally, and fear of responsibility. In January of 1983 Allan met Stella. She was married with a ten year old daughter, but wishing to leave her husband because of his infidelity. Allan had never worked with dreams in this way before. He described what happened as follows:

'Though attracted to her, my conduct was of the nature which respected her marriage. I learnt several months after she returned home that she had also thought a lot of me and would be coming on yet another holiday in the April.

'We talked of our feelings on the first night of her arrival and agreed that whatever developed between us had to be kept on a basis of honesty to ourselves and each other, and that we should endeavour to maintain contact with our feelings.

'On the 27th, some six days after Stella had left for her home, I became fearful of the responsibilities I may have to take on, should a relationship develop, and how restrictive it might be. I was feeling scared! Yet I knew that if I was going to be strong enough to take on a relationship should the situation arise, I had to look at this fear. Tony suggested I asked my dreams for help in understanding how to meet the fear and the relationship.

'I went to bed with one question in mind, "How was I going to resolve this conflict and find the strength which would enable me to enter into a relationship." A restless night followed, tossing and turning whilst images of my childhood home impressed themselves upon my mind. They were grey, inactive stifling and intensified my feelings to run away. This was followed by images full of colour and activity – I saw people I "knew" working and enjoying the things they were doing. I then became involved in a conversation with my dream in which I debated the two situations and how I could, if I wanted, choose between the two. Of course I wanted the richer and more fulfilling life. I awoke feeling that I had not slept and yet feeling strong and confident.

72

'Shortly before noon Stella phoned and said she wanted to move in with her daughter and asked what I felt about it. Having some understanding of her situation at home I said that I felt good and would await her arrival. From our first week together Stella has been like a mirror; reflecting my strengths and fears which has, I feel, helped us both with the problems that a broken marriage brings forth.'

In conversation Allan explained that the images of his parents showed a grey, unchanging, unhappy condition. He was frightened any relationships he had would be like that. The second set of images showed an alternative. The comparison set him free of his fear, because he saw he need not be trapped in a deadly relationship as his parents were, so he felt free to enter the relationship with Stella.

Another person, Michael, working with dream incubation had the difficulty of finding a wife. He is a mathematician, meets mostly men at work, and was beginning to feel there was no woman who was interested in him. His question was, 'Why can't I find a wife?' That night he dreamt he was unsuccessfully looking for something in his office, his car, and then at home. At that point he awoke feeling frustrated and disappointed. On going back to sleep he then dreamt he was singing in a mixed choir, as he had during college days, and he felt wonderful.[1]

On waking he realised the dream was showing that he was looking in all the wrong places. There were few women at work, he couldn't find a woman driving around, and at home he spent his evenings alone reading. He took the dream literally and joined a choir again. There he met a lady who he began to date regularly.

Both these incubated dreams deal with relationships, but of course one can incubate a dream on any subject that is important to you.

Gayle Delaney reports a woman designer who regularly seeks and receives dream ideas for cover designs for the news magazine she works for. The members of many dream groups which meet regularly, seek answers to business, family or health problems from their dreams as a matter of course. My own experience of dream incubation has been deeply satisfying in the area of research into the dream process itself.

An important question many people face concerns what direction to take in life. Mrs. M.G. describes a dream which helped her in that situation. She says:

'I have been trying to decide whether to remain in a safe but boring job for several more years until I retire, or sell my house and take a course of study I have always wanted to do.

'My dream is, I am walking a path overgrown with nettles and have to walk very carefully. On my left is a low wall with a deep drop going down to smooth grass, on which my dog is running parallel to me. I consider jumping down. It would be much easier to walk on the grass, but I am afraid of the height. I continue on my path, and suddenly the nettles disappear. Ahead the wall has turned to face me, but there is a gate in it and my dog is waiting on the other side.'

The dream shows Mrs. M.G. experiencing tension and anxiety about her present way of life, as shown by the nettles. Yet to change her life to one which her instincts, the dog, enjoy, and which would allow more growth – the grass – is too much of a threat – the drop. But the dream goes on to show that if she continues her present way of life for a little longer, her circumstances and attitudes will alter, to allow an easier change.

Finding a happier relationship with the aspects of ourself, as shown in the dream above, may take time. We need to work on each dream as it arises. Bit by bit our inner conflicts are in that way reduced, and our enthusiasm and energy for life enhanced. When that occurs it becomes more imperative to find a relationship with other people and with the world, that is satisfying to our whole nature. Looking via dreams, at the way each individual relates to life and anxiety, there seems to me to be a fundamental need for giving and receiving. I do not believe that our nature is deeply satisfied if in some way we are not a productive part of the world. If we are merely a receiver, a taker, and not a giver, nature itself does not flow out to us, part of us does not find peace.

On the other hand, I do not find in dreams any narrowness about what or how we need to give. In fact I find the suggestion in dreams that the ways we can give and receive are infinite. Basically, giving means that we fulfill some function, in the body of humanity or nature, that contributes toward the whole in some way. Dreams are very biological, and often see individuals as cells in a body, with the same relationship to the whole as our cells have in our body. In other words, each cell needs to be equally nourished and cared for, and there is a great variety of roles. The Bible sums it up in saying,

'Whatever you do to the least of one of these, you do to me.' It doesn't matter if we entertain, teach, heal, plan, feed, re-produce, care for, protect, define useful ideas, manufacture, or act as a mental or spiritual function in the vast body.

In whatever depth we have given of ourself, that is how we receive in the sense of satisfaction and happiness. But dreams do not suggest rigid morality, or masochism as means to happiness.

DREAMS AND WORK

There is again and again, a statment in people's dreams that each of us, no matter who we are, can have a place within this body of life. Each of us can have a work to do, a pleasure in that work, and sustenance arising from it. This is not a mystical promise, it is straightforward common sense and practical psychology. If we do something purely for ourselves which few if any others can share or benefit from, then we are the only ones who will benefit. But if we can find some activity which involves others in a way that helps them, gives them healthy pleasure, or fulfills their needs, many will share and will reward us. In that way we become an actual function, or part of an organ, within the body of humanity. For instance, doctors are part of the healing function in the body; comedians are the function of tension release and pleasure givers; scholars are brain cells; inventors a part of the evolutionary process of change; mothers the womb; fathers the provider; cooks the feeder, etc.

The difficulty in our present culture is that we are not helped as children to listen to our dreams, which put us in contact with the collective consciousness of the world, and enable us to define our relationship with it. So we are frequently moved by commercial, expedient, social pressures, to work, or be out of work, which only partly satisfies us. No matter what age we are though, from our contact with that wider consciousness in dreams each of us can discover an activity which will satisfy us and provide our needs. That wider awareness, symbolised by Christ makes us the promise 'In my fathers house are many mansions. I go to prepare a place for you.'

Jung has pointed out that even very small children have a sense of what they wish to work at in life. He says adults experience this as the earliest memory they have of their childhood. For instance my own earliest natural memory is of when, as a three year old I rode my pedal car along the street in which I lived, and watched a drain cleaner at work. With ladels and rods he dredged out the muck from the drain. Up with it came coins and other treasures. My excitement was so intense the memory stayed with me for a lifetime. And I remember in those moments knowing drain cleaning would be my work when I was adult. My driving fascination was in what I might find down the drain. What treasure, what lost things of value? In fact that fascination has led me to dredge into the realm of the unconscious, and help people clear inner blockages. What drives me on is the treasures I discover. This for me is continually satisfying and rewarding.

If you wish to find your own work within the body of life, you need to begin a program of dream incubation with that question in mind. This may take time to completely materialise, but is perhaps one of the most important things we can do in regard to personal happiness and reward. The reason it may take time with some people is that sometimes our abilities are latent in us, like the tulip flower is in the bulb. So we need to grow and flourish before the flowering can occur. If pains and problems in our life have held back that growth, then ones dream work releases it, and the flowering will follow. I will let Chris P. tell his own story of how this worked for him.

'My whole work history is of having a job that I worked at quite hard, but it was purely a means of earning money and supporting my children. That seemed to me what most people did and I didn't question it. I accepted work was like that, and only a few lucky people found a job which was a means of expressing their deepest ambitions or interests. My own love was writing about people. I did this too of course, in my spare time after work, but I could never support my children on what I earned.

'It was made worse because my wife and I moved to a small rural village where there wasn't much work anyway. So for nine years I worked in maintenance and decorating. At times my mind was so split because of my disinterest in the work, my employer would tell me what work was needing to be done, and ten minutes later I couldn't remember what had been said. I began at that time to think I was stupid or only fit for menial tasks. Yet really, my mind was so bursting with thoughts about the work I really loved, and with feelings of frustration, that I hardly lived in the world of painting.

'It got so bad two years ago I began to look to my dreams for help. I had already looked outwardly, but with millions of people out of work, most jobs had forty or so people applying for them. Also, I didn't want to move away from my children to work, as I was no longer married to my first wife.

'One of the first dreams in the series about work was that a tramp came to my house carrying a bible, and it had my name and address in it. In the dream I felt very sceptical about this, and felt my address couldn't be in there because I was uncertain about my value as a person, and the work I did. Exploring the feelings in the dream, however, I really cried because the feeling I experienced in connection with the Bible was of being loved by God or life, and yet I had been uncertain of that love. Although I'm not a church goer I cried when I came across those feelings in the dream.

'The next dream was that Christ came to me and simply said, "Leave your nets."

'To me this clearly meant leaving the work I was doing, but that seemed crazy. How would I support my children? How would I find another job?

'Maybe it makes it clearer to understand what happened next if I explain that the state of the world troubled me deeply. Yet the more I considered what I, with my limitations and my strengths, could do to help create a better world, the more enormous the problem seemed. Nevertheless, I wanted whatever work I did to be a constructive act in making a better world. So when I worked on this dream and opened to the feelings of Christ in me, I was overwhelmed by a sense of touching something which was the essence of all human efforts to create a sane world. I felt I was in touch with something (I say something rather than somebody because it seemed to be bigger than any person I could conceive of) which knew the problems of the world, and how we could each play a part in healing it. It seemed to me Christ stood before me, and it was a privilege just to be in that presence. So I began to wind up my work connections. I had to find out whether this was real or a happy fantasy, and if I never took risks I would never know. But I found it impossible to remain confident or clear, and got depressed at what I considered was my future.

'Then I had a dream, the one you used in the newspaper. In it I was taking part in a bicycle rally. Each participant started from where they lived. As I lived at the foot of a huge hill, I spent most of the day riding up it. It took me till past midday to get to the top, where I rested. Then I cycled on and I knew, because the area was flatter, that I would cover much more ground in the afternoon and evening than I ever did in the morning.

'The dream really encouraged me because I saw it was saying that the morning or first part of my life had been an uphill struggle, but the rest of my life would be easier.

'Just after that I collected my ex-wife from a station fifty miles away with my daughter to give them a lift home. During the ride they spoke of people they had met on their holiday, what great jobs they had, and how much they got paid. They were idly talking, but I was so strung up about work, and how useless and unproductive I felt, the remarks deeply upset me. I had now cut off most of my previous work, and had nothing.

'That evening, remembering the contact with Christ, and the feelings of touching a presence that encompassed everybody, I sat down with my wife and defined just what I wanted to ask in regard to work.

1. I would like not to move away from my children.
2. I would like the work to make use of my abilities, be enjoyable to me, and be related to creating a better world.
3. I needed a certain amount of public recognition for what I did, as I had noticed my enthusiasm waned if there was no support.
4. I needed to earn enough from my work to care for my children and have a reasonable standard of living.

That night I prayed to the encompassing presence and put forward my request. Unbeknown to me, my wife did the same.

'The next morning I was painting the outside of my house – I was out of work – and the phone rang. It was an editor who contacted me from something I had written ten years before. He asked me to attend an interview in regard to regular work writing about my own specialised area. I went to the interview and was offered the job. It had every one of the things I looked for, and to me seemed like a miracle. It still does.'

Chris's description gives all the information we need in seeking satisfying work. First of all seeking help from his dreams. Continuing despite difficulties. Attempting to apply what he gathered from his dream responses. He then clarified exactly what he wanted.

This may seem presumptuous, but it seems to me Chris knew himself enough to know he needed to be near his children and receiving some public acclaim. In seeking such inner co-operativeness, it is essential to wish the work to be part of the creative life of human beings, or nature. Chris fulfilled that aspect because of his feelings about the world situation. But it is also essential to state one's own needs.

Lastly, many people find a deep link of action between meditation, prayer and dreams. The dramatic result of this connection is not uncommon. I could quote many other cases, but this short one illustrates dreams and prayer in creative action. Mrs. P. awoke from a frightening dream. All she could remember was that a particular son was in great danger. Her emotions were so shaken by the impact of the dream she kneeled and prayed for her son's safety. The following day a telegram arrived from him. He told her that he had stayed the night in a hotel, and was woken in the early hours by a dream in which he heard her voice and felt her shake him. 'Thank you,' he said. 'The hotel was on fire and I awoke just in time to avoid being engulfed by the flames.'

Chris's dreams and experiences are about a major change in his life. Sometimes our happiness depends upon more subtle changes. Dreams are an ever constant guide here too. Through such dreams as those which follow, the dreamers were able to keep a steady watch on their direction, and steer away from the beginnings of unhappiness or despair. Like a radar scanner our dreams warn of what is looming in our life.

C.S. works in a medical laboratory. She had become unhappy at work and felt it necessary to leave. She dreamt:

'It is the last hour of work. My long hair is hanging in my face making it hard for me to work. I go home and cut my hair short. The next day at work everyone is surprised by my short hair. A nurse comes over and says they need some strands of my hair for a culture they are making. I can't wait for the experimental culture to grow. I am excited to see if it will produce the healing medication.'

The dream reflected C.S.'s decision to quit, it being the last hour at work. It goes on to show it is her dark or negative thoughts – her hair – which is getting in the way of her work enjoyment. If she restyles her way of thinking something healing will grow in her work. C.S. was able to make those changes, and became more useful

79

and appreciated at work, which brought greater satisfaction.[3]

Mrs. L.S. is divorced and works as a nurse, providing for her two young children. She was deeply worried about the children in this situation, and dreamt:

'I am working in a hospital on night duty. My two children appear. I know I must find them somewhere to sleep. I lay them on seats while I go to find them beds. I look for the children's ward but can't find it. I know I have been a long time and panic in case they are missing me. I try to take a short cut, but it's all changed so I go the long way. I pass a military meeting, get caught in crossfire, and shot in the leg. I am now terrified. What will the children be doing? When I do get back they are with night sister, perfectly all right.'

The dream dramatises the degree of distress this mother feels in connection with her children and work. The dream clarifies for her that the children are in fact well cared for. It is she herself who is injured – the leg wound – which means she has lost confidence about being able to support herself. So the dream points out the real direction for her efforts, in sorting out her need for support.

Real peace and happiness in life cannot be experienced while we are internally ill at ease with parts of our own nature. Usually people believe that real guilt and remorse can only be felt if one has acted destructively to other people or to one's children. We also feel deep misery if we have killed our own beauty and love. We feel pain if we have turned from the flowering of life's promise in us; we live with remorse when we have not fostered our own genius.

To remember our dreams is to hear the voices of earnest life in us. To work on our dreams is to place ourself on the side of life's growth and healing, and to find our place within the process of life's body on this earth.

Quite apart from its cosmic connections, dreams help us to be human too.

DREAMS AND OUR FAMILY
One of the happiest benefits of learning from our dreams is the depth of contact and warmth which occurs when we share our dreams with our family or other people. When a husband or wife share dreams, for instance, a deeper degree of understanding develops between them than is usual. Some of this will be described in the next few chapters, but here I particularly want to bring attention to the

communications and ability to help, which can come about when parents listen to the dreams of their children. Without such contact with our family and friends, our personal happiness is certainly less.

Hyone and I have both been married before. We have no children from our present marriage, but Hyone has three girls from her previous marriage and I have four boys and one girl from mine. So between us we have eight children. Hearing their dreams helps understand their fears, the maturing process working in them, and to be a wiser guide in their lives.

My youngest son Quentin told me a dream in which the babies of his pet mouse had opened their eyes and were walking about the cage. He had previously had a dream of pets, and he had remarked that he sometimes felt like a pet, because pets couldn't decide when to go out by themselves, or to make their own choices. We had talked this over and he saw the dream was about his own dependence on his mother, and his urge to start making his own decisions. So the second dream showed the vulnerable baby parts of him beginning to become independent. Seeing this sharpened my awareness of Quentin's need to be supported in his own decision making and independent expeditions. From the time of the dream he began to do more things for himself in the home.

Recently, Hyone's middle daughter, Shawn, told us this dream:
'I am sitting on a piece of driftwood on a beach. The beach is not sandy, but has smooth round pebbles in shades of grey. The driftwood is really beautiful, it is actually a dead branch, with bits of bark worn by the sea. There is a slight hollow, which makes a comfortable, relaxing seat. On the smaller branches hang glistening wet fronds of seaweed. There is no one on the beach and I sit watching the waves, and the sun warms me. Following the shoreline down the beach I see a dog leisurely running in the frills of the waves as they coat the pebbles with a layer of gloss. The dog is male in appearance with a soft shaggy mane of hair. It walks up to me and places a mermaid's purse in my lap. Everything is beautifully calm, and I feel immensely, peacefully happy.'

Shawn is eighteen and had a very difficult period during early teens. The dream, and talking about it with Hyone and myself, produced a visible change in Shawn. She says that, 'Working on the dream left me feeling a lot more satisfied with myself in that area. That is, in regard to relationships. Beforehand I felt very restless

81

inside myself, and now I feel more peaceful. It seemed to me I had made a hash of everything, like leaving school without qualifications, mucking up relationships and not doing well socially. I felt bad, or uneasy about that, but now I feel okay with myself.'

Technically the dream shows Shawn in contact with the major elements of her nature – the sea, sky and the animal. She is accepting her family history and the flow of biological life through her shown by the log and the branch. She is sitting easy concerning her female sexuality, shown by the mermaid purse. And the dog represents her readiness to start a relationship with the natural sex drive in a male partner. Overall the dream shows her in accord with her nature.

A dream gives a family an opportunity to talk about the really important issues in the lives of each of the members. Such talks together are the nourishment from which the inner health and growth of children and adults flourishes. It is a place of meeting where bonds are deepened or refined. It needs no great technical skill, only humanness. The only need is to spend time looking at the feelings and ideas raised by the dream, and offering each other one's own ideas or feelings about it. In the next chapter particular ways of understanding dreams are given which can be used where helpful.

For very young children I think the advice given by Ann Wiseman is excellent. Ann is a faculty member at Lesley College Graduate School in Cambridge, U.S.A. She has worked with children and their dreams for some years and says:

'As I started to put together a nightmare helper for parents and kids I decided I would do best to let the children themselves be my guide. Very little kids don't know what dreams are until you start asking about stories that run in your head while sleeping, or pictures we see in the dark. "Oh!" Jennie said, "Like the bad man who shakes my door knob, is that a dream?"

'We start every session by drawing our dreams, a perfect way to get the terror out of the head and into a safer position where it can't move unless we let it. As we were working with nightmares, the goal was to discover ways to empower the dreamer and isolate or freeze the enemy/monster/bad men/pursuer, without killing it in order to learn more about why and how it has such power over us. If we destroy the monster we will never learn what it wants or why it has come into our dreams.

'First the dreamers must protect themselves. Some of the ways kids found to protect themselves in their drawings were by drawing in cages, nets, police help, telephone helpers, super helpers, invisibility, etc., or by distancing, getting bigger or smaller, and calling upon the wisdom of specialists who have greater power.

'Once the monster was stopped and the dreamer was protected in the picture, we could feel safe enough to explore the situation. It turned out that Jimmy's ice-cream monster who bombarded him with sticky sweetness wanted his company. The bargain he reached with her was that he'd agree to play with her for half an hour each day if she would stop hitting him with things that sounded and looked nice but hurt him. That gave us a chance to discuss metaphors; ice-cream cones can be sweet sticky bribes that hurt when they are used as darts or bombs. Sweet promises can be as tempting as ice-cream cones but when they are shot at you from an ice machine they hurt.

'We don't kill monsters, we find out what information is hidden behind the image. We find out why it's haunting us and what it wants. What the child finds is that their monsters have an exaggerated quality of someone they know who is in an authority power position, not Mom or Dad so much as the quality of their power as the child perceives it. Mom may feel like an ice machine when she wants something from me, but the next question is "What am I doing that makes her act like an ice machine?" . . . "I keep away," Jimmy said. "She's always at me." Jimmy instinctively knows the dialogue of each of these images and as he plays its part he can better experience its feelings. As the ice machine he said, "People should love me because I give them treats and run day and night but when my machinery gets angry I use my cones as darts."

'By the time the images in the drawing have been allowed to "speak" it is clear that there are two points of view and a bargain for settlement is needed. Even if we never mention how much like Mom or Dad the monster is, the negotiation exercise empowers the child to better handle stress situations that are similar. We solve the dream and protect the identity. We have dreamed a metaphor because it is too risky to confront the issue head on.

'As we work in small groups and each child listens to the other's dialogue and negotiations, one's work helps another, and each nightmare gets our full attention. Courage to confront the enemy is contagious and there is safety in numbers. What seemed silly or embarrassing at first is not of real importance.

'Mark, when he'd finished speaking as his own lawyer to defend himself against the untrue accusations of his monster pursuer, opened his eyes and said, "You mean I have a wise judge living inside of me?" Who else supplied him with the judge's dialogue?

'We learn that we have wisdom far beyond our own experience. Working with dreams gives us access to an awareness of our potentials and helps us learn to use our powers of negotiation. Best of all it helps us to get in touch with feelings that we have not learned to recognise or articulate.

'It is astonishing how out of touch with their feelings some adults are. Children are in touch with their feelings, but need help learning how to articulate them.

'When I discussed my dream work with a professor from Harvard one evening, it struck him that a college graduate might be based on "our own material." I find one's own dreams are the most profound teacher. The learning is unforgettable.'[4]

Chapter Six

Finding Happier Emotions

EMOTIONS are, almost without exception, the major source of human misery or happiness. One can say that physical pain, difficult events, outer persecution are more certainly causes of misery, but this is only true where they stimulate agonizing emotions. The extraordinary nature of human beings shows that in even the most severe cases of physical pain or social deprivation, a swing of mood from depression to laughter and joy, actually reduces or removes pain and brings a positive attitude towards what previously appeared as impossible odds. Research has shown that the physical condition of our body also changes.

Norman Cousins was at one time the editor of *Newsweek* in America. He was invited to Moscow as the chief guest in a national conference. On arriving he was taken to his hotel and told that a limousine with chauffeur would collect him early the next morning to transport him to the conference.

The limousine arrived on time and they set off, only to arrive at the wrong hall. There followed a frantic search for the right conference hall which lasted for hours. As Norman was the main guest, when he finally arrived the assembly were still awaiting him. With apologies and explanations the conference then began.

That night Norman did not sleep well. On his way home he noticed a heaviness in his legs. This did not disappear once home and working, but became much worse. Medical examination showed that he had an illness related to the collagen in his body. Collagen forms the connective tissues in the body, such as ligaments and tendons, and gives firmness to the flesh. Norman's illness was severe, and he was hospitalised.

In the hospital his condition degenerated. One day one of the doctors on his case left a note for a collegue who was to examine him later. Being puzzled and troubled about his condition Norman opened the envelope and read the note. It said, 'I feel we are losing Norman.'

This was naturally a great shock to him. He had not realised how serious his illness was. Understanding now that the doctors felt doubt about being able to help him, he made efforts to help himself. He carefully considered his activities during the last year. It was obvious as he reviewed them that the year had been particularly stressful, culminating in the tension in Moscow. So his next step was to ask his wife to bring him books about stress. As he read through them he saw that in essence they were saying that during stress our glandular system produces substances which enter the bloodstream and have a destructive effect on the body and its health. During periods of pleasure and relaxation the glandular system produces substances which enter the bloodstream and are constructive to the body and health.

Norman was then faced with an enormous decision – whether to take his health into his own hands. He decided yes, and had himself discharged from hospital and taken to a hotel apartment. He was in such physical pain he could hardly move, so had to remain almost immobile. He had friends set up a cine film projector and screen near his bed, and had them show all his favourite comedy films. In his bed he chuckled, laughed and roared at the antics of the great film comedians, and he discovered that for every hour of laughter, he had an hour of release from pain.

Over the following days his condition radically improved. That is to say, even such fundamental things as the condition of blood, which was part of his illness, changed for the better. During this period he also took very high doses of Vitamin C, which he had been told aided healthy collagen formation in the body. In two weeks he was back at work, his pain and illness gone. He had fought the battle of physical pain and negative emotions and had won.[1]

In dealing with the destructive and depressive side of our emotions, dreams are a constant demonstration of an almost unbelievable fact. When we casually watch someone thinking or sharing their thoughts with us in conversation, a thought or feeling appears as a transitory, ephemeral thing. Yet in a dream, every thought, every shade of emotion is immediately a physical reality.

Even if we observe thought and emotion from the outside, they are not as evanescent as they at first appear. If we keenly observe the person, changes of facial expression, body posture, heartbeat, respiration and facial colouring occur as the thoughts and emotions shift. Norman Cousins shows how his mental and emotional life literally embodied themselves in his glands and tissues. So he could either destroy his body with his feelings, or regenerate it. All of us, in a similar sense, sculpt our body, its posture and overall condition, with our thoughts and emotions. Obviously this is a complex situation, because our sexuality, food, environment and genetic background are also powerful factors. The influence of mind must not be buried and obscured by these other factors though. And we must not forget either that there are few places we can gaze on that are not materialisations of human thoughts and feelings. Every house, car, building, road, article of clothing, hedgerow, book or film, even human society itself, is a materialisation of thoughts and emotions. The changes in society, fashions, architecture, are also expression of changes in the human psyche. All these things are first felt, thought and planned before being materialised. When we come to dreams, this is even more obvious and immediate. Research into the human mind, from various directions, demonstrates this.

This dream from Mrs. J.W. has the theme of not being able to put the light on while feeling anxious. She says, 'It started when I was six years old and living with my Mother and brother in my grandparents house, after my mother's divorce. In the dream I am alone in the house. It begins to grow dark but I switch on the light. It is very dim so I go to another room and try another light. This light is even dimmer. I carry on like this until in the end I am in virtual darkness and very frightened.'

On the same theme here is another of A.T.'s dreams. 'At the bottom of the hill was a lodge house. This was said to be haunted. I did not feel frightened, but I did feel the need for light. I found some matches, but they were very difficult to light. I tried to light candles, and eventually succeeded, but they were not very bright, and it was still dark. A cat moved in the darkness. It did not frighten me. Using a candle I tried to light gas lamps noticed in the light from the candles. They were as difficult as the candles, and no brighter. Then I noticed electric lights, found I had some money and put it in the meter and switched on.'

The obvious anxiety in the dreams manifests itself as the physical reality of the lights being dim. A.T. is able, step by step, to deal with his anxiety through the dream symbols. First matches, then candles, next gas, then electricity. the confidence generated by the money enable him finally to dispel his anxiety by switching the lights on. Or rather, his dispelled anxiety enables him to change the physical reality of the dream. This demonstrates one of the fundamental ways human beings have dealt with negative (and therefore dangerous to survival) emotions. They use some object, person or ritual exterior to themselves to help them stimulate their own pleasure or confidence. Norman Cousins used films. Doctors commonly use a placebo to help patients feel confident in face of anxiety about health. Religious symbols or personages have been perhaps the most widely used means of helping people meet the anxieties life confronts us with. Perhaps some people substitute power of money as their means to combat uncertainty and stress. A.T. gains his eventual confidence by that means. In many dreams, however, a loved or respected person helps us transform our dream world from darkness to light, or anxiety to pleasure. Or else realisation or a change of heart brings it about.

In earlier times, and still today in some cultures, the level of faith or belief was so high, that talismans, charms, holy relics, religious blessings and symbols were potent means of healing anxiety and physical health. It is quite ridiculous to laugh at the primitive as superstitious who uses these practical and effective measures. Perhaps we, with our use of tons of sedatives, millions of gallons of alchohol each year, laugh because since we are blessed and cursed with a questioning rational mind, we no longer have easy access to faith, and are thus a readier prey to anxiety. And unlike animals, who do not have the abstract symbols of speech to remind them of illness, death, failure and loneliness, we cannot forget them, but live with them always.

If, now we have the rational mind, we cannot find health and confidence so easily in the old type of faith and symbols, what can we do? Looking at the many primitive societies who have been robbed of their social and individual health by the white men destroying their beliefs, we must learn a lesson. Perhaps the first step is the realisation that we ourselves are primitives who have robbed ourselves of our old religions by daring to develop sceptical rational thought.

Hyone and I have received dreams from people in many parts of the world, and a huge number from people in Britain. A general summary of these dreams shows that people are frightened of their emotions and unconscious mind. We may laugh at a primitive frightened of ghosts, spirits and Ju Ju, but we are frightened of ourselves. Our rational mind may look at a talisman or St. Christopher medalion and see it as a useless piece of metal or material, which cannot heal us. How though, can we emerge from the prison walls of our own modern superstitions and fears?

Here is a dream showing one man's experience of transcending his past.

'I was in a large prison cell with three other men. The dream seemed to cover a very long period of time, and we were never allowed out of the cell. We ate, slept, lived and defecated in the one room. At first I was consumed with anger against everything and everybody who had put me in that cell. I would stand glaring out between the bars. Gradually I realised that all my anger was completely ineffective. The only person who was hurt or ill at ease because of it was myself. The warders only got delight from it. So I stopped being angry. After that, it became obvious that I was also the only sufferer of my other difficult feelings, such as that of being trapped, or unsatisfied without activity. I dropped these too and they felt like old ghosts melting away, no longer haunting me.

'One day as I sat on my mattress I felt the last ghost drop away. Everything, even my jailors were forgiven. It felt like a plug or block had fallen away inside me, and a great torrent of joy rushed up within me, filling me, pouring out of me. So great was this pleasure that I cried out involuntarily, and felt my face was shining as if alight. My cell mates were disturbed by the powerful feelings radiating from me, and called the jailor. They all stood at the door of the cell staring at me, while I sat motionless and radiating. I knew that nothing could ever be the same again. I was completely free, even though I remained in the cell. What had burst out of me had entered into each of the other men, and they were changed too.'

This dream of Tom's dramatises one of the basic ways of reaching psychic health, namely, self transcendence. The dream illustrates one of the most terrifying and yet amazing aspects of human existence, that we are forever the prisoners of our own mind or awareness. There is no secret door through which we can escape from our own being, perhaps not even by death. There is no otherness to travel to, no exterior to enter, no state to experience that is not, in the end, our own experience, our own self. Our own concepts and attitudes are our own prison bars or door to freedom.

Let us consider this by comparing the next two lucid dreams. To be lucid means to have, in the actual dream, waking self awareness and the ability to reason and direct one's activities.

The first is dreamt by Frederick Van Eeden, and reported in *A Study of Dreams*.

'On Sept 9, 1904 I dreamt that I stood at a table before a window. On the table were different objects. I was perfectly well aware I was dreaming and considered what sort of experiments I could make. I began by trying to break glass, by beating it with a stone. I put a small tablet of glass on two stones and struck it with another stone. Yet it would not break. Then I took a fine claret-glass from the table and struck it with my fist, with all my might, at the same time reflecting how dangerous it would be to do this in waking life; yet the glass remained whole. But lo; when I looked at it again after some time, it was broken.

This is reasonably typical of most lucid dreams. The person is aware they are dreaming, and can experiment or play with the situation. For instance they can fly, change the colour of a wall, make it disappear entirely, or create an object by willing it. This is interesting, but not very useful or instructive. Richard Corriere and J. Hart have pointed out that one can move beyond lucid experience of symbols into what they call the Transformation dream. Here is an excellent example of this type of dream. It occurred to A.T. during a period of light sleep.

'I am in a landscape and notice that everything is brown, the whole world is brown and lifeless. There is also a feeling of solemnity or dullness. I have enough awareness in the dream state to wonder why everything, the world of my dream, is so brown and dull. As I ask this I begin to become more and more aware of the feeling which the brown expresses. It is a feeling of seriousness – life is so serious and there is no room for humour or fun. The feeling deepens, real as a thing in itself, real enough, clear enough, to look at and understand. In fact I understand it is my father's attitude to life that I have unconsciously inherited. It is all so clear. I realise how anxious he always felt about life, and how I had also inherited this, which led me to be such a "brown" person, and so serious. I see too that I do not need to be either brown or serious.

'Then the landscape changes. There are trees, plants and animals in brilliant colour. I wonder what this means, and the landscape begins to spin until the colours blend and shimmer. Suddenly my body seems to open to them, as if they are spinning inside of me, and with a most glorious feeling a sensation of vibrating energy pours up my trunk to my head. With this comes realisation again. I see how stupid I have been in my brown, anxious existence, how much life I have held back. The animals and plants are the different forces in my being which blend into life energy and awareness. I have a sense of being able to do almost anything, like loving, writing a song, painting, telepathy, or speaking with the dead. This sparkling vibrating energy is life itself, and can, if I develop it through my desire and effort, grow into any ability or direction. I wake then with a wonderful sense of my possibilities as a person.'

Frederick Van Eeden remained within the symbols of his dream and manipulated them by being lucid. A.T. transcended the symbols into direct insight and personal growth by being lucid. Of the two, the experience of A.T. offers more practically useful possibilities than that of Van Eeden. A.T.'s experience also demonstrates very clearly the direct connection between personal attitudes, thoughts and anxieties, and the symbols, mood, colour and drama of the dream. The prison dream of Tom's, in a slightly less intense manner, shows the same thing. The prison, or the brown world, in the dream are physical realities in which the dreamer is totally locked; yet like the hero in a mythological adventure, the dreamer can transcend that world if they find a way of altering their habitual mood or attitudes. Tom did this by letting go of old angers, frustrations and feelings, and A.T. did it through having insight into the situation and allowing change to occur. If we consider that some people stay in self-defeating, self punishing, unhappy inner attitudes all their life, the image of the prison is very accurate. A very large number of dreams we receive are from people who have a recurring, anxious dream for

91

most of their life. While the attitudes, such as vengefulness and loneliness are still felt and accepted as necessary, in one's own mind they are as real as brick walls and steel bars to imprison us.

Often such emotional tones or moods are unconscious. The feeling state is so habitual we accept it as the reality of who we are. Having been in that situation all our life, we take it that the world *is* brown, non satisfying, without joy, or lonely. We accept the reality of our inner world as if it were as unchanging as the outer world. Yet the outer world is changeable. If our house is dull we can redecorate it, pull down a wall, move to another house. Our inner world is much more plastic. Here is a very strong dream showing how the dreamer, Maureen, was trapped and found change.

'I had made my home in a small disused stone cow shed. I had lived there for years and never went out. There was no toilet or washing facilities so I and the shed were in a terrible condition. But I wouldn't move out because I had a feeling of irritation and resentment against the world. I suppose I felt as if I were punishing the world for whatever I felt it was guilty of. Friends, living in a nearby house, frequently urged me to leave, but I wouldn't. But after years I began to soften. I could see the world got on with its business despite what I was doing. I was the person who suffered from my own squalor, so I agreed to leave. My friends were delighted and immediately took my clothes to put in a washing machine and I rather shyly began my new life. Shy because of what a fool I had been.'

In this dream, Maureen finds change in a similar way to Tom, by admitting to herself she is the one suffering, not 'the world'. Her own grubby and resentful emotions are shown to be physical realities in the dream, in which she has trapped herself for years. Tom and Maureen of course, are not alone in their suppressed anger and resentment against 'the world'. Many of us have this unfortunate habit, which consumes an enormous amount of our creative energy over many wasted years. If we accept the dream is an indication of what we are actually creating in our life – Tom was creating a squalid prison, and Maureen a rather crappy cow shed. In everyday terms their creative emotions were introverted, creating negative glandular products in their own bodies, and leading to no satisfaction. Seeing the transformation A.T. made in his dream, why should we walk when we can fly? Why live in a hovel when you can as easily make a place of beauty, or find home in a wood of glorious trees?

And why exist in symbols when you can transcend into direct insight?

In looking now at how we can begin this process in our own dreams, the points of importance so far are;

a) Norman Cousins demonstrated that direct conscious frontal attack brought real change.

b) The 'light' dreams of Mrs. J.W. and A.T. show how inner feelings produce a real world in our dream, and how we may be trapped in that, or may begin to change it. A.T. used the symbols of matches, candles, money, to change. Symbols can be very helpful to alter the inner feelings which are destructive or inhibitive in our life.

c) Because we have a rational mind, we may not be able to depend on a religious faith or explicit trust in others or ourself to heal us. The critical mind itself needs to be integrated into the process of change. Tom's prison dream and Maureen's cow shed dream show that this can be done by consciously recognising what negative emotions we have felt to be so important to us, and seeing them as destructive and no longer needed.

d) If we have no consciousness, nothing exists for us. There are no people, no world, no stars – nothing. Conversely, our consciousness is the whole world. If I have not transformed my own negative emotions, the whole world is brown, or a shitty cow shed. I cannot escape from myself, but I can transform myself.

A.T.'s brown dream shows one of the most powerful ways of making this change – insight into our situation, and through it understanding enabling us to transform ourselves.

e) Several of the dreams show factors which stand in the way of this. In most of them the negative feeling states were habitual. A.T.'s brown feelings were lifelong, having been inherited in childhood as an attitude to life in general.

Maureen's dream, and Tom's prison dream, show the feelings of resentment as a chosen action against the world. Whether they chose consciously or not does not matter. What is important is that such a chosen stand has meaning for them and is not easily or casually given up. Maureen and Tom are shown in their dreams, as making a very slow reassessment of their original decision to punish the world. As they do this they see

93

their anger as ineffective and only harmful to themselves. Once that is recognised, their step of positive change becomes easier.

In the 'light' dreams, fear was shown as an inhibitor of producing change. Many of us are frightened of ourselves, or what has so far not been experienced of ourselves, and this stands in the way of transformation.

The comparison of Van Eeden's dream and A.T.'s brown dream, illustrates another inhibitor of change. It is such a subtle one that most of us are prisoners of it. It is that we rest in the already known possibilities of our own being.

Van Eeden never asked himself the question – Why do I create just this world in my dreams? or – What does this mean? as A.T. did. Or perhaps he asked at some time but did not dare to discover direct insight into his own weaknesses and his own unlimited potential.

In this sense, Van Eeden's lack of curiosity, his possible doubts about his own abilities, or anxiety about his own depths are all, in the dream state, physical realities which stand in the way of change. In his writings, Van Eeden actually poo-pooh's the symbolic nature of dreams, thereby resisting his own insight into them.

Most of us tend to believe we are only frightened of life's negatives. The truth is strangely that we are as often scared of our own possibilities and also happiness. That is most likely because our sense of identity, the sailing craft already described, feels threatened by anything it does not already comprehend. It is probably one of the most primal of fears that some other form of energy will engulf us and make us a part of its being instead of us making it a part of ours. This, too, is one of the inhibiting factors of change.

In the middle of this century, tests were made on free grazing sheep to measure effects of anxiety on them. First a trailing wire was attached to one leg. This produced no observable change. Then a harmless electric current was occasionally discharged along the wire. The sheep were momentarily shocked, but there was no overall change in grazing or health. Next a bell was rung when the electric shock occurred. Still no change. Then the bell was rung before the shock. Now the sheep experienced *anticipation* of the shock and began to be ill at ease and less inclined to graze. Lastly the bell was rung frequently and the sheep stopped grazing, declined in health and began to show signs of dying. At that point the experiment was finished and the sheep were back on their feet, grazing and healthy within a few hours.

This shows that shock, unless severe, is not in itself dangerous. But anticipation of shock can be fatal if continued. When there is relief from this anticipation recovery occurs rapidly. As humans we do not need bells ringing to produce anxious anticipation. We have a thousand ways of doing this ourselves. It might be that we anticipate failure at work; perhaps we feel inadequate in competition and fear losing our job; we may live in constant anticipation of our marriage partner leaving us for greener pastures; anticipation of injury to our children; being punished for not complying to the law; being persecuted. These are just a few of the deadly bells we may ring. A.T. lived with a constant low level anxiety about what 'might happen'. As a species we need ways to stop the bells ringing, if only for a short time.

STEP SIX

The next question to use is:

9. *What is the Dream Telling Me?*

By asking this question we can define what attitudes or emotions are creating our dream situations and plot. Once defined they become easier to be conscious of in everyday life. Their unconscious habitual hold on us can then be let go of or transformed. We may at times need to experience those feelings and deal with them as described in step four. Or simply the insight into what we are doing and why, may produce the change.

Let us start with this rather long and complex dream of Jane's.

'I feel I am in a street somewhere and meet a younger woman. We hug each other in warm greeting. We both realise we are going to join what is like a great sisterhood of women. They are going to an activity where they will express themselves creatively. But we had no idea there would be so many women, and there was a huge queue. All sorts of women were in it; all ages, all types, and we joined the queue. There was happiness, friendliness and a good feeling, as none of the women stood out as separate or distinct. I felt it might be too

95

late to get in, as there were so many women.

'Then I felt somebody grab me playfully from behind, and they said, "Guess who?" I turned around with eyes closed, partly knowing who it was, partly guessing, feeling his head with my hands. He had crouched to make himself the height of a child. Then I opened my eyes and saw it was T, the husband of a friend. I also saw that the building, which did have open windows and doors, now had closed doors with solid brick walls.

'T and I walked away together, still playful. Then I began to feel anxious and guilty about my husband knowing if I have been with this man, and the pleasure I have. I notice snow is beginning to fall, and I stand trying to plan how we can meet without my husband finding out. Then I get into a terribly complicated thoughts of where I could go that would be safe. Next I am at a railway station with my husband and children. The ticket collector gives me a ticket. He is a friend of the man I want to be with. I am going to meet him once a month, and a slip of paper is concealed in the tickets telling me where we will meet – a different place each month.'

ANALYSIS BY KEY WORDS

Through our work with hundreds of people's dreams Hyone and I have developed techniques which enable us to cut through the complexity of a dream. This helps us see what may have given rise to the symbols in the mind of the dreamer. One of the techniques we use we call Key Words, another is Drama and a third, First Scene.

With Key Words we cut away, like massive pruning, all the words except those which are fundamental to the action or feelings in any section of a dream. So in the first section of Jane's dream, three words would sum it up – Warm, Creatively, Women. If we then extend these words we could say the first part of the dream expresses warm feelings to do with creative womanhood or femininity.

In the next section there are not many descriptive words, but we have – playful and friend. So we can say it is about having a warm friendly relationship with a male.

In the third section there are – anxious, guilty, pleasure, complicated, safe. This can be expressed as to be about Jane feeling anxious and guilty about pleasure with a man other than her husband. This makes her attempt complicated ways of seeking to do this safely.

If the *Drama* or plot of the dream is considered, what one attempts, is to view the dream like a small play or film. What is the plot expressing? What is the playwright communicating? What is the scene saying overall?

In many dreams, the First Scene is very important. It is like the opening scene of a film, which introduces characters and says what the film is to be about. The First Scene can also sum up the 'story so far' in one's life, or at least, state the theme of the dream.

Looking at the First Scene in this sense my impression of it is of expressing positive feelings about being a woman. She is also moving towards discovering something to do with female creativity, but in this dream she does not achieve that.

The second scene gives the feeling of playful pleasure with the opposite sex. And the third scene, over all is to do with deviousness to avoid admitting her pleasure.

Therefore, using this approach, the summary of the dream is that Jane moves toward her own creativity and acceptance of her womanhood. She finds herself capable of pleasure but is anxious and guilty about allowing herself this. Yet she wants this pleasure, and is devious and plotting to gain it.

When Jane had summed up her dream in this way and had watched for some weeks to see if the clearer view of herself influenced her in any way, she said:

'This summary made me see more clearly, and admit to myself that I am not relaxed in relations with males other than my husband. I see what a tight spot I get myself into over this. I feel also my full creativity is not available to me until I work this out.'

When asked to visualise the dream to provide a satisfying conclusion, she said, 'What I arrive at is making T. into a family friend, bringing his wife to meet my husband. In that way I have the pleasure of his company without the guilt.'

If question six is applied to her response – what have I mistakenly introverted? – she is treating the dream as an outer reality. She has introverted her outer moral and social rulings, and is not openly allowing herself emotional and sexual pleasure in the dream. After realising this, she allowed herself greater freedom in later dreams.

Understanding our dreams in the way Jane did, can be as positive in producing life changes, as in actively imagining the dream on to satisfying conclusions. So I will look at one more dream in this way to show what sort of new awareness about oneself can arise.

The dream was sent to us by B.T. She says:

'In my dream I am nursing, feeling very tired. I get up off a bed and pick up a huge bundle of soiled linen, and am confronted by Night Super. Actually she is very fat, but in my dream is slim and sexy. She has my exam papers in her hand. I could see they were beautifully written and had intricate drawings. She harassed me about them and said, "I will give you 2%." I replied that I was fed up, and all I ever wanted to be was a good nurse.

When I looked again she was a tall thin-faced man with a moustache. He said, "I'm sure we can sort things out." '

B.T. was a nurse, so the first scene – which by the way is not very distinct in this dream, not being separated from the rest of the action – says the dream is about work and tiredness.

If we prune away sentences to find key words, they are – tired, soiled linen, confronted, harrassed, fed up, sort things out.

These do not give as clear a picture as with Jane's dream. They obviously show though, that B.T. is confronting feelings to do with being fed up and tired about some aspect of her life, which she is trying to sort out.

In this case, the Drama of the dream is the most revealing aspect. If we ask ourselves what this tiny one act play communicates, there is a sense almost of giving up because of other people's judgements. Her own self evaluation, seen in the exam papers, is excellent. Yet in her own mind she makes an unattractive Night Superintendent into a glamourous powerful woman. Comparing herself in this way, with harsh judgements, she feels fed up.

The soiled lined suggests a messy situation she is trying to deal with. So she has a conflicting self image. In comparison with others she feels like the lowest – 2%. Yet she can see her work is excellent.

The clue to how she can meet this grubby bundle of negative emotions is shown at the end of the dream. The man can be understood by comparing him with his female aspect. As the female the expression is harrassing, expressive of value judgements and irritable emotions. As the male the expression is a rational offer to sort out the situation.

So if B.T. is aware that her own emotion-laden, self-critical judgements rob her of pleasurable motivation in her life, she can guard against them. The other aspect of herself, the rational problem solving self, promises much more stimulus to achievement.

With some practice, using these techniques on your dreams will enable you to extract from the symbols and the plot, something meaningful and useful. The dream does need to be written down fully first though, so one's descriptive language can be searched for clues.

Questions eleven and twelve need introduction at this point.

10. *Where Does the Feeling Arise From?*

and

11. *Am I Limiting Myself?*

The dream process is not simply a means of wish fulfillment. It is not just about anxieties or fears. Dreams also express our inner processes of psychological growth; they summarise what we are learning from our experience; they break through the boundaries of our own concepts and look at life with a new slant or new insight. They do so may things.

When we look at what the dream is telling us we can define which of these many areas the dream is a reflection of.

With question ten this is not necessary. The aim of the question is to focus attention on the main feelings in the dream in a way that will lead us to consider their origins.

This next example is a dream of Pete's, who had experienced a lot of pain long after the healing of a back injury. Pete felt the pain meant his back was still injured and he felt incapacitated by it. We worked with him for some time on his dreams and feelings, as a physical examination showed no bodily infirmity. Toward the end of working with us Pete reported this dream:

'I look over a hedge and see the back of a bull.'

In exploring the feelings of the dream, Pete recognised two. The first was fear or anxiety on seeing the back of the bull. The second was the feeling of enormous strength of the bull. He was then asked if he could recognise these feelings as appearing anytime in his everyday life. I asked him to take aside the symbols of the dream and just leave the feelings, and then ask himself when he had felt those feelings before.

Unfortunately I have to quote from memory, so cannot give Pete's exact words. But he recognised the anxiety as the feeling he had about his back. It was something which haunted him most of the time. At this point Pete had a look of amazement on his face. He had never before admitted to himself that he suffered anxiety. As a young male needing a good image of himself, he had dared not admit that he felt anxious about his own health.

The feelings of strength and power was also a part of Pete's everyday experience. He had the natural drive of a young man, to explore, to travel, to express himself.

With those two feelings defined the whole problem was clarified for him. He had injured his back at work. The injury had healed, but the pain remained. In fact, Pete's unadmitted anxieties about himself had been given a site or focus in his back, causing muscular tension. Through his unadmitted anxieties he had been conserving his strength and his urge to travel and explore, and had remained at home living with his parents. This holding back of his own enthusiasm and energy led to frustration and tension, which was the cause of the back pain. However, the pain caused Pete to fear he had real problems, which led to more anxiety, which led to more tension and pain, which led to more anxiety, and so on and on in a vicious circle.

Seeing and admitting the anxiety; having insight into the vicious circle, freed Pete. When the anxiety arose, he could counter it by thinking or saying – 'This feeling of tension and fear is because I am human and sometimes feel anxious. Everybody feels like that at times. It does not mean I am ill or my body is sick.' This released him from its negative influence. Pete finally left his parents, and now has travelled to various parts of the world, with friends, and on his own.

Pete's feelings of anxiety were focused by his back injury, not caused by it. Sometimes such feelings have their origins in the event itself. Here is another dream which illustrates this. It is another of Tom's dreams, and I will let him tell it in his own words.

'My sex life has always been a troublesome area, and I frequently cut off from my wife sexually rather than experience the extreme fatigue that arises some hours after intercourse. I was in a period of such cut off when I dreamt a doctor was talking to me. He said I ought to sleep with my wife. But I felt repulsed by the very thought of my wife's body.

'When I considered the dream and the feeling of repulsion, my first thought was that other people didn't find my wife repulsive, so why did I. So I asked the question about where the feeling started. It was a very startling experience because it was as if my mind went scanning right back through the years. That feeling had been a part of my life right the way back. Then I saw where it began. My mother used to threaten that she would put me in a home if I did anything wrong. One day when I was about six I had been late for school because I and a friend were picking flowers for the teacher. We got scared and didn't go in to class, but became involved in catching fish in a nearby river. Because I did not arrive home on time my mother said she was going to hurt me for worrying her. She undressed me, bathed me, put all my Sunday best clothes on, and said she would put me in a home. I remember screaming and begging. I also remember, looking back for the origin of the feeling of repulsion, that it began on that day. From then on, I can now see, I unconsciously decided I was never going to be hurt by the woman I loved again. I would withdraw my love from her. And the only way I could do that was to feel what a repulsive person she was, and how I didn't want to touch her.

'Realising this didn't stop me feeling tired after sex, but it did make me aware of why I had developed the habit of emotional cut off. I saw how, when I feel manipulated or when I try to be emotionally independent in my marriage, I use the feeling of repulsion. Seeing what a negative way of gaining my needs it is, helped me take the step of developing other more honest and positive ways. For instance, I can now say I need time to myself if I need it, instead of pushing my wife away as if she were loathsome.'

ANALYSIS BY STRIPPING AND BEING

The two basic ways of arriving at insight into feelings are to strip aside the symbols and see what feelings remain. Then consider where and how those feelings are experienced in everyday life. When this is linked with what the dream is saying, it gives a deep and useful insight into oneself.

Another useful method is to *be* the symbol. This can be done by two simple techniques. One is to relax with eyes closed, notice one's overall physical and feeling condition, then imagine oneself as the symbol, and observe subtle changes of feeling or tension. In being the symbol, it is helpful to imagine oneself filling the actual space of the person, animal or object. The aim is to explore imaginatively or be aware of with what feelings we invest the symbol. The technique is one I developed myself some years ago, and is based on the fact that our symbols are parts of our own feelings, processes and thoughts given form.

As we have already seen, a dream is a materialisation of our own attitudes and concepts. If a house or a person in our dream is an exteriorisation of an interior feeling, then by interiorising it again – by drawing the image back into blending with us – we can be aware of what feeling creates it. A person 'being' railway lines recognised the feeling as rigid rules and directions he aplied to his life all the time. A person 'being' a friend who appeared in his dream felt the feelings of sexual desire. The friend was a symbol of his own sexuality. A person 'being' a car felt it as their own energy or desire to get somewhere in life, their own ambition or drive.

The second technique is taken from Gestalt Therapy and is extremely useful. To use it we vocally express and feel ourself as the object or person, in the first person present. For instance, a man dreamt he was looking over a landscape with no houses or roads. He stood on the edge of a very large natural, tree covered bowl out of which he had just walked. There was an injured youth he had discovered, and was seeking help for. The dreamer used the technique by saying

'I am a place, away from people and houses, isolated and lonely. I am a huge and long depression, and in my midst is a hurt young man.'

Just those few words led him to tears, because he realised he was talking about his teenage. Suffering from acute acne, he had lived a life isolated from the opposite sex and normal social activities. In fact his teenage had been one long depression. The hurt young man was still inside him, because he had not released the painful emotions of his youth.

The points to remember are to describe yourself, in the first person, as the symbol. Notice and accept any emotions which arise, or insights which occur. If the symbol is a person or place you know in waking life, do not describe yourself as the known person or place. Describe yourself as the dream person or place, giving expression to what you feel like as that person, how you see your surroundings and relate to them, and your image of yourself. The insights you gain from using these methods, integrated with the other techniques, bring real positive life changes. They help to modify or redirect the visualisation of satisfying dream endings, and clarify goals we aim for in life

As this book is about methods which give us quick insights into our dreams, no attempt will be made to teach ways of fuller inter-pretation. This is already described in my book *Do You Dream?* and is out of place here.★

Working with question eleven – Am I limiting myself? – gives another way of bringing dramatic positive life changes. When Pete worked on his dream about the bull, he saw that he had a negative image of himself, which, if put into words, said 'I am inadequate as a person. If I leave home and attempt to become independent I will have a physical breakdown. Because my back is unhealthy I will always have to be dependent.' In Pete this actually produced physical pain and dependence.

In the early part of this century Emile Coué helped hundreds of people to find release from such negative input. He wrote that, 'When the will and the imagination are in conflict, the imagination invariably wins the day.' If we substitute the word feelings for imagination, it describes Pete's situation. He consciously wanted or willed to be healthy, but beneath that his anxious feelings were saying, 'I'm ill. I'm inadequate. I'll never be as capable as other people.'

When we realise that each thought and feeling expresses an objec-tive reality in the world of the mind in dreams, then we see how the negative feelings we have about ourself can become actual realities. This is true not only in the dream, but in the material world. Pete not only brought about pain in his body as Norman Cousins did, but he created in his life an unsatisfying situation. Not only could he not leave his parents or travel as he wished, but he had also taken a poorer paid job. Both he and Norman healed themselves of their pain. Of course thousands of other cases of even more dramatic life changes could be quoted. However, the important thing is to recognise what the major keys to positive change are.

CHANGING A NEGATIVE SELF IMAGE OR HABIT
Working on their dreams, Tom, A.T. and Pete uncovered negative self images or habits. If such habits or feelings are suspected through depression or anxiety, but not discovered in the dream, there are direct methods of defining them.

Ray Hodgson and Peter Miller, in their book *Self Watching*,

★ Published by Neville Spearman.

describe some direct ways of observing and changing negative patterns. Negative views bring about apathy and absence of motivation to attempt anything. The inactivity and withdrawal from involvement allow the negative patterns to remain unchallenged. In such feeling states we are liable to feel or say that there is no point in attempting anything, or that everything we do fails or creates more difficult feelings.

One of the first steps therefore is to challenge old patterns by testing their truth. For example, our pattern might be to feel sure we will fail if we try; or we may be afraid people see us as inferior; or, like Tom, there may be a pattern of pushing people away as he did with feelings of repulsion.

Using the technique of challenge, it does not matter whether the pattern has been set in place by a traumatic childhood experience. It is not necessary to unearth the experience. All that needs to be done is to move against the negative pressure. For instance, try to achieve, despite the fear of failure. Meet people despite the feeling of inferiority. Make contact despite the feeling of repulsion. In each of these cases, the negative feelings have become an interior and exterior reality, an imprisoning wall beyond which one dare not move. Moving through and beyond the wall is the quickest way to transform it, especially if we dare to do so without suppressing our feelings. The wall is made up of the fears, disappointments and pains of the past, but we do not need to hunt for them in our memory. They remain as operative forces in our present life, in the form of habits and predjudices. So when we dare to go beyond one of these walls, *we actually experience the emotions or anxieties which created it*, and have insight into original causes or traumas. The first time is the most difficult, but each successive time we challenge it, it becomes easier and easier, because we are building a new habit.

Another helpful tool is to realise that our negative habits usually lead us to assess ourself and events very rigidly, often in a self depreciating or self defeating manner. Our dream may show us as habitually relating to things in our dream as threatening, or too powerful to act against, or we make no move to stand up for our own rights. Such recurring dream themes show us as assessing the world as actively aggressive to us; alternatively we have assumed our efforts will always be fruitless.

In such situations it helps to recognise that every evaluation is only made from a standpoint of comparison. If we are sure we are a failure, this is only a comparison, and who are we comparing ourself with? Even the abject alchoholic, who may appear to be a failure to most, is a powerful survival success compared with those who died in the womb or in childhood.

Dreams which define the negative views we have of ourself usually portray us in an inferior relationship with others, or getting the worst of a situation. Here are two dreams which illustrate this:

'I was playing whist and was the gent; so I was dealing and it was all wrong. I either dealt a card which was face up, or there was rubbish, bits of cardboard, in the cards. I tried so hard, and got very upset. I went into the toilets and cried, thinking how could Betty, my friend, do it to me. I thought what a good card player my father is, and thought of what he would say, and I felt frightened.'

The second dream is:

'I am in the kitchen of my former house, and my two sons come to me while I cook. The youngest son looks at the soup in a disgusted fashion and goes away. The eldest son looks at the soufflé, which has wine in it, and is really special. In a tone of disgust he says he's not eating it, and goes away too. I look at it all and feel such a failure, burst into tears and wake crying.'

Both dreams portray feelings of failure despite efforts to succeed. In the first dream there is a strong feeling of comparison evident, with the father, for instance, and a sense of despair. In the second dream the drama suggests rejection as the trigger to the feelings of failure. Both the dreams help the dreamer to clarify what their personal, negative, emotional or mental reactions and habits are. It is helpful to put such statements as the dream dramatises, into words. If this is done for the first dream, it would read:

'I create an image of myself – in my dream – of being a social failure. In my thoughts I compare myself with other people and see myself as inferior.'

Verbalising the second dream, we have:

'In my own imagination I see myself as rejected and not appreciated. All my best efforts are of no avail, and my sense of failure causes emotional misery.'

The devastating influence of such habitual negative reactions is very deep. Therefore one needs to first define what the negative attitude is by verbalising or writing it down. Then one rephrases it to something which is life enhancing instead of self destructive. But it needs to be something one can believe, so avoid over positive statements.

Hypnotism demonstrates this to us in another way. A hypnotic subject who is habitually shy and withdrawn in company, has difficulty expressing himself in conversation, if given the suggestion that he is a confident and expressive orator, can immediately be confident and extrovert in front of an audience. What has happened is that their negative image of themselves, and their habits of failure, have been replaced by a confident, successful image and pattern. What is so important is that once we know how the negative feelings destroy our own happiness, then we can replace them.

There are several effective ways of changing our own negative habits and self image. They are:

a) Practising a new habit until a more satisfying habit or self image emerges. We can do this with the help of friends, or by ourself. If it is with friends, we need to practice the new role and have them give honest feedback, until we feel easy.

If alone, change in imagination each dream into one that satisfies. In imagination practice the new role until it becomes habitual. Tests with sportsmen showed that a group who imagined themselves practicing their sport each day, improved their skill only fractionally less than those who actually practiced.

b) Changing the script we inwardly suggest to ourself out of negative emotions changes the way we relate to ourselves and the world. The script of the first dreamer was basically, I am socially inferior and compare unfavourably with others. So in changing the script we must first become aware of it. Our dreams can help in this.

In the case of the script of the first dreamer, she needs to assess this carefully mentally. Is she inferior to everybody? If not, why play the thought over and over to cause anxiety? To people who can't play whist, she must be considered skilled. So she could change her script to ; 'I am as skilled as many people, so there is no need to chastise myself with a sense of failure.' This is not over exaggeration. Because she can believe in it, she could inwardly accept it.

It can he helpful to imagine oneself standing naked in front of members of the family and friends and in various situations, and take note of arising thoughts. This clarifies what our self image and basic social reactions are. By assessing the negative feelings realistically, we can see their untruth, change them, or do something about them.

c) Once we clarify the situation we can change it if there are apects of it amenable to change. If we see our image is negative because we are overweight, we can seek help to lose weight and gain fitness by exercise.

If we are lonely and are making no attempts to meet others, we can find activities in which we change this situation. The combined action of changing our negative attitudes, as well as the outer activities, works so much more effectively than change in just one area.

FORGIVENESS

Forgiveness is not a moral victory or a way of being noble, it is an incredible power to heal and free oneself. Tom's dream of imprisonment shows the way a human mind can be shackled and restrained by its own vengefulness and desire to blame others. The dream also shows how peace and joy are released in one's life by forgiveness. Problem solving dreams show forgiveness as one of the major tools of personal change to health and peace.

Dr. Maltz tells of the time he sat in on a discussion between clergymen on why Jesus was able to forgive the woman taken in adultery. What he points out is that Jesus did not forgive. He said, when pressurised by the group who wanted him to pronounce judgement, 'Let him who is without sin among you be the first to throw a stone at her.' When they had all gone he looked at the woman and said, 'Woman, where are they? Has no one condemned you?' She replied, 'No one, Lord.' Then Jesus said, 'Neither do I condemn you, go and do not sin again.' As we stop judging other people, so the pressure of self condemnation drops away from one's own life.

EXPRESSION OF EMOTIONS

All of us are born with amazingly free emotional expression. As a baby we scream with misery; we go purple with anger and thresh and bang; we gurgle, laugh and cavort with pleasure; all of these feelings fill our whole being. As social training occurs, we learn that certain behaviour will be rewarded and other types punished. Then we either comply or rebel. But in either case we develop habits – the habits of making our emotions conform, or the habits of stimulating our emotions into resentment and rebellion. If we remained at the baby level, with unrestrained emotions we would be a danger to others and ourself. That is the situation John Steinbeck explores in his story *Of Mice and Men*.

So we are faced by a problem with several facets.

1. How can we live successfully in relationship with others without suppressing major areas of our natural reactions?
2. If emotions need expression, how can we release them without detriment to ourself or others?
3. Can we find a way to relate to our biological reactions so as to minimise personal stress?

Because of the importance of releasing emotions, modern psychotherapy has made possible safe ways of expressing anger, frustration and pain. Instead of hitting the person, one hits a mattress or punchbag. The healing release is the same, but the social consequences are different. Psychotherapy has also pioneered the teaching of methods to transform raw emotion, such as anger, into satisfying but socially acceptable action. Therefore, if John is frustrated and angry at his boss because someone else got a rise and not he, instead of feeling shitty and going out to get drunk, or going home and being irritable, he goes to the boss and says what his irritation is. The energy to get drunk or to speak up is the same. One is self defeating, whereas the other could be self enhancing.

In taking note of our dreams we need to be aware of any situation where we do not freely express ourselves. In our dreams we can still be a total 'baby' without harm to ourself or others. In fact, freedom in our dreams is the safest area of self expression. Therefore, wherever there are unexpressed feelings visualise a full and satisfying expression. This gradually becomes a part of our actual dreams, and the healing release is spontaneous.

Here are dreams from one dreamer showing the various stages of release. The first, in fact, shows hesitation.

'A coloured chieftain, proud of his people, offered me three wives. Although they were beautiful, and I knew deep down we would love each other, I felt I couldn't marry them, or take them as wives. It wasn't the "done" thing.'

Second Dream

'I had been asked to run a mission hall, mostly coloured people. I asked them to work as a team to produce a book. Next week a woman gave me two books they had produced. They were photographs of themselves at work in all the basic industries. They were beautiful. I could see the effort and loving care in each page, along with team work and respect for myself, and what I was trying to do. I was overcome with humility and love for them. So much so I took the woman in my arms and held her while I wept. It was a most ecstatic moment of love between us.'

Third Dream

'Awoke in a girl's room. She was there. I made love to her after spanking her. I felt great peace.'

Fourth Dream

'Went with Ben to a woman psychiatrist. He sat telling her his problems about homosexuality while I stood undressing and dropping my clothes down a toilet. That is, all but my underpants.

'After he stopped talking she said "Why don't you go with him?' I was really shocked at first. Then I realised this was a dream, and realising how important it was to allow the fantasy I went to Ben and fantasied masturbation, or his penis in me. But I suddenly took hold of him and entered him from the rear – but fully. That is, we blended into one person and the dream ended.'

Fifth Dream

'I was walking along with a male friend. He kept irritating me until I felt really riled, and caught him by the neck and punched hell out of him.'

This series shows how the dreamer is allowing a wide range of emotions to be not only felt but expressed. There is shyness, humility, ecstatic love, sex, pleasurable aggression in the spanking, homosexual drive, and outright anger. Those are the constituents of a healthier emotional life. This does not in the exterior personality produce permissiveness, and that is not what is being aimed at. As the various shades or notes of feeling life are allowed to unfold, it is as if a delicate interior sense organ, that has been inflexible, closed and unresponsive, now opens and responds. I believe it is the whole feeling response of psychobiological life itself to the experience of living, which is allowed to function. Like a delicate living antenna, the petals of this sense organ open to our world and the cosmos, and produce a picture of life, it's meaning, and one's place in that meaning. But with our antenna closed by rigid constraints, there can be no wider awareness of life than can be gathered through our eyes and ears and touch.

Chapter Seven

Finding a Happier Sex Life

ANYONE who explores the unconscious life processes in any depth, discovers that within us, beneath the veneer of modern social training and culture dwells a beast, an animal – in fact the human animal. Unfortunately, until recent in-depth studies of wild animals occurred, Western culture regarded the lives of animals as bestial, governed by raw aggression, lust and lack of care. Now that animal behaviour is known to have deeply ingrained rules of behaviour which avoid unnecessary aggression, which act as an an expression of caring for the young and for group survival, we need also to revise our conception of our own innate naturalness.

In their book *The Human Race,* Terence Dixon and Martin Lucas give the example of a male Orang-utang at Chester Zoo which was said to have wilfully murdered members of its family. But studies of Orang-utangs in the wild show them to be peaceful creatures. The reason for the killing was that in their natural habitat they are monogamous, and the children leave their parents at sexual maturity. Sometimes the father drives them away. As the Chester Orang-utang was always confined in a small cage with his wife and sexually mature children, he tried to drive them away to be independent. As it was not possible to leave, his instinctive attacks continued and the children died from their injuries. Was it not the enforced and unnatural social situation which was the real murderer?

Within the unconscious most Europeans have a similar situation. Entering the unconscious is like entering a primordial world which has been formed by tens of thousands of years of survival experience by the human race. There are deeply rooted taboos, built by generation after generation accepting as true certain facts – such as the wrongness of inter breeding. Just as the Orang-utang is instinctively monogamous, and has this inbuilt morality, so we too have inbuilt moral codes. However, we have created a social system which in many ways ignores these basic needs and drives, and actually creates non-functional or socially-ill humans. So we have inside, not only a natural morality, sociability and sexuality, but also in many cases, an angry, perplexed animal, sick because it has been made to live in an unnatural environment like the Orang-utang. Our identity and our ability to relate to other humans sexually, develops out of our childhood experience of parents and family. Because we are human animals who live in conditions which have put us in a stress situation, we tend to damage the growth of our children at its very roots; at birth, at breast feeding and in the lack of close and long physical contact. The fact is that a 'great deal of the violence that occurs in modern Western society is directed towards children by their parents.'[1] The N.S.P.C.C. gives the figures for 1980 alone as, 65 children under the age of 15 killed by parents, 759 seriously injured, and 5,800 injured.

What tends to be overlooked is that the above figures only illustrate the obvious physical cruelty. But the vast bulk of infant cruelty goes on as apparently normal behaviour in modern society. In so-called primitive societies the baby is never separated from its mother until it is psychologically and physically ready to do so of its own accord. Separation is in fact the major trauma for a baby. Yet we think nothing of immediate separation at birth because of hospital routine; the separation of baby in prams and cots; no actual skin contact for many babies at all because they are bottle fed.

We see the results in our world today as increasing numbers of non-functional human beings. Many of us cannot maintain a bonded relationship with the opposite sex; we cannot enjoy pleasurable love making; and we have no joy in our children. Sexual deviation and homosexuality are accepted as part of our world instead of signs that as a society we are creating human animals who have lost basic human/animal traits.

We need to realise, of course, that it is not the right of every animal, human or otherwies, to be completely free of problems.

112

Even animals have sexual problems and anxieties. Fortunately human beings have a great capacity to re-program negative habits and make changes in themselves. Where changes cannot be made, such as altering physical factors, humans also have the ability to develop a different attitude to the same situation. Because of these abilities we do not have to return to the inbuilt patterns of morality from times past; nor remain in an unsatisfactory present-day social, sexual personality structure. We have the ability to produce change in ourselves, but not by ignoring or glossing over the unconscious processes of our being, their centuries long conditioning, and their millions of year old survival drives. We do not teach a dog to become a guide to the blind by simply talking to it. It becomes a guide dog by working with its reactions to punishment and rewards, and its natural feelings of love and herding. So our own drives can be directed to new levels of expression and achievement by understanding them.

DREAMS AND SEXUAL FULFILMENT

As a baby and child our sexuality is completely uninhibited. Here is a dream which shows this. It is the earliest dream the person can remember from childhood.

'I am lying face up cradled in my aunty's knickers. She still has them on, so my own naked body is pressed against hers. I am quite small, in that my head does not emerge from her pants, but at the same time I feel my normal size. My aunty walks around normally while I am pressed up against her, and I have an incredibly thrilling feeling of orgasm all the time, and very deep sensual pleasure too. Then my aunty passes faeces, and this is like being bathed in ecstasy. It is so strong it woke me up. I am not sure of my age at the time, but I believe it was pre-school.'

Here the child has no problems in using images and feelings freely to express intense sexual pleasure. There is no sense of guilt, wrongness or shame about any aspect of the dream.

This next dream of C.N.B. a Navajo Indian, shows a struggle with the whole process of desire. So much so that the dream never reaches direct sexuality.

'I dreamt a bad dream about a dog. I went to hogan, but I do not know who it belonged to. Then this grey dog chased me. He got hold of my pants and tore 'em off. Then Mrs. Armijo got hold of the

113

dog and pulled him away. The dog tore Mrs. Armijo's dress to pieces. We were then both fighting the dog. I was talking in my dream and my wife woke me up. I told my wife nothing was the matter.'

The dream suggests that C.N.B. strongly desired Mrs. Armijo, and she him, but he fought the wild desire even in his dream. This leaves him still unsatisfied. No matter what code he chooses to live by during the day, there is no point in frustrating himself at night also. In fact the first step in releasing one's sexual potential is to begin to drop the limitations we place on ourselves not only in dreams, but also in our fantasy life. In taking such a dream on to a conclusion, one should allow even the wildest fantasies.

In her book, *Myself and I,* Constance Newland describes her experience of sixteen LSD therapy sessions. Her given reason for entering therapy was frigidity, which led to sex being painful and unpleasant. Helped by the deinhibiting influence of the drug, Constance gradually allowed deeper and fuller fantasy experiences until she contacted the feelings and memories which led to the physical tensions, emotional feelings and distorted impressions which underlay her frigidity. During those sessions she fantasied such things as making love to her partner; eating a desert full of hard boiled eggs; being a long scream through a tunnel; tearing her mother apart in murderous rage; being a man making love, and killing her sister. Yet her most powerful and healing session she describes as:

'. . . a holy experience. During this hour, with no drug or stimulus other than music, I had uncovered forgotten emotions and experiences of unbelievable reality.' Later, describing how she changed from an overweight, unattractive woman to a slim and attractive female by finding her independence, she says, 'I would like to emphasise that I achieved this cure for myself. I believe one can achieve psychic health without recourse to therapy. It is only when one fights a consistenly *losing* battle against an important problem one needs help.'

Without any drug, by using fantasy and allowing her emotions to be felt, Constance plumbed the depths of her being, and brought about positive life changes.

FANTASY AND SEX

Fantasy is the language of the unconscious processes. By its use the unconscious thinks out or works out our problems or ways of further growth. By working with the unconscious in its labour, the process of problem solving can be speeded up enormously. As problem solving also relates to our growth, its improvement is akin to speeding up our evolution as a person. The unconscious cannot look back upon its own processes and analyse them, or ask varied questions as our waking mind can. In a certain sense the unconscious is like an amazing computor which although having enormous potential, only does what it is programmed to do.

Programs or habits are put into our unconscious originally by actual experiences and our thought/feeling reaction to them. Working with fantasy is a way of replaying these experiences and our reactions. Because we are consciously involved we can watch what is happening and ask questions or give feedback. It is helpful also to realise that fantasy is not simply a thing of the mind. A dancer who improvises is fantasying with their body. A singer who explores and idea for a song is fantasying with their voice. And an actor fantasies with his emotions, body and voice. In their cases we recognise fantasy as a highly productive tool of creativity. It is a means of exploring the new, the yet undiscovered. When we employ it with our dreams, it is also highly productive in self discovery and problem solving. By exploring a fantasy with images we can achieve a great deal. If we allow our body, voice and emotions to express in movement, sound and feelings, the pleasures, the pains, the joy, the uncertainty and the peace of our fantasy journey, the depth of discovery will be enormously increased. By allowing the body to move, we can release deep-seated physical tensions which are being touched by the fantasy.

Some important features of how to use fantasy are shown in this series of dreams and fantasies of Brian, as he explored his own sexual feelings.

'It started with a dream in which I was in the First World War in Germany. The Germans had taken a hill we had been defending, and I had been captured.

'I had learnt to allow fantasy which included my body and feelings, and when I continued the dream I fantasised, in a very deep sense, being a prisoner and being tied to a bed. German officers

115

tortured me by crushing my left foot, but I wouldn't give information. During the fantasy my body actually took on the position of being tied and tortured, and I cried out with the pain. It all seemed real to me, and knowing my name as that soldier, I thought it must be memories of a past life.

'Because I couldn't understand or feel conclusive about the first fantasy session I undertook another to explore further. The fantasy continued as if it was something very real. Because I would not talk I was strapped on the bed face down and a line of German soldiers came and, one after the other, buggered me. I lived this all out with my body and feelings too, and I really understood what people meant when they say "I feel buggered:" It was as if my personality had been smashed, broken, and I was just a body walking around. I had at one period relived incidents from my childhood using this method, and this experience was just as real and deeply felt. So again I concluded I must be remembering a past life. I was not happily married, and continually struggled with my sexuality, and I thought perhaps past-life experiences accounted for these inbuilt difficulties.

'On talking this over with a friend however, I noticed when I came to the past-life idea, I didn't look her in the eye, and I thought I must be avoiding looking at something in myself.

'I tried a third fantasy session, and the talk with P. must have gone deep because I seemed now to relive being attacked by two youths while I was a teenager in London. This was so realistic I had to ask my parents if I had ever come home bashed, as if I had been assaulted. They, and I, were mystified. How can one live out an event which never happened? It was so real, and I felt as if it had happened to me. I felt confused for several days.

'Then I had a dream in which an army was on the move. Some sort of national upheaval was taking place. The army was made up of teenage males. They were very "cocky" and were looking out for girls. I felt bitter about their herd feelings.

'After that I dreamt I went to look at some chickens in the garden of a house I used to live in. A large cockerel was amongst them, and to my amused pleasure began to chase the hens. They all ran madly away. My father came along and said the chickens wouldn't lay with that hen chasing them. I said it wasn't a chicken but a cockerel, and they would soon calm down. My mother now came and I said the chickens would stop running eventually because the cockerel was bigger than they. She said, no, it wasn't the size, but the manner and attitude of his approach which could cause an instinctive response in them.

'When I worked on this dream I fantasied that I was the cockerel, but I couldn't manage to give myself a real cockerel comb, or powerful neck. This showed me something from my unconscious was not going along with my fantasy. In observing the feeling I had a sort of explosion of realisation. Here I was, in a male body, yet in regard to most men I felt "chicken", subservient or as if I was trying to get them to like me. I was like a chicken in a cockerel's body. I realised I had developed that because I was always trying to get my father to give me some sign of approval or praise, and none ever came. So I had been going round trying to find an admiring father figure in other men. Also I could see the feeling showed me as "chicken", scared of being a sexual male with woman. Not only because I was uncertain of myself as a male, but because my mother had scared shit out of me about sex. From thirteen to twenty-one I never even had a wet dream, let alone a girl friend or masturbation, I was so scared.

'From that explosion of realisation all the other things fell into place. I remembered that as a teenager my uncle had given me a set of volumes about the war. I used to sit and look through the photos for ages. My dream and fantasy had taken the war as an expression of my own terrible inner conflict about sex. I had been a prisoner of that conflict, and had been tortured by it. My left foot was my inner feelings of confidence to stand up or support myself as a man. The buggery and the attack by youths were one and the same thing. Because I never masturbated, allowed myself a wet dream, or any flow of sexuality, the pressure of sexual drive had been introverted. Again and again I had felt that pressure as an attack which I resisted, until I was buggered as a youthful personality.

'The reason it had presented as past lives or a fantasy attack by youths was because I would sooner see it as several lives away, or as anything except feeling the fact that I had never properly turned into a man. I had resisted that so strongly my unconscious could only express the information in stories which represented the truth in the fantasy of past lives. It was only when I questioned the fantasy, and

117

would not accept it at face value because it never actually gave me insight into my present problem or resolved it, that it was connected with my everyday life of today.

'I had one more dream in this series which shows something of the outcome. I was in a small hall with my wife, C. We were in an area like a bar enclosure for serving drinks. The whole place was dimly lit. I touched C. then ran my hands under her clothes. She responded tremendously and we fell to the floor. She was really emotional and kept crying out for me to do "something" with her legs. I forget exactly what. Then some people slowly walked into the hall from another room. Apparently they were a group interested in spiritualism, and I believe I was supposed to give them a talk. I said to C. to hold it because of the people, but she was so deep into her desires she went on demanding I have sex with her. I fought to break free, and it was quite difficult. I walked out of the bar and confronted a youngish man. We walked into another room where we talked.

'When I began to work on this dream it was very difficult. After a while I dropped my efforts and my thoughts wandered. At first I took this to be idle day dreaming, then realised I was thinking about my time in the R.A.F. when I took turns to work behind the bar. There was also an N.C.O.'s bar, in which the sergeant often locked himself and had it away with various women. I realised this connected with the bar of my dream. It was at that bar I had met H . . ., my second girl friend, I took her on the Sussex downs and we just lay looking at the stars. She always looked so unhappy. No wonder she was so frustrated, I wanted to be seduced even then. Poor girl tried her hardest without actually losing her femininity and doing it for me.

The pattern of the dream then made sense. I had broken away, during those years, from sexual connection with women and turned to men, just as I did in the dream. All I wanted was to talk about philosophy and spiritualism. As I realised this, strong feelings arose in my abdomen, like warmth and sexual longing.

'A powerful urge to masturbate arose from this, but I wanted to share it with a woman. My wife was out. I went next door to see if my youngest son was okay there. Looking at the full breasts of P., the neighbour, I felt tremendous sexual longing, like hunger deep in my belly. I felt sex was like eating or sleeping. It had no great end solution or answer in it, and it was not a thing to aim for like a goal

FINDING A HAPPIER SEX LIFE

which would make one happy, but should be enjoyed for what it is.

'When my wife came home we made love. It was very full and lasted a long time.'

In drawing out the information here, several things need emphasising;

   a) Brian did not set out to work on his sexual difficulties. He simply worked on the war dream. This shows how the dream process is always looking at problem areas. By working with the process it was carried forward in a way it would not have been capable of without waking consciousness. For instance, there was a strong resistance for Brian to actually acknowledge his own 'hen' feelings. This would have prevented the area of feeling from being consciously known if he had not pressed on through the confusion determined to understand.

   b) The drive toward understanding and insight is one of the main safeguards against being lost in meaninglessness and confusion in the unconscious world of fantasy. Some spiritualistic and psychic researchers get lost in this labyrinth of fantasy because they do not recognise how personal problems are portrayed in dramatic plots, exterior beings and past lives by the unconscious. *We must never forget that the unconscious dreams. It is the great dramatist. At a moment's notice it can create a story about ourselves in any guise and any form, in symbols we will allow into consciousness.*

If it is dance we will permit – then we will dance out an expression of our own inner pains and wonder. If it is a paintbrush we wield, then we paint; or a dowsing rod, or a sword, or a past-life hope, or spirits of the dead; whatever it is, the master artist, the great dreamer, weaves its wisdom, sings its song, plays out its wondrous theme of life and death, its majesty of love and struggle toward becoming in the midst of being.

By always seeking to find the connection between the dream life and the objective world of waking experience, or common human experience, we integrate our being. Brian integrated his fantasies of past lives with his present day life of teenage sexual conflict, and marital difficulty. But if he had remained in the world of past-life fantasies, he would never quite discover insight and real change in his present-day life.

c) Brian worked out his new understanding of himself and a release of his deep physical sexual hunger, through a series of dreams and fantasies. Constance Newland also found change through a series. Both suffered confusion during the series. So if a dream cannot be carried to immediate satisfaction it is perfectly normal. The unconscious factors which prevent us from creating the satisfying images or feelings need to be honoured and explored.

d) At one point Brian nearly missed the relevance of his fantasy by thinking it was 'an idle day dream.' The unconscious is incredibly responsive to the requests of the conscious self. If it were not so we would be unable to remember the countless pieces of information we do during each day. Once we have set a question to the unconscious, such as, what is the relevance of this dream to my life, or what is it telling me, the unconscious will attempt to respond, so long as we will allow it to do so.

However, there is a problem. Imagine a friend who has an amazing amount of information about life in general and also yourself, and you ask him a question. Let's say the question is, Why do I feel irritable with my husband? or, What is this dream telling me?

Supposing also that having asked, you never stop talking in order to listen for the reply; that you have already demanded that any reply must not deal with anything to do with religion or politics. The reply must not stir your emotions in ways you do not like; it must not contradict your own prejudices about life; it must not mention your inadequacies; it must not use four letter words, and most important . . . etc., etc.

Brian was so busy trying to work on his last dream that he didn't give the unconscious a chance to respond until he gave up. So we need to be quiet and watch. If we are holding tightly to our emotions, imagination, sexuality and attitudes, how can it respond? What means has it other than our own being? Even apparently silly little things like a song coming suddenly to mind have meaning.

SEX AND RELATIONSHIPS

Brian's series of dreams and his work on them graphically depict what has already been said, that sex is not simply an isolated part of

120

our being. Sex is intimately connected in Brian's life with his self image – whether he is a hen or a cockerel; with his relationships, with his mother and father and with his philosophy of life, in which he sees sex not as a goal in itself but as a basic pleasure enjoyed for its own sake.

This dream of Barbara's shows the relationship side of sex.

'My husband and I were in bed together. I was feeling hurt as he had his back to me and was masturbating. I was thinking, "Why turn your back on me?" Then he turned over and faced me. He had his legs and thighs close to me, and with his legs apart he openly started to masturbate again. This time somehow I felt he wasn't cutting me off, and I could and did share the feeling of quiet peace and pleasure.'

This is a problem-solving dream in that the original feeling of being left out has been dealt with by the end of the dream. If Barbara's dream had ended before her husband turned over, it would have left a feeling of tenseness. The dream also shows Barbara feeling her husband does not need her to gain his pleasure. She resolves this difficult relationship situation by creating a feeling of being willing to share his pleasure. Perhaps that would have been the solution she would have found had she carried the unfinished dream on in visualisation. In either case she had found a way of relating to her husband in a satisfying way. Both Barbara and Derek agreed the dream was a clear summing up of the way they were relating to each other at the time. Where Derek turns to Barbara is the point of change in the dream. If we take it literally it is a turning point in their relationship. The turning point is that he offers and she is willing to share his pleasure in his sense of independence. This sharing within independence is a point of growth many couples meet, and some founder on. The turning point in the dream is so important that Barbara and Derek need to make themselves very aware of it, and use the feelings it expresses in everyday interactions.

STEP SEVEN
12. *What is the Turning Point?*
If we look at Brian's series of dreams in this light, there is also an apparent turning point. It begins when he is not satisfied with fantasies which do not complete the connection between his fantasy life and his lived life. But the change really occurred when he had the sudden insight into his feelings of looking for a praising father and

121

being scared of sex. When he saw how he had pulled away from a sexual relationship out of that fear, and involved himself in philosophy and spiritualism, he was able to drop the tension in his abdomen and felt his sexual hunger. Brian's turning point, therefore, was in recognising what had been an unconscious choice, of avoiding sexual relationships because he inwardly felt female and was frightened of sex.

These turning points are like keys which unlock habitual feeling responses to a situation, allowing satisfying changes to be made. Because habits do not usually disappear overnight, these keys must be used many times in the relationship, until a new habit is formed. Therefore, the key needs to be made very conscious, written down, and frequently remembered. Or, better still, practice the change from the locked, unsatisfactory feeling state to the unlocked satisfying one. So question number four – Is there something I need to practice? needs to be used here.

THE INTIMATE SIDE OF SEX
Dreams often portray the ceremony of marriage as a purely social act. This does not belittle it, because a respect for the power of the group, and a regard for social requirements is sensible. But actual unity of two people in marriage, as far as dreams are concerned, begins or ends in the flow or withdrawal of loving intimacy. In this sense, a couple who have had the church ceremony, but who cannot share this intimacy, or are actually destructive toward one another, are not married. Dreams are extremely frank about this, as is the following:

'My wife and I were in a hotel. She was lying back on a couch, and I had my thumb in her vagina. I asked her if it were pleasurable and she told me she couldn't feel anything.'

The dreamer, Don, worked on the dream in a group. His comments are:

'The course leader had asked us to tell our dream to the members of our group and notice what we felt as we did so. I began to tell my dream and immediately blushed because I knew exactly what it meant, and didn't like what it showed me about myself. It meant that sex was a kind of comforting thumb suck for me. Because it wasn't an act of giving, my wife received no emotional nourishment at all. I didn't actually love her, I was using her body for my pleasure only,

122

in a sort of no-handed masturbation.'

Dreams show that a part of our nature is deeply disturbed by loveless sex, in or out of marriage. This applies to men and women equally, although the following is a man's experience.

'I can't actually remember what the dream was, but I awoke from it in the early hours of the morning, with a tremendous feeling of being dirty. I got out of bed trying not to disturb my wife, and went into the bathroom and cried. I had to wash my genitals to get rid of the feeling of uncleaness because of the many times I had sex without sharing love with my wife. I'm Christian enough to worry about what that means, because I just haven't been able to rouse a love for my wife. Now I feel that adultery can happen within marriage. It doesn't mean having sex with someone you're not married to, but with someone you don't love.'

When that flow between a couple, whether man and woman, or woman to woman occurs, something very special, or even mysterious, happens. We comunicate and meet each other at levels which are often beyond our perception.

Peter and Chris had not made love for a while, and were feeling a sense of distance between them that they both knew could be removed if they met sexually. During the day Peter felt attraction for Chris and several times held her warmly. He did not continue the loving embrace because he had quite a lot of work to do at one point; he was also aware of a slight coldness on Chris' part, and also several friends called on them. When they went to bed the feeling of distance was still there, but during the night Peter reached for Chris, but she did not respond. Later Chris reached for Peter, and he did not respond.

When they woke up the next morning they still hadn't met, and the feeling of distance and coldness was an almost physical reality. At that point Chris told Peter her dream of the night.

She said, 'I was lying in bed with you. We felt close and warm with each other. You started to reach out to me to share our good feelings, and a woman come to the door and wanted to ask us something. You drew away from me and when the woman received her information she went away satisfied. I saw you had got dressed and were putting on shoes to go out. I sensed you had given up trying to reach out and I felt hurt and alone and cut off from you.

'Then I was aware of you being back in bed with me, but I still had

123

the hurt, alone feelings inside myself. There was no talking in my dream, and I woke up.'

Peter then said to Chris that the dream was an almost exact duplicate of what had happened the day before. He wanted to get close but people kept calling. Then he felt Chris' coldness and kept his distance. Chris' response was that she thought he just didn't want her. They were then able to clearly see the thoughts and feelings creating the difficulty and talk about them. All the feelings of distance disappeared, and they enjoyed holding and touching and pleasuring each other.

Marriages can be made, broken and mended, over and over, if both partners wish to *make* love. At first, love, or that warm gush of passion, caring, self giving and tenderness, may be spontaneous. But in most long standing relationships the delicate tendrils of feeling which are the links between the couple are hurt and draw back. With no inner links, the couple are now divorced, with or without any social agreement of that. But if they want to, they can repair the link. And in most marriages this breaking and mending goes on again and again. It is a healthy process, not a sign of failure. Dreams are of great help in this, because, as these dreams show, they frankly state the true relationship between the couple. This helps them to understand and repair any breaks, or intensify the bonds.

One can actually incubate a dream to show what stands between oneself and one's partner by mutually deciding to meet in one's dreams. The reason this works is because dreams do not lie, and they pictorialise the subtle feelings we have which block deep intimacy. To actually meet, not only in our surface personality, but deep in ourself, the hesitations, secrets and blocks need to be removed.

Here are the dreams of a couple who decided to meet each other in their dreams.

Husband 'I was with my wife Jenny in a room. It reminded me of the bedroom of a house I lived in with my first wife. Jenny asked me to move a wardrobe for her. I did so by standing with my back to it and pressing my hand onto its ceiling. I put it against another wall, and saw I had damaged the top. The wardrobe looked worn out and, I thought needed thowing away.

'To me, the dream suggests I am carrying something from my first marriage into my present relationship. It felt like something shabby. When I looked at the feeling it was to do with the process of

124

divorce. Part of me feels it is shabby, something ideally I would never do. Yet I have. I don't want go to back to my early way of life, yet I am carrying this feeling of shabbyness, of second best, into my relationship. I can see I need to get rid of it.'

Wife 'All I can remember is that it had something to do with very expensive toilets. They were all very clean. My impression was they were all tiled and unusual. As I looked and saw they were all low lying, I saw that jerseys were being washed in each one. I thought someone had been washing the woollens, and had left them in the water to soak. Then I went to a loo opposite to those, but a woman came to the loo at the same time. She squatted next to the loo I used.

'Then Terry – my husband – I, and another couple had arranged to meet. I was a bit anxious because we hadn't arranged exactly where we were going to meet. Though I felt deep in me that I knew where to meet if I relaxed my anxiety.

'What I feel the dream is saying is that I am holding back my creativity still. I have had a lot of loo dreams. In most of them the loos have been dirty, and I have been cleaning them. These loos are clean, which seems to me to show that a lot of difficult or unsure feelings about myself have been cleared.

'The night before the dream I saw a snatch of a program about woollen garments on television. I felt it to be very creative, and so the dream is saying I'm removing difficulties from my creativity. That's why I'm not meeting Terry completely, or why I'm unsure of myself in that meeting, because inside I don't feel complete yet. I see the other couple, making the foursome, and meaning that each of us had a part of ourselves we do not express. To be whole we need to meet it. So Terry comes with his other half and I with mine.'

THE SPIRITUAL SIDE OF SEX

The question of whether we can merge with our flow of feelings as well as with our body is of first importance in a real relationship. The following dream dmonstrates this.

'During the night as I was holding my wife I experienced something which was not a dream. It was as if my whole body was full of feelings – not emotions. There was as enormous range of feelings, all the time changing. It was incredibly thrilling to be full of the feelings and pleasures one had always desired. It felt almost as though I were a group of people, and all our feelings were being poured into a

125

common centre, and we were all drawing from that centre. I kept thinking, I must remember how this is done. But I could never analyse it and woke up.

'I then held my wife sexually, waiting for that strange thing, total body feeling, to come into the act. It didn't, so I waited for the act to arise out of a common flow of feelings between us. That didn't happen either. Turning away from my wife, I felt the act would be completed inside myself. In fact, I then dreamt of an oriental woman with whom the orgasm completed itself.'

Just as we may dream of sexual experience before we actually encounter it, so we can dream of a deep merging with a partner before we achieve it in real life. Also, to merge in such a way need not necessitate sexual penetration at all. Mothers feel merged with their children; friends merge when their love overflows; great actors or singers merge with us during a performance, and our being experiences that merging when we feel the immensity and wonder of life. That is sex too.

At such times there appears to be a tangible exchange of energy, of feelings, of mutual respect and understanding, and of ourself. In this way a sexual act or relationship are a means of nourishment. We are slowly enlarged by it as a person. Something of the other person enters us and stays. Perhaps we partake of their humour, their wisdom, their impatient attack of life, or their piercing cynicism. I can look within myself and see still living in me something of a friend's generosity, another friend's eager exuberance and courage in love; and yet another one's questioning mind. In being thus entered by them I have grown to be a bigger person.

That is not only a law of life which brings health and change, it is also a practical fact for those who for one reason or another, find physical sexual intercourse untenable. Practical in that our life is still worth living if we can mate and love with our mind and heart, and share the essence of our life and wisdom with those who love us with a smile, an open ear or a held hand. Is there less love between a grandparent and grandchild than between two young lovers? Does a craftsman give less of themselves to a student than they? I know that my ability to write is born of a love thousands of years old. A love that was passed from teacher to student even through dark and terrible times, until it was given to me, still bright and eager. Remember, that also is love. And it demonstrates yet another of the great facts of loving and making love, that what we give of ourself to others lives on and is, perhaps, the only part of us life blesses with eternal existence.

Chapter Eight

Finding Better Health

DREAMS respond to a direct request for information about our health, and what can be done about it. In fact, dreams frequently deal with health hazards without our having consciously sought such information.

The following is an example.

'I had been taking a high protein diet, and I dreamt I was looking at a male athlete. I saw how spongy and unhealthy his muscles looked. They were very large, but looked puffed up. Then a voice or an interior sense of knowing, caused me to understand that the muscles were stimulated to this unhealthy growth by too much protein.

'When I woke I easily understood the dream, and stopped my high protein diet. The dream occurred in the early seventies, and it was some years later that I heard of research into protein in diet which indicated that too much protein overstimulated cell growth and could be a contributory cause of cancer. I was amazed that my dream could give me essentially the same information without research.'

Elsie Sechrist describes a similar type of dream. She says, 'In 1951, when I was suffering from a chest condition, the doctor gave me an injection of antibiotics. Just before wakening the next morning I saw a pile of oranges and the letters 'N.G.' next to them. To me the letters meant 'No Good'. It was my custom to drink a glass of orange juice each morning, so I assumed the dream was a warning against drinking it. Two days later I had another injection of antibiotics, and having forgotten the dream, I drank the orange juice. This precipitated a violent vomiting spell. Two years later I was ill with pneumonia, and when the doctor gave me the usual antibiotics he said, "If I were you, I would avoid all citrus juices; for we have discovered the combination of citrus and antibiotics makes some people very ill."[1]

In ancient Greece, many beautiful temples, such as at Epidaurus, had the sole function of helping sick people to dream a cure for their illness. These temples were extremely successful, and there are many inscriptions on stone tablets still preserved in them today, describing successful cures. One such inscription says that a man named Julian haemorrhaged from the lungs. In a dream he was told to go to the altar, mix pine nuts with honey, and eat them for three days. He did so and was cured.

These temples, devoted to the healing god Aesculapius, were an extension of techniques that had been used for centuries by healers, *shamans* and witch doctors throughout the primitive world. Anthropologists studying the healing practices of primitive tribes living today, discovered that the majority of herbal medicines and techniques used by a healer had their origin in the healer's dreams. Even treatments that had become traditional usually had their origin in the dream of a healer generations back.

The following is an example of such primitive dreams and their efficacy.

'It was at the time that many chiefs of all the tribes died of the great epidemic, influenza. Then we all saw Qu'lad was really sick for he was coughing all the time and yellow fluid was running all the time from his nose. His breath was short and he was not able to walk. Then he was informed of the death of many people. For seven days he was in bed. I mean Qu'lad. Then he slept for a short time. Then it is said he had a dream of a wolf which came into his house. Then it is said the wolf spoke to him and said, "Do not act like this Qu'lad, good friend, but go into the water of this river morning and evening. For four days do this if you want to get well, and take a bucket and dip water out of this river while you are sitting in the water, and pour the water in the bucket over both sides of your neck. Two buckets full of water in the bucket pour over the right side of your neck, and in the same way two buckets full over the left side of your neck." Thus said the wolf in the dream of Qu'lad. Then the wolf left.'

He followed the instructions and was cured. All those who acted according to his words recovered. Only Awalos later died. There were many witnesses.[2]

Alexander the Great is recorded as having had such a dream as his friend Ptolemaeus lay dying from the wound inflicted by a poisoned arrow. Watching over him, Alexander became exhausted and fell asleep. He dreamt he saw a fish being fed a strange root by his mother. The fish suggested the same roots should be fed to Ptolemaeus, and showed where it could be found. Alexander found the roots and gave them to his friend, who recovered.

In recent years, some of the great European drug houses have turned part of their research facility into investigating the properties of such herbal remedies. The results show that many of the remedies contain active ingredients which do what they were originally claimed to do. And, of course, many well known modern drugs, such as aspirin, belladona, quinine, thymol, etc., were originally herbal remedies.

To understand how a dream can give such detailed information, often previously unknown to us consciously, we must remember that consciousness or mind, is not separate from the biological and physical processes of our body. For generations the Western world have held the idea of the soul entering the body at the first breath, and leaving it at the last. Perhaps this deep-rooted conception arose from the Bible story of God breathing the soul into Adam. However it arose, and however much we feel we are not influenced by such a view our whole cultural attitude is that of consciousness having no deep interweaving with the unconscious processes of the body. Yet the body has arisen out of the natural processes on this earth, as it relates to our solar system, and mind has arisen out of the body processes. If the earth did not relate to the sun our physical existence could not have arisen. In this sense, personal consciousness has its roots, not only deeply involved in the body, but also in the earth and the cosmos. If consciousness is turned inwards to examine its roots, what might we find?

Dr. Thomas Verny and John Kelly, in their book, *The Secret Life of the Unborn Child*, show the possibility of degrees of consciousness existing in the unborn baby from the time of conception. My own research into the unconscious suggests that a form of consciousness exists prior even to conception, while insights into this, and experience of it, can be gained by our waking and sleeping self.

130

I believe such memories can become conscious because they are stages of awareness. We can observe them in our growth from infancy to adulthood. The first stage is pure physical sensation and emotion in early babyhood. There is no speech and no sense of selfhood. The next stage is speech and self awareness, but without the ability to reason fully, or verbalise inner feelings clearly. Next come the ability to reason, although, in many adults, this is still undeveloped.

W.V. Caldwell, writing about Van Rhijn's model of the stages of development in consciousness, gives four levels.

1. The deeply unconscious physiological process. Problems which cannot move more fully in consciousness, but are held at this level become psychomatic pains or illness. This is the earliest infancy level.

2. As the physiological or psychobioligical process moves nearer consciousness, its next level of expression is postural or gestural. Thus we may express our deepest, hidden feelings, in an unconscious body posture or movement.

3. Next, the unconscious content arises into the dream level, where consciousness, or our personal consciousness, can look at it. This stage is still symbolic or mythic, and the content is only partially known to us.

4. Here, what was deeply unconscious, as it rises from the other levels, emerges into verbalisation, is consciously known, and can be analysed. Assuredly this is not the final level of awareness. New levels are still being developed as the race discovers its potentialities.

In recognition of the way an unconscious content needs to emerge through the stages, I have developed a technique called co-ex, to aid in bringing to consciousness what is still in the psychosomatic or gestural level. This aids body movements and fantasy to bring about a flow between stages of unconsciousness and waking awareness. It is briefly described at the end of this chapter.

By allowing the content of dreams and body postures to unfold into waking awareness, we can know what was previously an unconscious body process. We can become aware of experiences we gained in babyhood prior to verbalisation and memory based on images or words. Our first memories are completely non-visual and non-thought or word structured. We can also gain access to the areas

131

of our present experience which remain outside thought, visual or word structures.

What is important here is the possibility that our consciousness, in dreams or while awake can have access to areas of our body, and information, usually unconscious and/or not a part of our memory. Also important is the fact that we can consciously direct this process, just as we can direct the process of walking or gaining access to our general memory.

The evening before I started to write this chapter, and in order to test this once again, I made the decision to give my body a checkout to see what basic health needs were required. In the early hours of the morning I dreamt I was talking to a man analysing my body needs. This was verging on a lucid dream in that I experienced having insight into my body, almost like looking into it. I finally arrived at the realisation I needed more calcium and Vitamin C in my diet.

In this case I had no means of finding out whether this information was based on actual body needs for the mineral and vitamin. It could simply be a dream which satisfies my demand for a 'health dream'. Because of my past experience with dreams, however, I trust this information and shall use it.

Many more examples of dreams dealing with health could be quoted in attempting to 'prove' the argument, although I do not believe that such a case could actually be proved in this way. What I hope to communicate is that dreams are not haphazard; they frequently relate directly to our health, both physical and psychological; a helpful dream can actually be stimulated by conscious decision, and there are techniques we can learn in order to achieve this.

I can be positive about such claims because of personal experience of my own dreams, other people's dreams, and reports of other writers investigating this area. Hyone and I receive so many letters from people good enough to describe their life situation and their dreams, and because of this opportunity we have been able to see the connection between the two. I would like to quote just one letter to demonstrate this.

Dear Tony and Hyone,

Some months ago I read in the *Daily Mail* of your research into dreams and have been following the dreams featured in the paper ever since with considerable interest.

For as long as I can remember, even way back as a small child, I have had graphic, often terrifying dreams. Most of them concerned falling from heights. As I grew older, I realised that these dreams occurred during stressful periods of my life, and that the 'falling' was my own fear of failure (and I must confess, I am a perfectionist). Some of my dreams have been so vivid that I can remember them in some detail, even years later.

Two of my dreams, in particular, I would like to tell you about because they occurred some distance in time apart, yet the second 'finished off' the first.

Some background, first, because I think it would be useful.

When my husband finished his nine-year contract in the Royal Navy we bought a small, rather run-down shop in West London because he had no trade or training and needed a job, we needed the accommodation above the shop, and it was not far from his father, who was supposed to be coming into partnership with us (he let us down at a point when it was too late for us to back out). It was a very unhappy time in my life – at one point we came close to going bankrupt – and I found myself working physically very hard in the shop, which was not my *metier* (I had previously been a senior secretary with BBC television), doing a part-time office job outside, caring for my husband and two small children and looking after my home. After five years of this, we had to sell up and move away as I was by this time suffering from chronic duodenal ulcers and was being treated for a nervous breakdown. We moved away, bought a house, my husband got a job, the children settled in well at school, I found a part-time job and recovered, but unfortunately the marriage never recovered. Eventually, my husband suffered an early 'mid-life crisis', ran up debts and an overdraft and after six or seven months of great unhappiness for us both, left home to 'sort himself out', promising to return when he had done that. Immediately after Christmas and New Year (part of which he spent with us), when he had been away for five months I realised he did not intend to return, and, having found myself a full-time, very demanding job, cleared all the outstanding money problems and coped with my own and the children's problems, I suffered what my doctor called 'a severe reactive depression' – whatever it was called, I was rather ill for some time – and it was at this time that I had the first of my two linked dreams.

First Dream

I dreamt that we had only recently taken the shop and while washing the floor I found a raised square where a trap-door of some kind had been hidden by the floor covering (oddly enough, I recognised the floor covering as the one we had ourselves laid in reality, though in fact there

133

was no cellar and therefore no trap-door). We lifted the floor covering and carefully raised the trap-door, though my heart was thumping and I knew I was afraid of what might be down there. As the trap-door was raised, an awful stench came up from the blackness, as if it were putrifying flesh, and I knew that something really evil was down there. We closed the trap-door and I told my husband to go the chandler's shop to buy some quick-lime so that we could throw it into the cellar and seal it up. I even told him that if the assistant in the shop asked why he needed quick-lime he was to say he was going to whitewash the back-yard wall (my Dad white-washed the back-yard of the Liverpool terraced house I was brought up in every summer and always put some lime in the mixture!). He went to the shop, got the lime, threw it into the cellar and we covered up the trap-door.

The dream then moved through time and I was aware that we had sold up and moved away. I was in the house by myself reading a newspaper and came across a piece which said that the row of shops (including 'ours') had been sold to developers and plans had been submitted for the whole block to be demolished and an office complex to be built in its place. I felt panic, knowing that the workmen would find whatever it was we had sealed up in the cellar, and jumped up from the table to go to phone my husband at work to tell him and ask him what we should do. At this point, I woke up, absolutely panic-stricken, to find myself out of bed and actually on my way downstairs to the telephone (it may be significant that my husband had mentioned in one of his frequent phone calls that he was on night duty and would actually have been at work if I had phoned him, even though it was about two or three in the morning).

Second Dream

This was a long time after the first, when I had come through the depression and quite a lot of physical illness and had at last, though very reluctantly, agreed to divorce my husband. I was again in the shop, standing in exactly the same spot as in the first dream, but this time *alone*. I didn't want to, but I knew I *had* to pull back the floor covering and lift the trap-door. I could feel my heart hammering and my mouth dry as I bent down and lifted the trap-door – but instead of darkness, a vile smell and the sensation of evil that I had in the first dream, there was light, warmth rose from the opening, and I could hear the chatter of people's voices and I watched from above people going about the normal business of running – a Bank: Nobody saw me, but I felt such a sense of relief at the feeling of normality, warmth, reassurance and human contact so close. I woke up feeling I had in a sense 'laid a ghost'.

I hope these dreams may be of interest to you and may be of use in your research.

With best wishes. Mrs. V.G.

The cellar is a generally accepted symbol of the unconscious process. Looking within herself through the trap-door the dreamer senses what are almost certainly the painful emotions, the destructive self images and the conflicts regarding the relationship. The husband going was the quick-lime which began the process of healing. But quite without any subtle attempts at interpretation, the dream indicates that something very wrong needs attention within the dreamer. Whereas the second dream gives her a clean bill of health.

Dr. Bernard S. Siegel and Barbara Siegel B.S., have worked with patients using dreams and drawings. They report their work as follows:

Physicians are generally trained as mechanics, with very little attention paid to the relationship between pysche and soma. Due to a personal search and growth process, as well as a congenial relationship with Elisabeth Kubler-Ross, I was exposed to the work of Susan Bach, an English psychotherapist and student of Carl Jung.

As a practicing surgeon, I explored the active role of the mind in illness and was astonished at the information available via dreams and drawings. I became aware that patients knew their diagnoses. The mind literally knew what was going on in the body. When I shared my beliefs and was open, the patients began to share with me their knowledge of future events and the outcome of their diseases and treatments. Now, I routinely ask for dream material and for drawings as part of their care and as part of the diagnostic testing process. As examples:

Dream 1. Patient with breast cancer reported dream in which her head was shaved and the word cancer written on it. She awakened with the knowledge that she had brain metastases. No physical signs or symptoms until three weeks had passed and diagnosis confirmed.

Dream 2. Patient had dream in which shellfish opens and worm presents itself. An old woman points and says, 'That's what's wrong with you.' The patient, a nurse, sick with an undiagnosed illness awakens with the knowledge that hepatitis is her diagnosis. Con-

135

firmed by physician later.

Dream 3. (Personal dream at a time in which I had symptoms possibly due to cancer). A group was present in dream. Others had cancer but I was pointed out as not having it. I awoke with the knowledge that I did not have cancer, which was verified by later tests.

Dream 4. (Patient with leukemia and bone marrow aspiration, reported as normal). She had a dream of termites eating away at the foundation of a house. (Imagery was utilized and exterminators brought in.) Next dream was of maggots consuming potatotes at her feet. She died in three weeks.

Dream 5. A patient dreams of seeing a picture of her son under water and the next day her son drowns.

Dream 6. A college student dreams of two stones being dropped from a bridge, rising up as spirits and writes a poem about it. This student while on vacation mails a postcard home of scene of California surf and he and a friend drown at that spot the next day. His poem was used at his funeral service.

Dream 7. A woman dreamed that DEATH came and said, 'We're taking your husband tomorrow!' She answered, 'Everybody always gets two weeks notice!' An agreement must have been made. Her husband died exactly two weeks later.

In view of my own limitations as a dream analyst, I have turned to drawings, which like the unconscious material in dreams can be interpreted for diagnosis and appropriate therapy. Drawings have predicted accurately the time and cause of death. As examples:

Drawing 1. A four-year-old draws a purple balloon floating up into the sky with her name on it, multicoloured decorations around it plus what resembles a cake, and dies on her mother's birthday.

Drawing 2. A symbolic drawing of an operating room with two lights, blue drape on the table, white drape under patient, and four figures around the patient is done by a seven-year-old one hour before her surgery at an outpatient facility, never seen before by the child. Caring for her in the operating room were two nurses, the anesthesiologist, and her surgeon, when she was taken there one hour late.

Drawing 3. A child draws a special picture for her mother, the night before her mother's surgery. On one side of the drawing is a little room with the number (6) above it. The next day mother is taken to operating room (6).

Drawing 4.   Patient draws X-Ray therapy as black and red spraying his body, and has a terrible reaction to the therapy.

Drawing 5.   Patient draws X-Ray therapy as a golden beam of energy and has an excellent result and no side effects.

The future results of chemotherapy and surgery can also be revealed in drawings. If patients see their treatment as an insult, assault or as poison they react accordingly. The unconscious mind believing in and accepting the therapy alters the side-effects and produces a better therapeutic result. This information is important so that we may alter any negative beliefs before treatment.

One of the most significant examples was a man who left his doctor's office when he was told the treatment would KILL his cancer. His drawing had been of little men carrying away his cancer cells because he was a Quaker, a conscientious objector and never killed anything! He is alive several years later using his mind and Vitamin C.

Elisabeth Kubler-Ross emphasised the importance to me of, 'Thou shalt not kill' as a commandment in our conscious and unconscious minds.

What I learned was that to heal we need to love ourselves. The love stimulates our immune system and white blood cells to fight for us. The effects of love and despair have been verified in many studies of immune responses to various stimuli.

'Mechanics' do not realise the importance of patients' belief systems in the outcome of therapy. If we are to achieve exceptional results, however, we must start working to unite the team of mind, body and spirit.

A patient listening to his inner voice often receives instructions via dreams or during meditation as one man did, requesting that he take injections of Vitamin C and utilise computor images for positive subliminal stimulation. (Exploration of these techniques has just begun by orthodox medicine.) It seems the inner voice preceded the medical profession in exploring the path to self healing or participation with the physician.

These experiences have shown me a new path as a healer, teacher,

137

care giver and have reinforced my beliefs. My patients now feel free to share experiences they would never share with a mechanistic M.D.

In summary, may I say, that this exposure has led me to believe that the psyche and soma are communicating and that somatic problems can be brought to conscious awareness via symbols. Also, I believe as Carl Jung did, 'The future is unconsciously prepared long in advance and therefore can be guessed by clairvoyants.'[3]

To use this power of our dream process to give us an assessment of our own health the following techniques can be used.

STEP EIGHT
13. *What is My State of Health?*
The simple concentration on this question during the day, and just before sleeping is usually sufficient to produce a dream in response. However, I have recently defined a modification through information I garnered from a dream, which increases the likelihood of success.

Most of us have a physical notebook or a mental memo of articles we need to buy, jobs planned, or activities we wish to do. For instance because I am engaged in writing this book, I have already got a mental memo that tomorrow, unless anything pressing needs to be done, I will sit and write. Because of the attitude behind the memo, because I look forward to the work, my faculties are deeply involved in the work. So much so that during periods when I am not writing, things I hear in conversation, see on television, think or feel are all assessed for their possible use in the book. Also, when tomorrow comes I will simply get up and carry on with the work automatically.

I am suggesting that if we put on our mental and physical memo a note saying 'Dream Check up on Health', our inner processes automatically move to complete the task. Most of our activities from cleaning up house, to cutting our fingernails are done in this way. Our dream process can be stimulated to respond by just the same process. During the day, and prior to sleeping, either write down, or make a mental note of having a dream check of health. Then forget it. If it occurs that night, tick it off your list. If not, remind yourself that it is still on your list of things you want to do.

It is a good idea to plan such a check about once a month. Changes in health and energy fluctuate all the time, and checking one's health is more important than checking the petrol in the car, what food is in the house, or whether we are in the red at the bank.

The suggestion is not being made that one checks health in this way to see if one is ill, but as a means of preventative medicine and general extension of one's life. Elsie Sechrist reports a warning dream in which she is told to be careful to avoid a lung infection. She took no notice of the dream, had several late nights and was exposed to cold weather conditions, and developed double pneumonia.

In using this question we must not use it as a means of avoiding regular medical care. But personal responsibility for health can certainly prevent many illnesses. Also the unconscious often has insights into our condition the doctor might not, as described by Bernard Siegel. It must be remembered, however, that the dream process nearly always symbolises. Many people dream of having cancer who have no physical illness whatsoever, and who never develop cancer in later life. The dream process often uses cancer as a symbol of destructive attitudes and emotions existing in us. Such dreams need to be worked out in the ways already suggested.

Most health dreams are very logical and give direct information. For instance, at a time when I suffered a great deal of acid indigestion I dreamt I was looking into the stomach and could watch the action a raw onion had. It cleansed and balanced the processes. Later, in using the advice, I found small amounts of onion and especially the leaves of chives, cleared the indigestion.

If the dream is not directly understandable use Step Six to clarify its meaning. Also continue seeking the dream response until it becomes clear. Many realisations take time to become clear even in waking life. This is also true of the processes of the dream. It is akin to a growth process which adds cell to cell to produce a limb or a leaf or to emerge through the levels of awareness described. Jung calls it a process of meandering in which themes emerge, disappear and reappear later, producing a process of psychic growth. Many insights can only be built step by step, like a logical argument, and we could not understand the final statement if we had not understood the foundations.

14. *What Can I Helpfully Do?*

139

If you are already ill, or if the dream is not clear on this point, seek a dream, which gives clearly what you can do to aid recovery or health.

If you are involved with someone else who is ill, either as a relative or professionally as a doctor, dreams can still be a source of help. Alexander the Great has not been the only person to dream helpfully for a loved friend. The dream at the beginning of the book shows how dream information helped save the life of a baby.

Some years ago a doctor in Texas had a dream in which he received a telephone call during the night to say a patient's condition had deteriorated. He dreamt he quickly dressed, ran to his car and reversed it up the incline from his garage. His brakes failed and the car smashed back into the garage. He was delayed and the patient died.

Some nights later he actually received a call to visit the patient as their condition had deteriorated. Backing up from his garage the brakes failed. Through the delay the patient died.

WHY WAIT FOR SLEEP?

Hyone and I have both been married before we met each other. When we got together we looked for a place to live which we could afford, and were lucky in being able to buy the premises we presently occupy. Prior to our purchase it had been used as a commune because of its size, and was in a very run down condition. During the period of renovating the building I developed a permanent pain in the forearm of my right arm. I talked about this to a doctor who is a friend, and he diagnosed it as tennis elbow, and told me there was nothing much I could do except avoid exertion. The pain continued for about six months without any change, and I decided to ask my unconscious if there was anything I could do to help the condition. I did not wait for sleep, but remained conscious, asked the question and waited for the responses to arise from within as I knew they would from past experience. Soon spontaneous fantasies and ideas bubbled into awareness, almost as if someone was explaining the situation to me. What I was led to understand was that during the past year I had not only been working hard physically, but because of the stress of divorce, family conflict and change of home, I had also experienced much tension and anger. These, in

140

part, had been discharged in the sawing, planing, and hammering I did while working with my right arm. But the work had broken down the cells in the arm, and the anger and tension had prevented the cells regenerating properly.

As I received this explanation I could see that it was a shrewd summary of what I had been unconsciously doing. The emerging explanation went on to say that each cell is a tiny individual, but in the body takes on a particular task. There it depends upon selfless sharing on the part of other cells for food, oxygen, protection and pleasure. What I needed to do then was to regularly and consciously allow my arm to share the pleasures of eating, music, love making and so on. The muscles didn't mind hard work, but they did need pleasure and relaxation too.

I used this information as well as I could, consciously letting pleasure flow to the arm. Within a week it was completely free from pain. The problem has never returned.

Some time prior to that, during a very bad virus attack which laid me low for several days, I developed a painful cough. Gradually, what felt like a toothache of the chest occurred. It kept me awake at night, and did not lessen despite pain killers. It then spread to both arms also. Unable to sleep I got out of bed to walk about the house for relief. At that point I decided to ask my unconscious what I could do. The response was very quick, my body badly needed Vitamin B. I had brewers yeast in the house and ate about twelve tablets. After swallowing them I felt a real hunger to eat more. I ate another ten, then another, until I felt satisfied. I then went back to bed and the pain disappeared within ten minutes or so, and I slept for the first time in several days. The pain never returned, and I realised I had read about the need for B vitamins in neuralgia years previously, but had forgotten the information.

How is it possible to have such a clear and detailed response from one's unconscious without recourse to sleep, drugs or unusual states of mind? It is through the practice of a simple technique which enables our conscious self to relate more fully to the unconscious. The technique allows the dream process to break through into conscious activity. It can then become much more direct and specific. It can respond to particular questions as dreams themselves do, but much more quickly. It tends to express in symbols still, but

141

can be led to transcend into direct perception or verbal expression. In the two examples I have given above, the expression was quick, to the point and effective.

In essence the technique is ages old. There is very little new under the sun. In the past, however, the method and its results were usually described in symbolic, sectarian or mysterious terms. Therefore, to be understandable rationally, the technique needs some explanation in today's terms.

In January of 1972, Mike Tanner, Sheila Johns and I started a small experimental group. At the time we were not very clear about exactly what we were looking for or how to find it. Looking back, however, I can see clearly now the pieces of information and experience which we eventually put together to find the waking, lucid dream. I had already noticed, as most of us have, that during sleep animals and humans make spontaneous movements and sounds. It is easy to recognise these as connected with the process of dreaming. Because most of us wake ourselves at sometime by talking or shouting in our sleep, we can see that the talking and the movements are expressive of what we are doing in the dream.

The important point is that we have not *consciously* decided to make such movements or sounds. They are spontaneous, as is the dream itself. Our conscious personality may be amused or even anxious about such movements. What they point out is that there are at least two parts of our nature which motivates actions, movements, speech and ideas. These are the waking self and the unconscious. In general one rules the day and the other the night. Considering that the unconscious directs all the non-volitional functions such as digestion, heartbeat and metabolism, and it creates very cohesive patterns of thought and action in dreams, it is far more in charge of our being than our conscious self is. However, many people feel that if they gave up their conscious self, with its likes, dislikes, ideas and decisions about which arm to move, and which eye to wink, there would be no other directing or creative centre to their being. Yet each night in sleep the other centre takes over and lives its own life, complete with speech, relationships, emotions, sex, movements and so on.

So the next question I asked was, why doesn't the unconscious break through into the day, and direct what is happening? Could in the fact, the movements, sounds and ideation from the unconscious centre be allowed expression while awake? After all, it has fuller access to memory, the regenerative processes, body functions, genetic coding, and other actions in our being which at times would be extremely helpful to use.

Sometimes the unconscious or some drive in it does take over from conscious volition. When a person sleep walks, the actions in the dream are being allowed full expression. Also, people who have a vision or intuitive hunch, are experiencing the breaking through of the dream process into waking consciousness.

As an experimental group, our interests were to see if we could extend the effectiveness of the self regulating or therapeutic function of dreams by tapping it consciously. Also whether we could extend our waking mental abilities by greater access to full memory via the dream process. I was suffering a great deal of ill health at the time, and hoped to find ways of improvement. As such, sleep walking, hallucinations and visions would not be helpful, even though they might be interesting material from the unconscious. What we wanted was a tool which would enable us to work with the unconscious. To do so we needed to find how to release the normal inhibiting factors which prevent the dream process during waking.

We outlined the inhibitory factors as:

1. An inbuilt process which inhibits full flow of nervous impulses from the brain to the motor-muscle nerves during dreaming.
2. An attitude which, during waking, is assumed in order to direct activities, i.e. we assume nothing is going to happen with our voluntary muscles and our speech, unless we will it.
3. Muscular tensions which inhibit spontaneous movements, tics, and others.

We assumed correctly that the inbuilt inhibition of movements while sleeping could be altered by a learning process. An interesting point here is that I recently came across a research project into animals dreams by Adrian Morrison at the University of Pennsylvania. He says that usually a neurological safety mechanism prevents the limbs from responding to signals from the brain during dreams. While investigating a condition, called narcolepsy, in animals, which causes them to lapse uncontrollably into real sleep, he discovered a surgical way to release the safety mechanism. He found that a small area of the pons, in the brain, played a part in suppressing the nerve impulses during sleep which activate the muscles. When this area in the pons is damaged, the animal expresses full movement while dreaming in rem sleep. Thus cats were observed jumping, playing and stalking prey while they dreamt. In our own experiments we had the same results without the surgery. We found we could learn a different response to unconscious impulses.

The way to do this is to create a similar mental and physical state to sleep, but remain awake. When we sleep we let go of our conscious decisions, our directed thinking, our desire to move, our rational criticism and we surrender ourself to unconsciousness. In a sense it is like handing over our body to, say, a physiotherapist to move and direct, while we remain limp. We also surrender in some degree our inhibitions about expressing irrational social actions.

We found in hundreds of experimental sessions on ourselves and other people that as we learnt to have a permissive conscious mental and physical condition, movements, feelings and sounds, from a source other than conscious volition occurred. Observation of this phenomena over the last eleven years leads me to believe there are certain well-defined features.

1. Although the movements may at first appear haphazard and irrational, if allowed to continue without conscious criticism they usually express a defined theme or even a dramatic event.
2. Like a dream, the theme or drama often symbolises the person's life situation, creative thinking or problem-solving faculty.
3. There are obvious stages or depths of the experience as Caldwell described. Movement is most often the first phase. It can then extend to include emotions and fantasy. This can, if met in the right way, lead to insight or realisation of what the theme is expressing. In other words, the symbols give way to rational understanding.
4. If left entirely alone, the movements and theme appear to express what are habitual energy patterns. For instance, if we have a habitual pattern of turning our anger inwards upon ourselves, the movement or theme might express as banging one's chest aggressively with one's fist.
5. Because we can consciously observe the themes and come to understand them, these habits can be worked with and transformed.

6. The basic action is self regulatory. So, in these movements, themes, fantasies, our organism attempts its own healing and growth. In the sleep state the process is only partly successful. When united to conscious observation and cooperation, the effectiveness is heightened. My own illness was dealt with in this way.

7. The process is also amenable to direction. It is a learnt skill allowing the unconscious to express in a controlled and meaningful manner. Therefore, skill at directing it increases with degree of ability in allowing depth of expression. Some of the possibilities of cooperating with the unconscious will be considered in the next chapter.

Because the overall result of this process is an expansion of self awareness, or consciousness expansion, I have called it co-ex for short.

From the point of view of health, there are simple methods for using co-ex. Because one of the main features of the dream is self regulation (homeostesis) which aims at physical and psychic health and growth, almost any degree of expression of co-ex is helpful. It is primarily helpful in releasing nervous tension and in allowing the body to heal itself.

Some years ago I met a very heavily built young man who told me his own experience of spontaneous co-ex. He had suffered lower back pain for some time, and was standing in a pub with a pint in his hand telling a friend about his problem, when he realised his body was moving spontaneously. His hips were circling. During the following days he allowed the movements to occur regularly, and after some time the pains ceased.

Prior to using co-ex I suffered a great deal of pain between my shoulders, especially when driving. A friend massaging the area pointed out there were many small nodules there. When I started using co-ex some of the first movements were shoulder circling. I used co-ex about an hour each week, and I was amazed that for a whole hour my shoulders could continue their spontaneous movement. If I attempt to consciously exercise, an enormous effort of will is needed to continue such a movement for even a few minutes. But in co-ex many people find such movements effortless. After some weeks my shoulder tension disappeared, and I can now drive long distances without pain.

145

To use co-ex to improve your health, practice this simple technique.

1. Choose a time and place in which you can feel free to express any form of movement or sound, and when you will be undisturbed by outside intrusions. Make sure there is sufficient space. A body length and both arms width is about the minimum you need.
2. Sometimes it can be helpful if two or more people practice together, although many prefer to use the technique alone.
3. Wear loose clothing, or undress if you wish. Not tight or restrictive jeans, etc.
4. Give yourself at least half an hour in which you will allow what might usually be thought of as meaningless or irrational expression of yourself. During this period do not interfere with what happens by judging, criticising, directing or attempting to understand.
5. Let your body express its own needs in movements, sounds, feelings and quietness, and stand in the middle of your space with eyes closed. Slowly circle the arms. As you do this be aware of the shape in space your hands are carving. When you have this awareness, allow yourself to carve any shapes in space which arise out of the flowing expressive movements of your hands and arms. Let the rest of the body enter into this.
6. Now allow your body to doodle. Don't think up movements or irrational activities, but allow your body to relax and stretch or move in any way which suggests itself without conscious thought. You may have an urge to yawn, scratch your head, stretch, curl up and sleep, move or make sounds. Whatever arises allow the pleasure of expression.

Many of my own early sessions resulted in movements which expressed and stimulated various parts of my body.

A woman who experienced co-ex for the first time at a seminar in which I explained the technique, describes her initial experience as follows.

'When Tony came to explain co-ex to the group, I had just reached the point of despair with my marriage. A few days before I had taken the first step towards breaking it. From the first my experience of co-ex wove itself, directly or indirectly, into my outer life. It was never a separate thing going on inside only.

'Tony explained to us about letting whatever came, come. I did not understand too well, but lay down with the others and he came to each of us briefly and moved our arms, and left us lying. (In that group I was using the release of muscular tension to start co-ex.)

'Perhaps two minutes had passed when I felt a distinct twitching around my brow, which was repeated, and then it spread down my face, a downward pressing movement. My face was involved then in a big muscular movement, pressing down, seeming to flatten the face, and then spread down the body towards the feet. Gradually my whole body became involved in big waves of pressing movement which flowed down, lifting and tossing my legs, so that my heels were banging on the floor. Wave succeeded wave. I did as he said, and let it happen, using the skills to relax which I had learnt in practice. I wasn't frightened, although I couldn't imagine what was happening to me. Instead, I felt happy and elated, warmed through.

'I knew I had found something of great significance, but it was many months before I could put words to it. It remained an intriguing mystery, like a dropping away of chains, or a touching of promise, while I passed through the pain of divorce. I feel that my experience that day released considerable energy. It did not break my marriage – that would have happened anyway. But I received strength which I used for my needs at that time. Months later it came to me with the force of revelation, that I had been born that day.'

Co-ex has been a magical experience for me too. It has healed me of ills, taught me, shown me new vistas of mind and human possibility. It has at times faced me with my own problems and disturbed me. I have come to see that health is not simply eating the right foods or jogging occasionally; it depends upon how we relate to our work and our companions, how we regard the universe.

As Dr. Oliver Sacks writes: 'All the operations in coming to terms with oneself and the world, in face of continual changes in both, are subsumed under Claud Bernard's fundamental concept of "homeostasis". We have to recognise homeostatic endeavours at all levels of being, from molecular and cellular to social and cultural, all in intimate relation to each other.'

As we allow the self regulatory or homeostatic process of co-ex to work in our life through regular weekly practice, its expression matures. From physical movements we progress to movements with feelings as that area is enlivened. Out of feelings insight emerges. From being a passive observer, we graduate, as we gain insight into the process, into an enquirer, and a cooperate director of our own resources.

Chapter Nine

Finding New Dimensions of Your Mind

W E live in an age when exploration of space without a vehicle is not only possible but perhaps essential. It is unlikely that any craft can transcend the speed of light to make interstellar exploration possible. But the human mind, free, of its boundaries, can and does make such leaps. The future of humankind, or whatever we evolve into, has a physical boundary in our solar system created by the life of the sun. When the sun dies we die, unless we can find another environment.

Charles Lindbergh, the great leader in our age of flight said in *Life* magazine, when asked about the future of rocketry, 'We will discover that only without spaceships can we reach the galaxies; that only without cyclotrons can we know the interior of atoms. To venture beyond the fantastic accomplishments of this physically fantastic age, sensory perception must combine with the extra-sensory.'[7]

The sun is not the most pressing and immediately important of our boundaries. We have a very real and present inbuilt boundary created by our propensity for aggression, manipulation, anxiety and our past. This boundary of war and self destruction, or loss of self through the manipulation of totalitarianism or capitalism, draws nearer each year as our technology develops. Our own nature, still largely immersed in sexual, territorial and aggressive drives, leads us to acts of terror and destruction *now*! Like an individual who is beating his children but who will not pause to examine his own

149

motives, his own urges, to see if they can be transformed, we as a race shy away from self examination. Nations, rather than admitting their own interior social sickness, develop enormous fangs of aggression to ward off the threat of social revolution they see in others.

We cannot, any longer, remain unconscious and complacent in believing that natural selection and evolution will lead us through our difficulties. It is imperative that we open the bonnet of our vehicle to see what makes it keep running off the road. Another crash may be the last. Unless we begin to accept personal responsibility, and learn to direct our own vehicle, we may not have another chance to learn from mistakes.

Dr. Salk, in a recent interview with Bernard Levin on television, said; 'I think we need a new way of thinking and new thinking tools in order to ably meet this new challenge. This is unprecedented in human evolution. We are really being challenged. We are being tested to see if we can make it, so to speak.

'I think we may very well see, in the future, the emergence of a transcendental human being, in the sense that it will be a human being who is natural but suprahuman; someone who is capable of the kind of consciousness, the kind of self restraint, the kind of discipline, the kind of participation as a human being in the fullness of life and, at the same time, is capable of influencing and directing those negative forces, those destructive entropic forces, that are constantly operating . . . I think that man is noble, that nobility is genetically inscribed, if you will, but it needs to be evoked. The potential for all that has emerged in the course of evolution must have pre-existed. It needed to be evoked by circumstances.'[2]

Even as I write, the problems facing humanity gather round us like giants, walking in our midst, often invisible except where some life is crushed, some nation is attacked, some group oppressed. War never ceases somewhere on our globe; our social systems no longer fulfil the needs of people, and are breaking down; the monetary system places human beings second or third in line to finance, factory production and corporations. It no longer serves the needs of people. They serve it. Education is preparing square people for square holes which no longer exist. Millions of people, willingly or unconsciously, are manipulated or farmed like cattle, through

150

shrewd techniques of indoctrination. A war is being waged throughout the world between the Haves and the Have Nots; between people who are in control of finance and resources, and those who are not.

When one goes through the doorway of self into the unconscious, it is not only personal dramas concerning work, love and survival that one finds. Beyond the personal lies the collective arena of human experience, and it is here one discovers the battle, the hidden forces of manipulation, the conflict between human beings, principalities and powers. Fortunately one also discovers wonder; naked glorious potential, and the figure of collective human love.

Here is a dream which is an example of a person becoming conscious of the internal battle.

'I am in a field with my mother and my son. It is in the village where I was born, near two large elm trees. As I watch I see that sheep are on the topmost branches of one of the elms. I wonder how they got up there, whether they climbed or were lifted. Then one of them jumps and crashes to the ground throwing up earth and dust. I am sure it is dead, but it gets up. I watch to see if its legs are broken, but it is unharmed.

'Now I expect another sheep to leap after the first, but at that moment a cow is lifted completely into the air, as high as the tree, then drops and smashes to the ground, dead. A bull also is lifted and smashed by an unseen force.

'I shout to my mother and son . I have to get them away quickly because something unseen and dangerous is happening. They start to hurry with me, but suddenly a huge sound fills the sky. I look and see flying organs (saucers). Music and singing of a religious nature fills the sky. I shout to them to keep their eyes on the ground, to concentrate on actually seeing the ground. In fact a sort of mist or fog swirls suddenly. I know instinctively that if one doesn't concentrate on the ground, the music will hypnotise one to follow it, like the Pied Piper. In fact, my mother decides to be one of those "lifted up" by the space craft. I feel she has been influenced or taken over by aliens, but I do not argue, only concentrate on getting out with my son.

'We turn around a corner, and are standing on a wide path half way up a canyon wall. Below me, moving towards the aliens I see a

151

group of people who believe they are the chosen ones being led from on high to live in a special way. They are driving magnificent cattle to the space crafts.

'I then walk back and look into what is now a huge ampitheatre filled with people lined in groups like soldiers. I feel they have lost their will to the influence.'

The dreamer used the method of 'being' the different symbols to discover what feelings and associations underlay the dream. He says:

'The sheep are people who are led into an impossible relationship with their environment by the social attitudes and political views they have accepted, grown up with, but not questioned. I am actually one of those sheep, but I jump down from my sick position through working on my dreams. Literally I have come down to earth. I expected others to follow but they didn't. The music and noise is the insidious and pervading influences, or political, religious and commercial forces, which try to "farm" human beings. They violently disrupt the natural forces of parenthood and social activity – the cow and the bull. My mother is my emotional nature which is swayed by them. But by continually looking at events and what is actually happening in the world we can remain our own self – we can make our own decisions from what is apparent in the world instead of what we are pressurised to decide.

'The group of people represent religious manipulation. By being presented a God which is exterior to us, we are opened to manipulation by what we are told this exterior Gods tells us to do.'

Is this one of the ways we become the suprahuman people Dr. Salk talks of? Namely, by becoming aware of our own unconscious and thereby having insight into those 'negative forces', those manipulating corrupting influences which have entered into us which we frequently accept as normal. Certainly, if we are to find a way through the problems of our own humanness, individually, socially and globally, we have to pull ourselves up by our own bootstraps, we have to find forces of transformation.

The dreamer describes one of these transformative forces – the watching of events.

But here is a dream which portrays another such form of transformation. I will call it the Helper to avoid negative associations. Maybe it is what Dr. Salk described as nobility.

'I was getting married and arrived at the door to the Quaker

Meeting House in Euston Road. My bride was with me. We had to produce a ticket to get in. My bride produced hers, or her half, but I didn't have my half. Instead of turning left into the Meeting, I went straight ahead into the Euston Road. A terrible battle was going on, bullets were flying, and people were being killed. I immediately thought, "Blow this, I'll play dead." So I dropped down as if I had been shot.

'I don't know if the battle was still going on, but as I lay there I saw a man walking toward me dressed as a soldier. He didn't have a gun or any weapon, but he had no fear at all, and came and knelt beside me. There was a thing like a limpet shell clinging to my back. I hadn't realised it was there until he touched it. Carefully he pulled the shell off, but its tentacles were in my flesh, and he told me that by service to others these would be dissolved. Then he left me, but I knew I had met a very great man.

'Afterwards, thinking about the dream, I realised he was telling me by his actions, not to be afraid of human conflict, my own or other peoples. I am still emotionally moved when I think about him now.'

Because such dreams, and the message they give, arises from the unconscious so often, to some extent one must see scientific laboratory type tests of such things as ESP and telepathy as somewhat blind and missing the point. If a fire chief knew that the person ringing the alarm was doing it only as an experiment, he would not mobilise the force. The unconscious is life itself. It is concerned with survival, with concern for the species or the group, and its basic drive in its interspecies relationships is self giving. Life gives itself all the time, as food, like a gift from one species to another, so each survives. Its secondary drive is cooperation, as in symbiosis. In this way cells work together to form living creatures. Living creatures work together to form an ecological system.

Any consideration of inner faculties or dimensions of the mind which overlooks these fundamental processes is in a cul-de-sac.

The relationship of our conscious self with our own interior, yet universal, life processes of self giving, cooperation, reproductive care, and love of infant life forms is, like everything else, an exterior symbol in our dream. The symbol directly dramatises or personifies the psychobiological events it portrays; and in the case of these universal processes, it does this in the symbol of the Helper; the Big

153

'Un, as Billy Connolly says, and the Christ. In other cultures other names are given. Life is ever involved in and interested in its life forms. Today as ever, life walks with us and talks with us in our dreams.

So what are the dimensions of the mind in which we and Life can talk, play, discover, love and rest?

BODILESS AWARENESS

In 1953, when I was sixteen, and already deeply interested in the possibilities of the human mind, I took a course in deep relaxation. I practiced every day for three months, tensing my muscles, relaxing them, then passing my awareness over and over my body, dropping the feeling of tension. After three months I was quite proficient. One evening, after coming home from dining out with friends, I went to bed thinking I would leave my usual practice, but in the end decided to practice even though it was late. After going over my body several times I suddenly lost my right arm. I had no sensation of it other than space, hugeness. Then I lost my left arm, and – my whole body. It was like falling through a trap-door into the stars. I had no sense of having a body. Thoughts had ceased, except for a murmur apparently a thousand miles away. Yet in blackness, in immensity, in absence of thought I existed vitally.

After that day I could repeat the experience almost any time I sat down and used the relaxation technique. I felt at the time, and still believe it correct, that I had fallen asleep yet remained awake. Waking, critical awareness, had been taken through the magic doors of sleep into a universe it seldom ever sees.

Waking consciousness exists as a tiny part of the total being it manifests in. Maybe I am exaggerating, but in its tiny room it has a few buttons it presses and the voluntary muscles move. There are a few screens which, through *some* of the body senses give a view of a tiny range of the phenomena of the universe. The rest of our being, the remainder of the universe, we give the cover-all name of unconsciousness. It simply means – *we are not aware of it*. The unconscious is not a thing or a process – it is a mass of functions, processes, actions and reactions of which we are not usually aware. We frequently make the mistake of believing that anything we are not aware of does not have consciousness. Because of that we assume that one could never be aware of the intimate details of, for instance, liver functions, or brain-cell activity. But we are used to the idea of a part of our body being anaesthetised, or going to sleep because of a circulation block. These areas, which were devoid of awareness, can become conscious again. Could not anything which was entered into with waking awareness be considered conscious?

I do not think, in my experience of bodilessness, that I had 'left' my body. Rather, the connections with the sense organs had been switched off so that I had no body awareness.

The experience made me certain that waking consciousness could have a completely different experience of itself, other than the 'normal' one which is dominated by body sensations, emotions and thoughts. There were, I realised, other dimensions of mind to experience. Being of a practical nature I wondered what could be done from this new platform of experience. However, at that time, despite some months of experiment, I could achieve nothing more than bodiless consciousness. It is a condition most people can reach with a little regular practice.

EXTENSION OF AWARENESS

Two years later another dimension opened. I was living in Germany during two years of national service in the Royal Air Force. I felt very homesick, had no girl friend, and was still experimenting with states of mind. I wondered if I could reach my home in London by relaxing and concentrating. I went to bed early on a July night and tried the experiment. I could imagine my parents, the rooms of our house, but it remained mental pictures. I gave up and fell into sleep. Then I was suddenly aware of a rushing upward feeling, and a sense of great release or escape from pressure. This occurred in blackness, but gave way to light, and I found myself suspended above my bed, looking down on my sleeping body. Immediately I was overcome by panic and terror. Then the thought came that this must be what I had been trying to do, and I was now succeeding. With this the terror gave way to a burst of uncontrollable laughter. I believe this was the release of tension due to the terror. Spontaneously, and without thought, I was next flying high in the air, with my knees drawn to my chest, looking down at the German countryside. I noticed at one point radiations emanating from areas on the ground, and wondered if it were people praying. Then I was over the sea, noticing ships far below; and suddenly I was

155

in our sitting room at home. It had all happened so quickly I was still in amazement, and looked down at my body, to take stock of myself, as if I were experiencing some sort of magic. I noticed I was dressed in civilian outdoors clothes, I looked and felt completely solid and real, but I felt much more awake, alert and in control of myself than I had ever felt before. Although solid, I felt as alive and quick as lightning; as if my very thought was a huge power which could transport or change me.

The self examination was over in a moment and I looked up to see that I was standing behind the sofa in the middle of the room. On my right my mother sat in an armchair alone, knitting. In front of me, our alsation dog Vince lay asleep by the gas fire. Thinking I must be easily visible, I called to my mother with great joy, to look at me. She paused in her knitting for a moment as if some thought had struck her, but didn't look at me. This led me to feel as if there must be a barrier of some sort blocking our communication, so I shouted to her as loud as I could. The part of her I watched, carried on knitting, but a deeper part of her seemingly unknown to her con- scious self, enveloped me in her love and care. Also, Vince seemed to have heard me shout. He looked up from his sleep and *saw* me. He leapt up and bounded to me behind the sofa. He whined, barked, yelped with love and pleasure at having me near again. Then the scene faded and I gradually awoke in Germany, my body feeling as heavy as lead compared with the fleet self I had just experienced. Consciousness, too, seemed dim, as if filtered.

Like the bodiless experience, this out of the body awareness is not uncommon either. Surveys at several universities in England, Australia and America suggest that up to one in four people have had at least one such experience. So here is another dimension of human experience. In my own case, my mother told me by letter that she had been alone that evening, my father being out. She had the sensation at one point of 'someone walking over her grave', but she didn't see or hear anything. The dog, however, appeared to see something behind the sofa and ran barking and yelping to the spot.

Such experiences are not as simple as they might at first appear. Does one, for instance, travel out of the body? Without taking into account the mass of information from other cases, there is a great deal to be deduced from this one example alone.

a) In bed I was clothed in forces issue pyjamas. In my OBE (out of body experience) I was dressed as a civilian. Unconsciously I never thought of myself as an airman, but always as a civilian. This suggests that my OBE body and clothing are not a sort of extracted version, a subtle counterpart of my physical self. It seems more likely that my OBE body is created, as in dreams, by my unconscious habitual thoughts and feelings about myself. If that is correct, one could assume any shape, or be a bodiless consciousness, a musical note, a colour, or anything.

b) The experience was largely spontaneous. The direction of its action appears to have been conditioned by my conscious attempts to reach my parents. While I slept, unconscious forces in myself took up this 'request' and completed it. This leads me to believe that to achieve this condition easily, one must have a very good working relationship between conscious self and the unconscious; or else a neurotic quirk brings about a relationship which enables it to occur easily.

My recent attempts to understand the process more fully, done subjectively by entering the unconscious itself through dreams and co-ex, suggest powerful blocks against easy access to this faculty. It seems from this work that the faculty is a stress and death response developed very early in the evolution of land animals. There appears to be a connection of consciousness between individuals and the collective experience or consciousness of the species. I believe the faculty was a survival trait which, at the moment of intense stress, but primarily at the moment of death, transmitted a full sensory impression of death or danger to the consciousness of the species or related members of the species, i.e. siblings or parents. Thereby the species could acquire a knowledge of a cause of death to further its survival chances.

The problems which arise in using this faculty are that it is like the emergency telephone number, we only use it when things get tough. We have deeply inbuilt inhibitions against hitting the death-message button unless we really need to. This suggests why so many people fear they are dying when they have a bodiless experience in deep relaxation; or my terror; and the stress people have in seeing a 'ghost'. Most OBE's actually occur during war, or at the moment of death. They usually communicate the event of death to relatives. So if we are to use

157

this faculty we have to defuse its connections with the death signal, and re-route it to other purposes.

c) The OBE occurred during sleep. It is, in some ways, akin to a dream, except that in this case it connects up with objective events, such as my mother being actually alone knitting, and the dog barking. Dreams are a common doorway to OBE. Much research is being done in England, Russia and America to explore this possibility.[3]

Unlike a dream, consciousness is fully alert, can direct events, and has critical reasoning ability.

d) The travelling was not continuous. I did not have to travel, because near the end I was instantly there. This raises the question of whether the travel, like the body, was necessary at all. Perhaps travel also, as in a dream, occurs out of habits of thought. How can one be somewhere very distant without travelling? Of course it appears impossible while we introvert the idea that we are a physical body which needs to be transported through physical space and time. Maybe we also introvert the idea, gained by having our input from body senses switched on too long, that we are our body shape; that consciousness is the same shape as the impressions arising as body image.

It seems likely that I travelled because I believed I had to, and travel is irrelevant. Maybe consciousness is already everywhere, and one never goes anywhere, so is not out of the body, but tunes into a particular part of the overall awareness.

Sir Auckland Geddes, talking to the Royal Society of Medicine, told of an extensive OBE in which the person, while apparently out of the body, realised that simply by thinking of a friend, they were observing the friend, and at the same time aware of events, occurring in their own house. Wondering how this could occur, they looked at their body, and saw that consciousness is not immersed in the body, the body is immersed in consciousness, and the brain is only a receiving or condensing plate.

e) Where my mother responded to me at one level but not at a conscious level, led me to theorise that each of us have a subliminal appreciation of other people's mental presence or attitudes. If these cannot be brought to consciousness, however, then it appears to our conscious self that there is no such thing. If the dead do continue to exist in a world similar to the one I experienced, where thought and unconscious attitudes create environment, unless we were able to be conscious of the unspoken thoughts of the living, we would believe the dead had no existence.

WAKING UP IN SLEEP

At sixteen I had learnt to remain awake while falling asleep; at eighteen I woke up while asleep and experienced extending my awareness to a distant point; but it wasn't until many years later that I experienced yet another dimension of sleep experience.

I had been working very extensively with co-ex, exploring its possibilities and found the process would respond to questions about dreams. In this way I could ask my own unconscious for an insight into my dreams. With two groups of people I experimented with this technique. During that period I had a dream in which I observed the leaf of a fern unfold. As I watched the unfolding I was at the same time aware of experiencing a sensation of something unfolding in my own body. I felt excitement even in the dream, because not only was I observing a symbol, but I was at the same time directly experiencing what the symbol represented. I had suspected for a long time that dreams are a part of the process in which the deep unconscious forces in our being rise into awareness. In this dream I felt I was watching it at work.

A few days later one of the most important events in my life occurred. I went to bed, fell deep into sleep, and *woke up while my body was deep in sleep*.

I want to make it clear that I did not have a lucid dream. In lucid dreaming one wakes up, is aware while the body sleeps, but is dreaming, in that one exists amidst symbols and visible surroundings. In my own case there were no symbols, not even an image of me in a body. I was simply wide awake without any shape or form. I had direct experience, without any symbols, of the action of the energies in my body. I had no awareness of body shape, only of the processes working in my body. I experienced them, but did not see them. I was again very excited, and checked over what was happening in my body. I noticed that a tension in my neck was interfering with the flow and exchange of energy between the trunk and head. I

159

could also observe that the tension was due to an attitude I had in regard to authority. I realised that having become aware of the attitude I could begin to change it and remove the tension to improve my health.

A little while later I developed a chest infection. During the infection I once more woke during sleep. Again I was aware of direct observation of the body processes. I watched with fascination and wonder, the forces of my body working to heal the infection. My main feeling was how plant like or gentle the action was.

The fourth of this series of experiences was the doorway to another dimension of awareness. I awoke, observed the ever flowing and changing body processes, and in this state tried to understand what had happened. I saw that usually I and everybody else dream in symbols. I had gone behind the symbol into an entirely different level of experience to view directly the processes from which dreams arise. This level was one of continuous movement and change, and I wondered what was beyond that. Immediately I penetrated behind the body changes, just as I had penetrated the dream symbols. This new level was one which transcended opposites, and in which no change was observable. I was no longer an ego, and was without identity, yet at the same time I existed. It then came like a revelation that the changeless and changing coexist. Only in our thoughts do we separate them. Later I remembered the words of Blake, that 'Eternity is in love with the productions of time.'

This type of experience is not new. In 1923 Rudolph Steiner's book, *Knowledge of The Higher Worlds*, was published, containing a chapter on sleep, and how to wake up and explore in just the way I describe above. Ouspensky and many others experimented on the ability to remain awake during sleep. Mostly they do not consider waking beyond symbols. They do not describe the possibility of exploring one's body functions in this state, or see the real practical issues this raises. For with the ability to consciously examine the processes of our being, the prevention or cure of disease takes a new turn. My feeling on viewing the powerful effect of one simple attitude was that many chronic illnesses have their original beginnings in long established disruptive attitudes. These attitudes, because they disrupt healthy functional flow over a long period, cause trouble spots in the system.

In other cultures such as those in the Far East, the possibility of waking in sleep was recognised, and training procedures, like yoga, used to attain it. Claims have been made by such gurus as Sai Baba of Shirdi that they had continuous awareness throughout waking and sleeping.

My own opinion is that here is a whole world of experience and possibilities which our culture has not explored or made its own. Because we wake up for hours each day to what we call the real or objective world, we have time to develop a personality, build relationships, undertake work, explore possibilities, and play at this level. Consider what might happen if we woke for several hours during each sleep period to this other world. We could also explore and develop relationships with others, and undertake some project or line of work. Dr. Rebbecca Beard, describing her change from dealing with patients at a physical level, to finding ways of healing their inner life, says that in fact she woke each night and developed a new life in sleep.[4]

HUMANITY AS THE AWARENESS OF NATURE

Although it is now popular to talk to plants, in general the seriousness of the undertaking is overlooked. Perhaps this is because we talk to the plants instead of attempting a communication. Humans have always believed that communication with nature and its forces was possible. Rain dances, crop fertility rites, hunting dreams, are very ancient. Until this century, however, many of these practices were considered ineffective superstition. Luther Burbank, one of the world's greatest horticulturalists exhibited a special contact with his plants, and was said to talk with them.

Experimenting with this ourselves, Hyone and I attempted communication with a sick New Zealand tomato tree we had. It was in a large tub, well fed and watered, but had the greenfly, and was also wilting. We had sprayed, but the general debility of the plant seemed to attract the fly. I used the technique of co-ex to see if my unconscious could asses the condition of the plant. The first thing I felt was an unexpected wave of love, as if the plant was wordlessly saying thank you for caring. Then I had the sense of my consciousness meshing with the consciousness/being of the plant. My impression was that the plant was an entity, a form of life and awareness, but it did not have a focused consciousness which could formulate the idea – what causes this sickness? Because I could ask the question, and

161

because I allowed my consciousness to consider the plant, a new situation arose; the plant could be aware of itself. The difficulty of the process was that everything was direct non-verbal experience. As the experience of plant life was new to me, I had to spend some time allowing the sensations to soak in and be analysed by my rational mind. What arose out of this was the understanding that the root system of the plant needed to spread sideways, not down. We therefore put the plant in a sack, with the same earth spread thin. Within a week the greenfly had all gone, without spraying, and the plant grew strong and luxuriant.

Obviously no hard and fast facts can be drawn from such slender evidence. Considering the ability to extend awareness to a distant place though, I feel it may be possible for consciousness to extend to anything, and thereby analyse its functions. But if I am honest, because of the information arising from many people's dreams, I believe nature itself is conscious; that matter itself is like a battery of consciousness. Dreams suggest that dreaming itself is a link between the living forces of nature in our being and our conscious identity.

I realise that, to some people, what I am about to say may sound naive, but it is an important part of what I have found in considering a large number of dreams. When an individual works on their dreams over a long period of time, in a way that aids the self healing action of our system to release stress, heal past pains, and achieve greater well being, the dreams express a sense of gratitude or thanks. It is as if the deeply unconscious life processes say, 'Thank you for helping us/me to be rid of these agonies. I/we love you for that.' Perhaps this is what the story of Androcles and the lion illustrates.

This has led me to believe that human beings can, if they choose, develop a symbiotic relationship with the rest of nature. By lending nature our consciousness, by extending consciousness to plants, animals, the biosphere itself, we could aid nature in its healing and evolution. Instead of polluting and destroying a new science of integrative process could develop. If that were to happen I believe nature would allow individuals consciously to enter more fully into its wider life. We would no longer be prisoners of the body as we now are.

Some observers tend to see the forces of nature as elementals, devas or fairy figures. Of course, if we remain at the symbol level of the unconscious (dream maker) process, every reality is expressed as an exterior form. We can transcend this if we wish, to have direct insight and empathy. To achieve this with nature is, I believe, a valid relationship humans can have with the cosmos. Dreams, and waking dream consciousness are the easiest doorway to that possibility.[5]

THE DREAM AS A COMPUTER

The human mind, unconscious or otherwise, has a number of functions seldom mentioned outside specialist literature. In a sense we all know our mind has the ability to form *gestalts*. When we look at a newsprint photograph or a T.V. screen image, or even a cinema screen image, we see an integrated picture, not the dots, the lines or the separate flickering pictures. That is a *gestalt*, a whole made from many separate parts. Despite this being common knowledge we seldom teach our children, or stimulate ourselves, to see the *gestalts* in the thousands of bits of everyday experience, body sensations, sense impressions and emotions of our life.

In 1969 I attended, in a supportive role, therapy sessions a friend was having with a well-known psychiatrist using LSD. To aid my ability to help and understand the therapy, I was given the opportunity to experience the drug in the clinical setting. During the first session two very important things occurred in connection with *gestalts*. The drug enables a readier flow of associations and experience from the unconscious to the waking identity. As I watched my friend, I realised that the many tiny movements of his body were being put together by my unconscious into an overall meaning. I did not know the idea of *gestalts* at that time, but I was able to observe the process taking place in myself. I felt at the time that through this I had a deep insight into my friend, and his body. I saw that many aspects of his experience, such as schooling, parental relationship, and national culture, had been taken into his being, but never digested. This caused two very stressful situations in him. The different parts of his experience were in conflict with each other, and most important, much of the experience was in conflict with his own basic life process. Also, his identity should have been something like a plant, which by feeding upon the minerals in the soil, grows, transforming the minerals into a living system. That is, the schooling, parental experience and culture should have been like the minerals which were integrated and transformed into a living, growing identity. But instead they had been plastered on him, and no *gestalts* had

163

been formed to create living personal realisations. In a similar sense the human system in eating, casts out the food it cannot use in its growth. He had not excreted the unusable parts – unusable in his personal life and work – of his schooling and experience.

Since that time I have tried to consciously use the ability to form *gestalts* of experience, and to understand what people are saying non-verbally with their body, and to use it with my dream work. At times this has very unexpected results. While working part time in a hotel I was standing watching the proprietor, who was in his sixties, talking to one of the staff, a lady also in her late fifties or sixties. They were conversing idly about the weather and how much trade there was, and suddenly, as in the case with my friend in therapy, I understood the overall meaning of their many tiny movements, facial changes and breathing patterns. What it told me was that while on the surface they appeared to be idly talking, at a deeper level, an enormous flow of feeling and contact was going on between them. This contact had been originally formed because they had made love at some time, and this acted as a bond between them.

The insight lasted for maybe two or three seconds and was gone. Being curious to check my impression I asked the lady if she had ever had a relationship with the boss. Looking surprised at first, then with a twinkle in her eye, she said they had made love, and not so very long ago.

Those experiences, and others like it, convinced me that if the ability to see so clearly into human beings was well established, our insight into politicians, church leaders, union officials and others who attempt to sway our decisions, would lead us to a revolutionary new relationship with society. Not only does such insight cut through the often pompous facade of people, but it also gives a view of their humanity, the terrible inner world so many live in, and the beauty and love which flows out of others.

My attempts to understand this ability suggest it is not a new faculty humans can develop, but an ancient one they have allowed to become dormant. It was developed over millions of years from non-verbal communication in which our ancestors read body signals. I believe this also applies to the signals of natural events, which early human beings needed to read to survive. The mind had to be able to form a *gestalt* from such diverse pieces of information as dust rising on the horizon, silence of birds, movement of animals, a drought in the area. Was the dust caused by an enemy or food? Survival depended on having a clear response. But prior to the use of words, and until recent times, there was no ability to reason. The creative solution had to be reached by intuition, a feeling response or a dream.

It is very likely that our forebears dreamt during the day. That is, their method of thinking and problem solving was a spontaneous rising into consciousness of mental images or even visions. The stories in ancient cultures of how the gods showed human beings how to write, grow plants and weave illustrates this clearly. Our dream process always embodies ideas in images or people. The Norse legend of how the weaving of flax was taught to humans by a goddess is almost certainly a waking dream experienced by the person who invented weaving. Unable to reason, but having already noticed the separate pieces of experience of the flax growing, rotting to reveal its fibres, the unconscious formed a new *gestalt*, maybe with the help of seeing woven baskets. So the person, while awake, has a vivid 'dream' or image thought process, in which the new idea is expressed as a goddess showing point by point how to weave.

Despite our amazing technological understanding, our culture is almost grossly superstitious and primitive in its view of such phenomena as clairvoyance and ESP. We still look for mysterious explanations, when every one of us has this incredible insight into each other and the world around us. Perhaps we have mostly buried this ability with our 'native past' or animal nature, and it only spontaneously expresses now in people who have not highly developed their intellectual faculties. But, in fact, it is the intellectual who can best use it, and can develop it, and dreams are our readiest means of tapping it. Dr. Ann Faraday, in her book *Dream Power*, tells of a dream following a conversation with a woman staying in the same hotel as herself. The conversation had been about the widespread use of medicines and drugs, and how necessary it was not to depend upon them. The woman agreed strongly, and said she herself always avoided their use. That night Ann dreamt she watched the woman in her bathroom, standing in front of a shelf full of bottles, swallowing dozens of tablets. Later the next day, while alone with the lady's husband, she told him her dream. His reply was, 'It's funny you should dream that. I keep telling her that if she takes any more pills or things, she'll make herself ill, but she takes no notice. She's a real

165

hypochondriac – always something wrong with her.'[6]

Ann Faraday says she is still not sure how she knew the truth about the woman. I believe it is a simple expression of the deep insight into body language we each have at an unconscious level. In some seminars I have taken, knowing that each of us have this ability I have taught people how to ask for information from this function when it is needed.

These cases seem also to be connected with the ability to dream while awake. Religious visions, creative intuition, ESP, extension of consciousness, and the ability to have insight into others or oneself, have a definite connection with the functions of the unconscious dream process. Many of these seemingly clairvoyant abilities arise from three basic functions.

a) The computer-like action of the unconscious to collate, cross reference and form *gestalts* from thousands or even millions of pieces of information.
b) The ability to read body language or, as it should really be called, the language of the living bio-organism.
c) The ability to extend awareness and make conscious the object of our perception.

These basic unconscious functions are unified and expressed by the dream process, in communicating its experience to consciousness in images or impressions, while sleeping or waking.

THE DREAM AS MICROSCOPE, TELESCOPE AND TIME TRAVEL

It would need another book to properly explain and document the abilities of the human mind. All that can be done in this chapter is to explain briefly some of what I believe are latent possibilities.

The dreams already quoted give some idea of the ability to look into the cellular processes of plants, the human body, and machines, to see delicate processes and functions in a useful manner. I do not want to quote further information or labour the point, but only to draw attention to or catalogue this aspect of the dream. I believe that the unconscious can be used as a research tool, just as we use a microscope or telescope. Most people never focus their unconscious abilities by directing their dream process to consider specific questions. When this is done, however, the results can be amazing. I am not suggesting that the unconscious will show us the 'truth', whatever that is, but it will certainly extend our sources of assessment and information. Such information should then be considered with as much care and criticism as information gathered by any other means.

The fact that the unconscious can be used as a telescope or research instrument can be seen from historical information alone. For instance, Babylonian astronomers have left written records of the movements of Venus, Mars and Jupiter. Four thousand years ago they described the positional changes of Jupiter's four moons, which are invisible to the naked eye. Telescopes were not invented until 1608.

Also, how could a small African tribe, the Dogon, tell in their folk wisdom, about the star Sirius, being a double star? The companion star is a white dwarf, and is invisible to the naked eye. It was only seen through a telescope in 1862.

In a similar vein, Fritjof Capra, in his book, *Tao of Physics*, shows how the subjective exploration of past mystics matches the findings of modern physics.

In 1977, before I had ever seen a computer simulation program or heard of one, I was questioning myself deeply about human misery. At the time I had met a lot of young people who appeared to be broken in mind and body, and attempted to explore my unconscious in a waking dream, looking for answers. I had that day met a young couple, disturbed in not being able to care for their baby, frightened even to ask for a piece of string they needed for a parcel, he an alchoholic, and she a disturbed young woman born from a mother who had herself been in and out of mental hospitals. Let me quote from my journal of the feelings and images arising from within.

I felt the deep pain such as I have felt of late when seeing broken lives, shipwrecked smashed people like Frank and Diane. This morning as I walked by the sea I had looked at the huge ocean, then at the rubbish of tins, bits of wood, shoes, junk the sea had washed up. Now feelings rose in me that people, me, you, my children, are like that. Life just throws them aside like they're nothing. Earthquakes, floods, social pressure creating human wreckage, broken bodies, nothing. It might be your mother, your child – dead. Just so much more human wreckage. Spent human beings washed up on the shore.

As I cried over the vision of human carnage and death I went deeper in an awareness of the whole cosmos, partly visually, partly in imageless awareness. It was as if I stood at a huge distance, watching it, yet

167

somehow in the middle of it too, seeing and experiencing the whole drama of life. All was movement, whirling, sweeping energy. Like eddy's and currents in a huge surfaceless sea of energy, patterns, waves, whirls, blending and parting. There seemed to be no spaces, no gaps or emptiness, just thicker and thinner whirling and movement. It is so difficult to describe. In the immensity of the cosmos, the ebb and flow, pulsing, dancing energies, create and destroy constantly. The world and humanity are just a tiny incomprehensible microscopic part of it all.

As I watch I try to understand just what place humanity has, what is their future. I see they are an expression of a part of the flow and existence of one part of the cosmos. They are a part of the living movement of the huge, twisting, dancing mass of energy. I see they were not planned, not created on purpose. They just are. There is no great destiny for them to fulfil, no plan for them, no real beginning, no real end. Nowhere to get, no aim, no point, just existence. It doesn't matter that they exist. It doesn't matter if they do not exist. They are simply part of the being and movement of the hugeness. But that is amazing, because it gives them freedom to create of themselves what they wish to be.

Here it was that I had an image of this great sea of energy moving in the form of a joyous person running through darkness and space; running like a dance. And I saw that if a hair fell from that lovely form, or a skin cell dropped, it might look back in wonder and say, 'Oh yes, I was so absorbed in the joy of my running I didn't notice. But yes, how lovely; what a beautiful thing. Nothing that I am, even if it is crushed and torn, is not a part of my wonder.'

As I watched, I understood the image to mean that each one of us, no matter what our life, was always a part of the whole. The cell might drop off, but the essential consciousness still existed eternally dancing as life itself.

A flow of insights arose then without attempting to think, almost as if I was simply listening, and my inner consciousness was teaching me. I saw how our idea of God or the eternal is an abstraction. The word itself – abstraction – means to take out of, to make an idea or symbol out of a real thing. I saw that God is a symbol or abstract which our unconscious creates to communicate what it gathers from thousands of everyday experiences and perceptions of things which occur over and over. Eating, sleeping, going to the toilet are some. But also we see processes which are not only going on all the time, but going on at the same time. Someone dies, but we see someone born the same day, even the same moment. We see growth and decay going on, youth and age; and out of this an abstraction arises. It is a sense which our unconscious gains, when it puts all these pieces together, of the whole process of life which is neither birth nor death, growth or decay, but is the whole, unchanging, because it is the opposites both at once. I felt there was no timeless or God outside of ordinary everyday experience. As humans, because we have this faculty of putting images to what we sense unconsciously, we had created a God outside of ourselves, and a devil too. This divinity was, in fact, ourselves. We were ourself, now, the very incarnation of the cosmos, discovering itself. In the very midst of everyday events, such as work, love making, family life, eating, birth and death, the mystery of life existed.

Since that experience I have watched a computer simulation of a galaxy whirling, and seen the realisation gained from recent advances in photography and computer science that space is not empty. That between the galaxies there is evident contact and flow of matter. As I watched I realised what an amazing computer and tool of exploration we each have, and how our own abilities to simulate and thereby understand, is even greater than modern computers. Like the computer, our dream process can put together masses of information to give us an overall view. It can look at a star, or consider the sub-microscopic.

There are many instances of creative dreaming, such as that of William Blake, who, when looking for a means of more cheaply engraving his songs, dreamt that his dead brother, Robert, came to him and explained a way of engraving copper. Blake tried it and it worked. Or the dream of Otto Loewi which led to his winning the Nobel Prize for his work in physiology and medicine. In 1903 he had the idea that the transmission of nervous impulses was chemical rather than electrical. At that time it was believed that the transmission was electrical. Despite his idea, however, Loewi could not think of an experiment to prove the theory and he forgot about it. Then, in 1920, he awoke from sleep one night and wrote down some notes. But in the morning he could not remember what it was he wished to note, nor could he read his writing. Describing what occurred next he says: 'The next night, at three o'clock, the idea returned. It was the design of an experiment to determine whether or not the hypothesis of chemical transmission . . . was correct. I got up immediately, went to the laboratory, and performed a simple experiment on a frog's heart according to the nocturnal design.' The result proved the theory.

But perhaps one of the most astonishing of creative dreams, showing microscopic, X-ray, even time-leaping qualities, is that of

169

Herman Hilprecht. While working as the professor of Assyrian at the University of Pennsylvania he was analysing two small pieces of agate which he believed were Babylonian finger rings. He worked late into the night, and classified one piece as of the Cassite period. He could not classify the other piece and went to bed still wondering about both pieces. He dreamt:

> A tall thin priest of the old pre-Christian Nippur, about forty years of age and clad in a simple abba, led me to the treasure chamber of the temple, on its south east side. He went with me into a small, low-ceilinged room without windows, in which there was a large wooden chest, while scraps of agate and lapis lazuli lay scattered on the floor. Here he addressed me as follows: 'The two fragments which you have published separately on pages 22 and 26 belong together, are not finger rings, and their history is as follows: King Kurigalzu (c 1300 B.C.) once sent to the temple of Bel, among other articles of agate and lapis lazuli, an inscribed votive cylinder of agate. Then we priests suddenly received the command to make for the statue of the god of Nihib a pair of earrings of agate. We were in great dismay, since there was no agate as raw material at hand. In order to execute the command there was nothing for us to do but cut the votive cylinder into three parts, thus making three rings, each of which contained a portion of the original inscription. The first two rings served as earrings for the statue of the god; the two fragments which have given you so much trouble are portions of them. If you put the two together you will have confirmation of my words. But the third ring you have not found in the course of your excavations and you will never find it.' With this the priest disappeared. Next morning I examined the fragments once more in the light of these disclosures, and to my astonishment found all the details of the dream precisely verified in so far as the means of verification were in my hands. The original inscription on the votive cylinder reads: 'To the god Ninib, son of Bel, his lord, has Kurigalzu, pontifex of Bel, presented this.'

USING THE POWERS OF MIND

One cannot separate the operation of mind from the intricate natural activities of which it is a part. To understand how we can make use of faculties lying dormant in us we need to understand basic facts about nature. In his book *Cosmos*, Carl Sagan tells how the Heike crab from the inland sea of Japan may have developed the Samurai type face on its shell. Crabs which have a face-like image on their shell are honoured and thrown back into the sea. Crabs without such a clear marking are eaten. As this had been going on for centuries, imposed hereditary selection has occurred, producing not just a face, but a scowling Samurai image.

In a sense, the crabs with markings similar to a face were rewarded by being allowed to survive. In a similar sense we have rewarded cows which produce large milk yield, and wheat which has yielded many large seeds. The amount of milk given by a cow before this directed selection took place was about a few hundred cubic centimetres, now it is a million.

The basic stimulus to produce change in a life form is reward. The reward might be survival, food, pleasure or the avoidance of stress. In the latter case an animal may learn an action, such as jumping through a flaming hoop, to avoid being hit. For humans the reward might arrive by achieving recognition, and success.

My work on dreams has suggested that to stimulate new or unusual responses from our system, the realisation that we are dealing with biological and feeling responses as in an animal is very important. Self doubt, over criticism of one's performance, ideas of futility are definitely put-downs to the subtle feelings and energies which we need to rouse into cooperation. Recent research into ESP has shown that if a subject is given regular feedback on their performance, the ability increases in effectiveness. Biofeedback experiments have a similar result. The subject learns more quickly when there is a positive feedback from successful efforts.

So the first rule toward success in mobilising one's abilities is not to chastise oneself for failure, but to allow pleasure feelings when successful.

Most dreams which transcend normal ability occur within a set of particular circumstances, because the transcendental dream arises out of basic relationships between natural forces, just as do other mental and physical phenomena. The bonds that develop through kinship, sexual relationship, mutual help, therefore also act as forces of contact at the psychological level. Our problem-solving reactions are also more fully stirred into action by real challenges than by idle speculation.

What this means practically is that a mother concerned over her sick child is much more likely to have a helpful dream if she sought it, than if she idly wondered about a friend's sick child. Because work involves us in relationships, with our family, work mates and

171

society, and because it may also involve us in challenge, it frequently stimulates helpful dreams.

This dream, from Mr. Kai DeFontanay has these qualities.

'Last year I programmed my dreams to give me some help on stock investments. I awoke from sleep, knowing I had dreamt about a stock but couldn't remember the name other than ROB – something. I consulted the paper and immediately recognised it as 'Robintech'. I called my broker for information on it. As he had nothing particularly good to say about it, I interrupted him and just said, 'Buy' – completely on faith. I transferred the money out of another stock. I bought Robintech at $12. It is now $19.50. The stock I sold for this transaction was then selling at $12. It is now $6.'⁷

When directing one's dream response, it is therefore helpful to choose a subject which is important and emotionally involves us, and actually needs an answer. Another factor is how much conscious thought and investigation we have given the subject. If, like Mr. Kai DeFontanay and Herman Hilprecht, we are deeply involved in the subject during waking hours, we are more likely to experience a transcendental dream while we sleep.

For those who do not simply wish for simple answers to problems, but wish to discover their life and work in relationship to the cosmos, and to find the intimate details of these in this wider view, there are problems which need to be understood and accepted. Our life is an unfolding process, and to learn its connections with society and the cosmos needs a fascination which continues through the years. Yet I believe it is this fascination in regard to one's own potential and its relationship to the whole, which can lead to the discovery of the suprahuman life referred to by Dr. Salk. This new life in sufficient individuals is the foundation of the world we have to create, if we are to emerge from our own conflict and destructiveness.

In 1981 I had a dream in which I was in Italy, deciding to learn the language and immerse myself in the way of life. The dream opened a doorway which led me to arrive at a new view of what it is to be an individual. My father was born in England of Italian parents. The dream showed me exploring this side of my origins. As I allowed myself to experience the feelings in the dream, I recognised them as attitudes I had learnt from my father. These attitudes had been largely unconscious, and, until the dream, I had not seen how deeply they penetrated my life.

In trying to understand how I learnt these attitudes, summarised by the phrase 'keeping one's head down', I saw they had not been transmitted verbally. What I had gradually uncovered was that these deeply pervading attitudes, which had led me, amongst other things, to avoid voting all my life, had been learnt through a process which is, I now believe, basic to all mammals. Naturalists have long noted it in animals, but it is seldom seen as an important factor in human life. It is the response a young animal learns from its parents. In this way young animals learn to react and run from such dangers as human approach, snakes and so on without having to learn by mistakes.

I had learnt from my father that one never disagreed with authority; that one should always be placatory; and that the anger one inwardly felt in being a subdued man should be directed at one's children to teach them the same awful lessons. And because these lessons are taught at a subliminal, non-verbal level, they are almost an invisible – to oneself – structure in one's personality.

The next step in my investigation was the most staggering. In looking at where my father had learnt these attitudes it was evident he had learnt them from his father, and he from his, and he from his. In fact, as I allowed the feelings behind the attitudes to arise, I felt a definite sense of experiencing the essence of my male forebears going back hundreds of years. Remember that the unconscious puts into images and feelings the subtle energies from deep within our being. It was as if the blended anger and pain of my forefathers poured out their lives to me as I removed the bars of restricted attitudes.

Truly I was learning the language of Italy. What I experienced was that my forebears were peasant farmers. For generations they survived by caring for their land. But they lived in a political and religious climate which was murderous and suppressive. To put it into words which rose out of my unconscious; 'Just because a man had a good piece of land and he becomes rich he calls himself a king. Not only does he call himself a king, but he wants everybody else to call him a king and bow down to him too. And if you don't they send their armed thugs to destroy your crops. Our children have been torn limb from limb before our eyes. If you want your sons to live you teach them to keep their eyes down. They even took our god, and used him to subdue us with fear of death, telling us what we must believe, what we must do. If we didn't, they killed us in the name of God.'

Seeing life through the eyes of my forefathers allowed me to see that even now, hundreds of years later, not only am I still deeply engraved and shaped by their experience, but so are the 'kings' and 'queens' of this world, who still employ what they sometimes call police, as thugs to impose upon the people. That such 'original scenes' can continue for centuries is terrifying in considering humanity's future.

How can we move out of these centuries old patterns of personal and social behaviour? How can we avoid being unconsciously manipulated or manipulating? I believe there are several ways. We can gradually penetrate our own unconscious to discover what was previously hidden to us. We can be helped to see these patterns by those who are aware of them. We can directly act against the old habits to create new ones.

The suprahuman individuals of tomorrow is one who will expand his consciousness to the point of discovering the forces and struggles of the past and present which produced them. The work of the real social reformer is to help individuals raise their awareness so they become above manipulation and manipulating. Vance Packard, in his book *The People Shapers*, shows the enormity of the present struggle between the 'kings and peasants' of today. He looks at such methods as using drugs to pacify school children, the use of television cameras and computers to maintain surveillance, and psychological techniques in commerce and politics to manipulate people *en masse*.[8]

From the analysis of thousands of dreams it doesn't seem to me that it is the Devil who wishes for our soul. What we find over and over again is the influence of leaders who, by gaining a large following, create a self perpetuating role, which rests usually upon such statements as 'You need me to:

a) Tell you what to think.
b) Tell you what God commands of you.
c) Protect you from the attack from other countries or groups. This is the well-known protection racket, which even governments use.
d) Protect you from illness.
e) Give you certainty in an uncertain world.
f) Tell you the meaning of life.

That dreams extend our awareness of ourself and the influences which are moving us, makes them one of the main bastions against manipulation or subliminal influence. Earlier in this century, P.W. Martin, through his work with dreams, saw them as a protection against totalitarianism, and the means by which individuals can learn responsibility for their own life, as well as finding a path between such opposites as self interest and group interest.

One of the greatest difficulties in claiming our suprahuman abilities then, is that in doing so we discover not only our own imprisonment and bondage to old pains, original scenes and fears, but we also claim our own mind and our own sexuality from their past fixations. Overall the process is one of expanding our awareness, taking it beyond its present fixation in the voluntary muscles, limited thinking patterns and unconscious responses.

A dream may be thought of as a journey by someone who has always lived in their home village, and imagined that the whole world held the same religious, political and sexual views. On the journey the traveller learns completely different ways of living and being. Part of his difficulty in partaking of the new is his old attitudes, which might tell him that the strange is wrong, that it is foolish, that it is alien.

For countless generations the unconscious has been linked with the idea of sleep, death, madness, spirits and the irrational. In Carl Jung's book, *Man and His Symbols*, under the heading 'Approaching the Unconscious', the very first illustration in the text is the entrance to an Egyptian tomb, the land of the dead. Before we can even enter into our own unconscious, we must meet and recognise these cultural taboos and guardians standing before the unconscious and engraved in our nature. Again and again, in helping people take awareness into their unconscious, I hear them saying such things as – Will I go mad? – I feel like I'm dying – What's the point of this exercise, because there's nothing of value to find – This is against my religion. These are actually the forces of cultural, even racial, taboo. I believe they are largely the result of ancient attitudes which looked upon the unconscious as a holy place of power into which only priests and initiates were allowed to enter. These feelings are still commonly held today. Unfortunately, even the priesthood now seldom enter to learn and worship.

The unconscious was also the source of the triggered death response, and there seems to be an element of taboo here also, that one should only enter under the direst need. But in many older

175

cultures, the unconscious was called into daily waking use quite frequently. Our lack of daily contact in the Western world allows the forces of the unconscious to lie unused for years on end. Like a body which is not exercised, it becomes ill and putrid from disuse. Much sickness, individual and social, arises from this inner decay in the West.

If we recognise and pass these taboos, our expanding awareness will usually first re-experience the essence, the pleasure and pain of our present lifetime. The essential process of expanding awareness is the integration of experience. The growing suprahuman self feeds on the events of our life; the experiences of love and hate; the tiny events of everyday existence. It feeds by deeply experiencing each event from birth and conception, with consciousness. Perhaps our outer self cries and moans during the process, but that is how the divine in us grows. The stories of people near to death re-experiencing their whole life illustrates this fact. To survive in the world of death, or the unconscious, one's whole life must have been penetrated by consciousness, for the realm of death is disembodied mind – consciousness itself. Dr. Moody, summarising these near death experiences in *Life After Life*,[9] describes how a great number of people during these encounters with dying, meet a Being of Light who asks – What have you brought? In other words, what harvest of life experience do you bring?

When we enter our unconscious we meet this figure – created by our own image-forming capacity – without having to die. We meet it because we are entering the realms of death, of transcendence of the body's boundaries. Steiner calls this figure the Guardian of the Threshold.

Summarising my experience it seems that only fragmentary and intermittent experiences of our inner world, and only partial ability to tap our inner resources can be gained if we have not fully met this process. The reason for this is perhaps explained by this dream. The woman who dreamt it had been seeking a response from her dreams as to why she could not be more fully active in the sleep state. She says:

'I was met by a being, actually a presence, not a person with a body. The presence spoke to me as we stood in a garden. I was told its name was Father Li or Faster than Light. I thought this was funny, especially the 'Fatherly' name. The presence then led me to a greenhouse. I understood the greehouse was like the inner world I wanted to enter. As we opened the door some young hooligans dashed in and careless of their movements trampled and broke tender plants. I could see what it all meant even as I dreamt. The hooligans were my own emotions From Father Li's point of view I was like a careless young adolescent. My emotions still could lash out angrily on occasions. If I entered this inner world where the delicate processes of life exist, I could do terrible damage to people and myself. Father Li said, "You see, we must be careful who we open the door to".'

Another important point is that the inner world is quite different in some ways to the outer world. If someone, for instance, enters within to look for truth, if they go once they may come back with wonderful insights. If they enter again, they may come back with insights which completely contradict the first ones.

The inner world is so vast, so much without beginning or end that we need to enter it in a specific way to avoid becoming lost in it. Before we attempt to penetrate our unconscious, the interests and restrictions of our waking life protect us from the mass of possible experience which could arise from within. There is less protection when we persistently penetrate sleep with wakefulness. We need then to decide exactly what we wish to discover, what work we wish to undertake; we need to build for ourselves a house or centre in that dimension which epitomises our way of relating to others. From that centre we can begin to wake up, work and grow. In other words we need to define for ourselves some function, such as healing, teaching, learning, experimenting, exploring, loving, nursing which is the main theme of our desire to enter the inner world. This is important because the most powerful drives in the unconscious are those to do with interelatedness. It is possible that the unconscious itself is created out of the countless creatures that have lived. The pattern of experience each creature left is blended into this vast pattern of energies and life forces which we call the unconscious. The statement in the New Testament which says, 'In my father's house are many mansions . . . and I go to prepare a place for you,' refers to the place we inhabit in the inner world. I believe such statements express the deepest forms of psycho-biological truths which we do not yet fully understand. They are describing in a symbolic sense, activites, in the subtle areas of nature.

Lastly, it remains for us to practice, to re-direct our energies, to work upon our very being in order to transform it. Areas of the brain, and the spinal cord itself, are increased in complexity by use. The more we use a function, the more the area of the brain dealing with it develops. So many dreams deal with this theme that it is impossible to give a clear picture of what occurs in a few words. But our individual dreams teach us the necessary details of how to alter the flow of our mental, emotional and sexual energies.

Useful Exercises.

1. If you have practiced the exercises given for co-ex in Chapter Eight, choose one dream per week, hold in mind the main symbol, and allow the co-ex fantasy to flow. Let the fantasy spontaneously deal with the symbol. Allow feelings within the dream, to be a part of that fantasy, i.e. remember the feelings prior to practising co-ex, and allow the feelings to express if they arise in the co-ex action.

   This practice begins to forge closer links between our conscious self and our inner life. One's early practices may be unsatisfying and lead to no insight into the symbol. But if practice continues week by week, the inner contents of the dream will begin to emerge. It is necessary to let the spontaneous co-ex action produce the insight. The function of the intellect during the exercise is to remain open but unconvinced until real insight is arrived at. If the intellect does the work of looking for insight, one has remained in the conscious self. By looking to the fantasy for insight, we are stimulating our unconscious to function creatively.

2. Something which became clear while working with co-ex over the last eleven years, is what I call the 'pendulum effect'. Briefly, it is seen when we hold any form of pendulum in our hand, and give our unconscious a consciously agreed symbol. For instance, the common parlour trick claims that if the pendulum swings in a straight line over a pregnant woman, the baby will be a boy. If it swings in a circle it will be a girl. In doing this we are actually giving the unconscious symbols to work with. Through tiny unconscious movements, the arm then swings the pendulum. If we do not consciously influence the swing, our predominant feelings or intuition will influence the way our arm moves. It must never be thought that the

response expresses 'truth'; it is merely moving in response to our inner feelings or unconscious perceptions. This may be correct or incorrect, but it is a means of tapping the unconscious through a readily understood symbol. As in biofeedback or ESP experiments, we can train our unconscious toward a higher score of correct hits, if we give feedback on results of such experiments.

Once the technique of giving the unconscious consciously arranged symbols is understood, a larger range of symbols than yes or no, male or female can be used. If you gain fluidity in co-ex, then you can even ask it how it will symbolise yes or no through the movements. Gradually, however, in the practice of co-ex, the need for symbolic body movements is transcended. Just as the unconscious can produce spontaneous conscious body movements or dance, so also it can produce spontaneous vocalisation, imagery and feelings as these areas are freed by its action. Then the unconscious has a whole wealth of tones, words and ideas it can play upon, like a keyboard, to lift to meaning or consciousness the play of its own experience.

3. A very helpful exercise to develop insight into other people is similar to the one used to find insight into a dream symbol. First one is aware of what tensions and feelings exist in one's own body and self. Then you imagine that you are within the body of the person you wish to understand. Imagine you are filling the same space as they, and notice what feelings, images and body changes occur. Do not rush this. The impressions usually take time to permeate through us and come into focus sufficiently to be understood and put into words. However, there are certain rules of privacy which the unconscious respects and sometimes, if permission is not asked, or the exercise used outside of need to help the person, real rebuffs may be felt.

This technique can also be tried on plants, animals and children, if their condition needs to be fathomed. As with the pendulum effect, correct insights arise with practice. Also, due to the nature of the unconscious it works best when there is real need.

4. Sitting with a partner and watching and expressing just what

arises in relationship to them is an excellent awareness exercise.

5. Patient long-term work on one's dreams is one of the most gentle and thorough means of extending awareness into the wonderful mystery of unconscious life in and around us. It is an adventure akin to reaching the stars. It is a cultural education one cannot find at present even in our great universities. It is a loving relationship between ourself and the cosmos.

6. Sincere prayer has always been one of the most healing and effective was of relating to the wider life. Our real needs, when expressed in this way, are powerfully active in helping us to find satisfaction. The questions we wish to ask of our wider awareness seem to produce more response if expressed in prayer. But prayer is complementary to meditation. As the seer Edgar Cayce said, 'Prayer is talking to God. Meditation is listening for the reply.'

The overall need is to practice, extending ourselves beyond the barriers we usually impose upon ourselves. If we are ambitious in that area, we need to practice daily, or at least several times each week. If we do not, the psychological and brain activities which need to be developed will lose tone, just as muscles do. Therefore, we need to include our wider abilities in our everyday life, using them to solve problems, gain insight and extend the range of our view and sources of information.

Chapter Ten

Finding Your Spiritual Life

THE spiritual life is a stance which places us in an effective relationship with the cosmos and ourself. Thus the spiritual life is also a journey. We are a traveller because we move from virtual unconsciousness of what we are and how we came to be to a wider awareness, and this enables us to arrive at a different view of life. The spiritual life is a process of waking up; a taking of light or awareness, into the darkness of our body and sleep. In this process and this life we also become a parent. Out of our body, its sense life and limited awareness, grows a child who is the native of a different dimension. This child is the new ability we have to live, work and love in the dimension of expanded consciousness. Until the birth of that child from our life we were a prisoner within our own limitations. After the birth we become a citizen of a wider life.

In the Old Testament the use of the word spirit was similar to that of soul in the modern sense, i.e. 'there wasn't a living soul there.' In the New Testament the word spirit is translated from the Greek word *pneuma*, and the word soul from the word *psyche*. *Pneuma* refers to the principle of life in all created things. It pertains to the universal character of life and creation. *Psyche* refers to the individual, one's sense of being a person and to personal experience. From these definitions to say we have a body, soul and spirit is to say that we have a physical organ through which we are aware of other physical objects. Through this awareness we have individual, personal experience and have developed a sense of selfhood. This sense

181

of selfhood exists within universal processes of the cosmos, and has a relationship with them. In fact, it is irrevocably a part of them. In this sense we have a body, soul and spirit.

As a person we can choose whether we shall attempt to become more conscious of the universal process of life in the cosmos which has given rise to us. We can choose whether we wish to live in harmony or conflict with life, or be an unconscious participator. We can certainly never be outside any relationship whatsoever, which is why the spiritual life is a stance, because the stance is the way we relate to the whole. If we improve our stance, we enhance this relationship.

Our relationship with the cosmos might be that we fail to recognise that we have such a relationship – like those who failed to recognise that the one they walked with on the road was the Christ. We might wish to reject any personal responsibility in the scheme of things, like Pilate washing his hands. Or we might recognise in the simplest experiences our involvement with all things – like the Magdalene recognising her loved one in the gardener.

Because we are an integral part of the cosmos, the spiritual life is starkly practical if by spiritual we mean an extension of the boundaries between our conscious self and the rest of our being that is the universe. The spiritual life then means a liberation from the prison of our own limited concepts of ourself, and the illusion of our own separateness. This makes a person like Buckminster Fuller a pioneer in a new age of cosmic citizenship.

In 1927 Bucky Fuller stood on the shore of Lake Michigan contemplating suicide. He said to himself: 'I've done the best I know how and it hasn't worked.' He was still grieving the loss of a daughter who had died five years earlier; his business had just failed, he was penniless and 32 years old. He wondered how he could support his wife and newly-born baby, but, after struggling with his despair for hours in the dark and the freezing wind, he decided to live the rest of life like an experiment. He wanted to discover whether the golden rule of life was dog eat dog. He would find out by seeing what could be physically demonstrated. To free his mind of conditioned thinking and reflexes he stopped talking for a year. Korzybski had convinced him that language structures caused conditioned associations or mechanical reactions which lock us in fixed perceptions. When he began to talk again he refused to use the words up or down, because there is no up or down in the universe. He also saw, as one of his insights gained through experience, that the golden rule was 'that if I worked always for others and only for all humanity, I would be optimally effective.'

Bucky Fuller went on from there to design the Dymaxion House, which is mass producible; the Dymaxion world map, which is the only flat map with hardly any distortion; the Geodesic Dome; the Floating Breakwater, and to be one of the world's great prophets of a sane, human future, coining the phrase 'Spaceship Earth.'[1]

Hans Selye, known for his enormous research into stress, offers the golden rule of gaining optimum life slightly differently. He says, 'We are all the children of nature and cannot go wrong by following her general rules in conjunction with whatever personal ideas or convictions may guide us. . .' Those who follow this doctrine, he says, will greedily gather wealth and strength, not in the form of money or domination of others but by earning the goodwill, gratitude, respect and love of those who surround them. Then, even if they have neither money nor power to command, they are unassailable, for no one would have a personal reason to attack them.[2]

Whether we accept Bucky Fuller's or Hans Selye's statement, it is reasonable that the more people who benefit from, or request who we are, what we do, what we produce, the more physical, emotional and mental wealth flows to us, the more opportunity we are offered, and the more a part of living huumanity we become. There seems to be no other secret to fame, wealth or spiritual greatness. Looking through any list of great men and women, the one thing that links them all is that in some way they gave something to others – so others gave something to them.

Even if we wish to give ourselves away, in one of the many ways in which it can be done, how can we move from an unsatisfactory stance to a satisfying one? Or how can we improve an already effective stance?

After attempting to understand the human condition for thirty years, and being at least old enough at forty-six to have opinions of my own, I believe our improvement of stance does not come from following the path laid down by other people. Certainly we need to learn from others, try out what others present, even stand upon their shoulders; but our vision, our insight and our stance, needs, like Bucky Fuller's, to arise from digesting our own experience. I feel that each of us also have a destiny which leads to particular life situations and a role in the cosmos.

By destiny I do not mean something pre-ordained, but something ingrained in the basic stuff of our nature from the physical, family, social and cosmic forces which .ntegrate to form our being. Like the difference between a diamond and ordinary carbon, through the different pressures of environment which bring human beings into existence, there is a different quality in each of us, along with basic similarities. This quality leads us, even if we have failed to recognise it, into circumstances and opportunities which relate to it. It also had in it the seed of our own personal giving away of self to life. And, in turn, it is only that giving away of self which gives us entrance into the wider life of the cosmos, and continuation of consciousness within it.

It must be said, though, that I cannot see any narrow restraints into the manner of just how we give ourself away. The only fact I have discovered is that our personal self has no continuance after death, no extension of experience and pleasure during life, no escape from the prison wall of self, except via sharing oneself with others. It is a basic cosmological, biological and psychological fact; it is, inescapably, a part of us. A cell gives itself to a cell in reproduction. A teacher gives himself to a pupil for continuity. The sun gives its energy to our planet, and the body of our planet gives itself to that energy, and from that giving their continuity occurs in living forms. And it does not seem to matter if our giving is as a giving prostitute, a musician, or a social worker. The factor which matters is whether we give ourself.

My own delight in looking at dreams is to see how free they are of dogma and prejudice. I have come to see them as the communications from the cosmos itself, with all its wonderful variety, paradoxes and gentle humour. And in seeking the quality of our own destiny, of the essence of our own experience, dreams are a teacher without equal.

Something of this humour and razor-sharp perceptiveness is shown in this account of a dream by Ann Faraday.

'When I first met my second husband he was well known as a presenter of Christianity in modern scientific terms on radio and television. His basic belief was in the divine power of love, and he interpreted the doctrine of the Trinity as a revelation that all love

184

involved three aspects – giving and receiving between lover and beloved, and the overflowing of their relationship to others.

'Shortly after we had begun our affair I dreamed of being in bed with a stranger whose name was Christian, and a former colleague of mine called Miss Locke. Christian started to make love to me and suddenly stopped, saying, "Excuse me, I'd better make love to Miss Locke first because she's getting married in a fortnight." I accepted this in the dream on the grounds that if Miss Locke were really going to be married in a fortnight, I had nothing to lose by being magnanimous. Unfortunately he showed no signs of returning to me, and I awoke in distress.

'Miss Locke was a real person who indeed was getting married in a fortnight, but I had no special relationship of any kind with her. When I associated her name, however, I was reminded of the time many years earlier when a young Swiss boy had rowed me across the Lake of Lucerne, and solemnly pronouncing that one woman was very much like another in bed. '*Lockist lock, und fertig,*' he said, which, translated means, 'A hole is a hole and that's all there is to it.' Obviously then, Miss Locke represented 'woman' to me in a specially sexual context. Associating to Christian, I was easily led to the Christian aspect of my new boy friend: the dream revealed I had an underlying suspicion that the overflowing of the Trinity in his theology might possibly mean he would overflow into other women!'[3]

The dream appeals to me because it cuts away the wrapping, whether it is theological or lustful, and sees through to basic relationships. A recently received dream shows this in a quite different way. It was sent by Mrs. P. I have already quoted it, but use it here to show another point.

'I decided to have a rest on my bed before going to Mass on Christmas Eve, and dreamt the following:

'The sky opened just enough to let Our Lord through. I felt calm, thinking this must be the end of the world. The Bible says our Lord will appear in the sky, and those not already dead will die of fright. He floated down to our dining-room window. I thought, "I'm still alive." Two nuns followed him dressed in white. One said to the other, "She gave me the sack." I thought to myself, "This certainly was not in the Bible, and it can't be the end of the world." '

The action of this dream is twofold. It puts the dreamer into

185

contact with her own spiritual life, the Christ. It also show her the funny side of her conscious ideas about what is true in regard to that spiritual life. I named this an 'It ain't necessarily so' dream. But there is also a message in the dream. In waking life she was about to go to Mass on Christmas Eve. She was going to share a meal with Christ. In her dream she is in her dining room, but Christ walks by, and she doesn't invite him in to share a meal with her.

Taken out of its symbols, the Christ represents our personal relationship with the cosmos. As it says in the New Testament, Christ is the son of man, and also the son of God. In other words, it is what comes to birth, what develops between our conscious self and the cosmos. The woman's dream shows her not only having ideas about the cosmos which her dream says do not apply, but also that she does not invite the wider life into her personal life. The dream is, in fact, showing her what stance she has in her relationship with life.

The importance of what stance we take in regard to our life is brought out by a dream told to me by John Clemence, a friend I worked for over a period of years. The dream occurred some years ago at a time when the media was full of news about the possibility of imminent nuclear war.

John dreamt, 'I knew that an atomic attack was soon to take place and wondered what to do. My two sons were at school in Tavistock, many miles away. I wanted them to be with us and thought of dashing down to get them. There did not seem to be time though, and going out into the streets I saw lots of people walking calmly about. It was like an Edwardian scene, with people dressed in their Sunday best, enjoying the day. Seeing this I realised there was nothing I could do about the coming attack, so I might as well join the people and enjoy the day.'

The dream shows John deeply concerned over what stance to take, not only for himself, but for his family under the threat of nuclear war. The people in the streets show him drawing from the national spirit of the British people. It is something he finds in himself as a heritage from his forebears, and looking at it he finds it good. He will not dash about uselessly out of fear; he will not loot and ravage, he will spend his life in quiet companionship and enjoyment. That is the stand he will take. That is his spiritual life.

In John's case, his spiritual life came to him almost ready made through the life, courage and endeavour of his forebears and countrymen. His own part in it is to make it his own in a time of crisis and to actually live it. In living his stance he passes it on to his own children and those around him. The spiritual life he receives and lives is a set of responses and attitudes in regard to life, its difficulties and pleasures. Everyone who is born into a family, social and national setting receives such a gift, usually unconsciously. How effective the stance is in facing the reality of experience has to be tested against events, as Bucky Fuller did.

Fundamentally, I do not believe human spiritual life originally came ready formed. It was gradually wrested from human experiences over very long periods of time. Perhaps this following dream explains how it may have had its beginnings.

'I was comfortably listening to the music of Sibelius; I believe it was his second symphony. As I listened I drifted into a reverie in which I had a dream. It appeared to arise directly out of the music.

'In the dream I was one of a group of Norsemen in the distant past. We were dressed in skins and lived amongst the rugged forests and rocky mountains. It felt as if our own souls were rugged, forested and misty like the land we lived in, and now were walking through to hunt. We had dogs with us and bows, to hunt the deer.

'Then we came across a magnificent antlered male and gave chase. We wounded the creature but it ran on and climbed a rocky crag several hundred feet high. It could not escape though, and the dogs backed it against a tall rock on the edge of a precipitous drop. It stood there fiery and keeping the dogs off until we approached it, excited and ready to kill. But as we neared enough to fire an arrow it paused and looked on us, proud and not at all cowed. Then it reared and leaped full into the void, falling down and down out of our sight to its death.

'The dogs and the small group of us men stood completely still and silent. It was a tremendous silence as if the creature had shouted a huge and wonderful defiance to us, understandable even to the dogs. It had leaped to break itself, rather than be broken.

'Without words we walked from the spot back to our dwellings, feeling as if we had seen a god who had spoken a great truth to us. We left the body of the creature where it lay, to honour its life and death.'

Perhaps that is how early men and women formed their spiritual life, through an intense experience of an approach to life and death.

Reading the Gospel of Matthew, I believe it is easy to recognise it

187

as a collection of folklore. It is possible that all religions are the unified essence of the experience of millions of people. It is the embodiment of the wit, life experience and wisdom of a particular culture. Perhaps a religious leader is a person who can tune in to the unconscious of a whole people, a race, and express the synthesis of what is there. Carl Jung has shown us through his own work with dreams how the unconscious of each of us, even without education, is the repositary for the spiritual wisdom of the world. Certainly each of us can tap that wellspring and receive something relevant to our own circumstances, and give something of value back.

During a period of my life when I was trying to come to terms with the Buddhist teaching of the Void, I had a dream in which I saw the Buddha. He was unlike any carvings or paintings I had ever seen of him, reminding me of one of the trees one sees on the edge of rocky sea cliffs, etched and shaped by the wind. His body and face was like such a tree, or like a rock, gnarled and shaped by the raw forces of nature, yet alive and vibrant with a quiet joy. As I looked at him I felt he could completely disappear and reappear again.

From the feelings and images of the dream I realised the Buddha had been an Oriental who had worked upon his being like the craftsmen of the East might work upon a piece of ivory. Every part of his being had been shaped by his craftsmanship. The result was a living stance that could meet all the raw forces of nature without being in conflict or destroyed. He could even disappear completely as an ego, into the forces of life, and then emerge again with the same quiet joy. That was liberation.

Each religious leader epitomises a different stance we can take to life. They are classical approaches to life defined by a particular race or geographical cultural response.

In dreams the grand antipodes of the mind are often symbolised by a cave or underground area representing what is past, what is already manifest or materialized in the evolutionary process; and the sky or an abyss which represents the chaos, the as yet unmanifest or defined. In the Christian story Jesus explores them both. He explores the unconscious in the cave and enters it completely by dying, always a symbol of entrance into the land of sleep and dreams. He then returns and later ascends into heaven prior to bringing the Holy Spirit. Like the dreamers of the Senoi, he brings something back from his journey for use in the lives of others. This is another classical stance.

Each of us can, however, find our own stance. Whatever we approach with, we find. If we craft for ourself a great mind, then life speaks to us of mighty realisations. If we run to life as a lover, it clasps us with its own passion. If we are a lost soul frightened and in pain, it is life weeping. If we arrive with the wonder of a child, then life is new and unnamed for us. If we approach as a worshipper, then life shines, for we have called upon it to be worshipful. If we approach with a question, it replies. I do not know of any artist, creative inventor or musician, or indeed of any great saint or reformer who approached life empty handed and came away laden. Even the child, Bernadette of Lourdes approached the grotto of her visions full of love and belief.

'I had been wondering how' says one dreamer, 'I could begin to find a fuller life through dream work. I dreamt I was standing before a shimmering translucent haze. It wasn't opaque, but I couldn't see anything in it. It was just emptyness or living nothingness. Very carefully I pushed my right hand into the haze to see if I could find anything. To my surprise a hand emerged to the left of mine. As I drew my hand back, so the hand also drew back. I felt the message was that whatever I put in I got out.'

Few people in our own culture have the sense of being an artist and crafting their own inner life. Yet if we are to gain more from life, the quality of who we are, what we are, and what we do needs to be improved. We are used to the idea of do-it-yourself home improve-ment, but not so much of self renovation. Yet the quality of our life, and quality of life in the world, is directly related to the improve-ment of our own inner life. A family who have never learnt to care for themselves and their environment can be given a beautiful new house and sufficient money, yet in weeks the house will become a tip if they do not change their habits. Real social revolution comes from within, not imposed from outside. There are only two problems in the world – me and you. If we can sort those two out the whole world will change. But if we are tempted to say there is only one problem – them – the force of regeneration and self responsibility is lost.

Whether our drive for enhancement of our life quality and the

189

effectiveness of our stance is towards personal achievement or global change, let us get the beam out of our own eye first. That will need commitment over a long period of time. Not only do we face the inherited wisdom of the world in our unconscious, but we face as well all the inherited ignorance, prejudices and pains. We face the difficulties of our own childhood plus the challenge of the human condition. Only long-term work on our dreams with patient craft will carve out the beauty and creativity of our life. It is a lifetime work, but the results of it are cosmic. The dream below gives a taste of this.

'I was in the garden of a large house. To the right of the house, my right, that is, I saw that the garden had been changed. I realised that I knew the garden from childhood, and there used to be a large pool by the house in which we all bathed when young. The ground sloped up from the house and was rough, but part of it had been dug over. The care and skill with which this had been done deeply impressed me.'

Joan, whose dream this is, worked on it and says:

'There were no direct associations I had with the house or pond, so I worked on it using co-ex, and allowing my own unconscious to tell me what the dream showed. I started with the pond, and had the most unexpected set of fantasies and feelings bubble up from within. The garden when we were children was the Garden of Eden. It was about the history of our development as human beings. It showed that in early stages of evolution all human beings lived in a state of awareness in which they had no sense of separation from nature itself. They had no sense of individual self either, so lived in a sort of paradisical state where there was no idea of birth or death or right or wrong. They felt at one with each other and the forces of nature. When I experienced this I understood at last what the story of Genesis meant. It was all about stages of psychological development, not physical history. Human beings had come out of the pool though, and at that point I experienced a mass of impressions and images I still cannot completely understand, but I will try to describe. The images were like maybe at first one or two human beings reached out of that pool, and they left a mark. They climbed out and put one stone on top of another.

I understood that this meant that one or two human beings had achieved self awareness. In that state they realised something about themselves, they could say, "I am". They could ask, "Who am I?" That had never been possible before.

'I need to say that what arose from the unconscious was not those words or memory or vision of definite events, but a sense of touching or experiencing an overall memory, an overall process. So I am trying to put into words what I sensed. It was such a wonderful thing to see that I want to put it in words. At the same time, it was an immense process and so difficult to capture.

'What I felt was that the pool was a collective consciousness, such as Jung speaks of, existing now in our unconscious. At that time though it was the everyday experience, but the individuals who attained self awareness began to build a new level. They left stone monuments, carving, paintings in caves, stone circles, pyramids; each person, each group realising deep down that this new level of awareness was a thing to be given and built.

'This is where words are difficult, but the dug ground in the dream describes it. If the son of a farmer takes over the farm, his work and achievement are built upon what his father did with the land. The father's work was also built upon, and was a continuation, of what *his* father did. Even if one were to take a piece of land which had never been farmed before, one would farm it with tools, experience and attitudes developed gradually throughout thousands of years of human effort. I saw that my self consciousness, although I am not usually aware of it, is formed out of the ideas, words, attitudes, pleasure and pain left to me as a heritage by millions of human beings. If I had not been brought up by self-aware humans, I would, in fact, not have developed an identity. My identity *is a gift* to me from the the great river of human beings who left a mark, one stone on the other, a concept enshrined in art, a struggle or love immortalised in stone, a realisation and transcendence depicted in a religious ritual or in a new word.

'The garden, the dug plot was my own self, my personality. But my personality, the attitudes and reactions of its very foundations and structure, the words on which my very mind realises its existence, are the living remains of countless other lives and their endeavour, their love, their ignoble failure, their genius and their prayers. That I have also dug that plot by working on my dreams, by

191

trying to transform the unwieldy loam of myself into finer stuff, gives me a place in the river of life, in the eternal process of continuity.

'Most important of all, perhaps, in such a simple act as writing out this dream, I leave a mark. I etch upon the world the sign of my own realisation, the changed lines of transformation. for self consciousness is a sort of collective consciousness which forever depends upon giving, and upon physical records or living beings to enshrine its existence. Without living beings who carry the words and responses gradually developed by their myriad ancestors; without books, paintings, music, science and architecture, we have no existence as people. In one generation we could be swallowed up by that pool, that sea of self forgetting symbolised by the waters that swallowed Noah's contemporaries. Even now, without the love of giving, that sea can swallow ourselves. That was my dream.'[5]

The waters of the unconscious – the monument of self awareness – the abyss of the as yet to come; these are the great areas of human life and spiritual experience. And in our personal journey into the hills, sea and sky of our wider life, we meet the Helper lifting us if we fall in battle; the Christ speaking from a hill-top as we listen; Krishna calling with his music the lowing animals of our instinctive nature; Buddha, smiling enigmatically.

The spiritual life is a transformation of, and an increased effectiveness of waking and sleep life. It is an expansion of awareness into our roots, hidden as they may be in unconsciousness. It is a penetration by consciousness into the void, and into the life of today, by long-term cooperative action between the conscious personality and the cosmic forces of which it exists as an inseparable part. This transformation and cooperativeness is not simply individual. Our individual life is an integral part of, and penetrates, the whole. Our naked spirit is that aspect of our being which is integral with the eternal cosmos itself. The spiritual life is the path of realising ourselves as that.

To make clear the main areas of this work let us look at them one at a time.

THE WATERS AND THE CAVE

The term the 'unconscious' is general. It covers everything of which we are not aware. Within that unawareness are body events, chemical processes of our being, subliminal impressions, memories, and so on. In dreams, however, the symbols of deep waters, a cellar or cave, are more specific. They represent the past; the already revealed but forgotten; the habit patterns and physiological processes developed over long millenia of evolution.

This area includes a group or collective strata of consciousness, out of which individual awareness developed, and upon which it rests. Penetrating this part of our being gives access to body processes; to the long imprinted patterns of reproduction, group interaction; and survival drives which underly our present social codes and responses. Exploration helps us to heal old wounds, recognise old vendettas, comprehending long-standing personal or cultural responses and attitudes; to see how the living process constantly rests upon, exists because of, death and decay; how consciousness itself is the result of the 'death' of living forms we eat. The cave and the waters are deeply biological, chemical and energy based. Dreams are a constant entrance into this area of ourself.

PENETRATING SLEEP

To wake up in sleep is not the same as dreaming. Our identity, forged in the three dimensional world of waking life, is now born in an area of experience in which it previously died. Despite the many books promising quick lucidity, I do not believe it is an easy task. Certainly, it is reasonably easy to arrive at an experience of realising you are dreaming, and to begin to move around consciously in the symbols. To actually arrive at insight, to produce transformation of deep-seated habits; to lift awareness to where it can scan the whole progress of evolution, or see the group soul of a family or nation and commune with it; or to undertake meaningful work and contact with other identities at that level requires the long process of self discovery and initiation. We need to cleanse our own childhood traumas and the pain of our family, since the organs of perception at that level are formed out of our mobile and freed sexuality and emotions, and from our digested and integrated life experience. The wider the latter, the more varied, the greater number of people whose minds and soul and body we have shared in love, the greater our vision. But to possess that greatness of vision we must have grocked – savoured, digested, felt – each pain and pleasure of our life

193

THE INSTANT DREAM BOOK

and the lives of those entered into us.

Waking up in sleep represents the real transition between a life bounded by physical senses and personal memories, and a life which shares the lives of all humanity, all earth, and is a citizen of the cosmos.

The following dream was experienced at a time when the dreamer had become impatient with his spiritual growth and his inability to extend his awareness in a real sense, into sleep and the cosmos.

'There were no images in my dream, only a sense of being in a particular circumstance. The feeling was of being in the sky or part of the earth and trying to break free, almost as if I were in a glass globe and was trying to be free of the restriction. Beyond the earth were beings. Again there was no shape or form, but they communicated with me. It seemed to me that they were free creatures and I was shut up in the globe of the world, and I asked them how I could get out. Their reply stunned me so much I cried out. They said that Earth was the prison, the penitentiary of the galaxy. Beings who had hurt, killed or been violent or destructive, were put in the bodies of earth creatures. The criminals of the universe were born as children of Earth. It was a humane prison, because there was no way to break out of it except by learning the lessons of life, of cooperation, of care and non-destruction. The prison was our own body, as we were actually non-physical beings who lived and worked as free agents in the universe. Being born in a body we could not go beyond its boundaries except by working with the forces of our existence and the beings we had previously trangressed against. We could only be free of our biological prison when we could stand before the other beings and say – "I claim my rights as a free citizen of the universe. I am a citizen of this Earth, this body, because I committed offences against life in the form of other beings and myself and I have been imprisoned here until I learn love. Now I have learnt to love and not to brutalise, and I claim again my citizenship." '

Whether we are in fact fallen angels, born in bodies of flesh – 'clothing ourselves in skins' remains for each one of us to discover for ourselves. What can be verified, however, is that nature does not allow us to consciously penetrate the vast reaches of its being without having learnt the lessons of harmlessness and respect for all beings. Nevertheless, the dream says something which appears to be at the heart of every major religion. Whether the reason for that is

194

due to an enormous unconscious fantasy on the part of humanity, or is the intuition of a long-past heritage I do not yet know. But each religion promises a release from the difficulties of physical life, or offers a wider life if the lesson of love is learnt, although I feel mutual respect is perhaps a better description than love.

A theory which has arisen in my mind in an attempt to understand dreams such as this and the near-death experiences of many people, is that a bridgehead has been built in the dimension of consciousness.

In sleep, when one wakes up and has a distinct sense of identity without any body awareness, it leaves one with the distinct conviction that personality can survive in the realm of consciousness despite the loss of one's body. In this condition of lucidity without symbols, there is a feeling that consciousness is as much a universal principle of the cosmos as energy or light. Just as an amoeba swims in water, so identity in lucid sleep moves about in a sea of consciousness. Like the amoeba, which is largely water and is formed out of the elements in which it lives and the dynamic patterns within cells, the identity is also formed out of the stuff of consciousness.

The experience and symbols of dreaming suggest that consciousness as we know it arises out of the process of reproduction and death on our planet. Death is important in the process because it is a break-up of form, which releases energy which can be known as consciousness. Dream symbols, as in the pond, portray consciousness as an interconnected area, a pool or ocean, within which the forms or bodies which become aware, are immersed. Dreams also suggest that consciousness holds within it not just the patterns of the body forms it expresses or knows itself through, but also the huge processes of biological creation and decay. So, interiorised self awareness sometimes meets a huge area of carrion forces which live upon death, as well as the powerful forces of growth. In this connection it is interesting that the Christian Mass is a banquet of the Body of Christ

I believe that early in the development of self consciousness, because of the emergence of conscious will, which could express in such acts as holding the breath, or resisting the urge to sleep or procreate, individuals began to direct their experience, and explore the roots of their awareness. This led some of them to wake up in sleep. Records of this are found in many ancient cultures, and, considering that some Eastern cultures had tens of thousands of monks and nuns experimenting with consciousness and dreams, it would be extremely likely that many individuals mastered the dimension of mind. Not only were they able to remain awake during each sleep period, but they claimed that at death they would experience no discontinuity of awareness.

Profane history makes much of the impact on humanity of the lives of such people as Attila, Marco Polo, and Alexander the Great. The impact of a human being achieving a new dimension of consciousness, however, is not mentioned. Yet its effects upon the future of humanity can be compared with the difference between an atom bomb and a squib. The first human being to attain this made possible a new era. Death was no longer the end of individual life; human beings need no longer be prisoners of a sick body or human fears and despairs; and the earth was no longer our tomb at the death of the sun. A whole new universe opened.

To gain an insight into this, imagine the early white settlers discovering a land where there were no other human beings. The first settlers might be nearly wiped out by the harshness of winter. But they survived and built a bridgehead, a settlement, from which the further reaches of the wilderness could be explored and claimed. Great travellers, like Lewis and Clarke, set out to map the land, and others followed.

I believe there is evidence to suggest that in the world of sleep and death a bridgehead was built by those who could maintain identity despite sleep and death. In the hugeness of an ocean of energy they created a settlement built out of mindstuff, as in dreams, and woke up those who died, who had enough love and life experience to enable them to exist in this new domain. And they in turn woke others and trained them to remain awake and how to live in this universe of consciousness. Prior to that, I do no think there was the possibility of survival of personality.

Isn't that the bare bones of folklore and religion?

'I dreamt that I was dying and I felt fear. All the figures of death appeared, in the form of skeletons, maggots in a dead body, the sense of saying goodbye, of final endings. I sensed the futility of existence, how I was simply a grub-like form which arose, mated and died, and to what purpose, what end? But I wanted at least to die with courage and strength, because maybe that was all the dignity a person had.

'Now I felt the whole finality of death. I saw and felt it as the great ending, the great parting, the putting out of the light of awareness – finish. There was fear, there was regret, there was awareness of futility, that it should end so, perhaps in rotteness of disease, or the soul destroying finish of senility, of the meaninglessness of fatal injury. The end.

'The fear subsided, and the urge to fight the indignity and the meaninglessness of it faded. I let go of my relatives and my children and died. . . .

'There was nothing. No body, no shapes, no up, no down, no objects, yet I existed. I was the fragile, naked thought and conviction of my own existence. All was darkness and quiet, yet I felt exhilaration. This was death!? No wonder religious disciplines lead the disciple to let go of worldly things. It was in order to get ready for the loss of everthing except Being itself. Then it came to me that I was only newly born into this world. I was just a paddler up to my ankles in a huge sea; and other humans had been here before me, and were now natives of this world.

'When I woke up I had a great respect for Christian traditions. The baptism represented the recognition of the great waters in which I had bathed. The giving of the name is also a recognition that the only thing which survives is our idea of ourself, our name. Without a name, if a baby or person died, they would be in the waters without a life-jacket. Spiritually children need those truths given by religion without dogma.'

THE MONUMENT

When I was fairly new to working with my dreams I experienced one which, for a while, remained a mystery to me.

In the dream I stand upon a small hill overlooking a desert type landscape. Not far from me, rising maybe a hundred feet in the air is a huge column of rock. At its base it is natural weathered rock, but near the top of the column, blending in with the natural shape of the rock are the most beautiful designs. So the overall impression of the column was one of rugged, powerful nature, rising and being shaped eventually by the art of humans.

Gradually I came to understand the rock to mean the raw material of life, of human nature, which is shaped by our actions, our love, our anguish and decision. The coloumn was my life, which I was shaping, yet respecting the forces of nature.

197

Recently, through *The Daily Mail*, we were sent a beautiful dream by a Mr. H.C. He says: 'This dream recurred until the age of six. I am now sixty three.

'I am walking along a narrow, shaded lane. The lane takes a sharp turn to the right, but directly in front is an opening into a disused sandstone quarry at the foot of a steep wooded hill. There are many big sandstone boulders lying around and, in the manner of dreams, I carry one of these boulders with great ease in an acorn cup, with the stalk between finger and thumb. There is no sense of weight and I never leave the quarry. There is a heavy, oppressive atmosphere difficult to describe, with a tinge of sadness and inevitability.'

Our comments on the dream which were published are as follows:

What a beautiful dream. It captures the endeavour of human life in a few images. The lane is your own individual existence, leading to expression of yourself as a person. The quarry is where humans have toiled with unwieldy nature to create something; have worked with their natural desires and fears to achieve humaness. In your hand you hold the acorn cup, symbol of something mighty growing from small beginnings. That is your childhood and the feeling of potential as you met life and growth. And the rock is the raw material, your natural being, to shape to beauty or ugliness, to work on or leave in the rough, to carve the lines of your pain and pleasures, wit or gathered wisdom upon. That is life as seen in the unconscious wisdom of your childhood.

M.L. von Franz, as one of the co-authors of Jung's book *Man and His Symbols*, says that some 'Australian aborigines believe that their dead ancestors continue to exist in stones as virtuous and divine powers, and that if they rub these stones, the power increases both for the living and the dead.'

From earliest times stones have been used to represent spiritual life, and to act as a monument to it. Jacob of the Old Testamant, after his dream of the angels ascending and descending to heaven, and his vision of God, 'rose early in the morning and took the stone he had put for his pillow, and set it up for a pillar, and poured oil upon the top of it . And he called the name of that place Beth-el (the house of God).'

Sometimes, as in the Ka'aba, the black stone of Mecca, the stone actually represents God, or our central Self. Dr. von Franz says that, 'The fact that this highest and most frequent symbol of the Self is an

198

object of inorganic matter points to yet another field of enquiry and speculation: that is, the still unknown relationship between what we call the unconscious psyche and what we call "matter" . . . In studying this still undefined and unexplained connection – it may prove that "psyche" and "matter" are one and the same thing.[4]

I believe, from my own subjective research, that this question is of the utmost importance in understanding what consciousness is, and what is human spirituality. In fact, my experience, gathered through co-ex and dream work, suggests that the prime creative impulse behind human life – God – is matter. And in saying that, I am referring to the prime human impulse, not to a cosmic wholeness, for mankind has more than one concept of cosmos or divinity. I believe that the original life impulse towards consciousness on our planet arose from matter. Obviously science already states something similar, and it may seem as if I am saying the obvious, so there is a need for clarification.

My supposition is, as the dream symbol of the engraved column implies, that life always leaves a mark on, and transforms, inorganic matter. The matter then carries in it the patterns of the experience of life. Therefore the millions of bodies of living forms on our planet, even if all life dies on earth, will leave the essence of their experience in the soil and rocks left behind. Should our solar system die and over unimaginable periods of time be dispersed and form other systems, our bodies, the essence of our whole race, will be the seeds for other life forms. As life arose on another planet which incorporated matter from our earth, the living forms arising would have as a very ground, our collective experience, which, as the beings arose to consciousness, would be experienced by them subjectively as a guiding influence, a parent.

Our own Ancient of Days, I believe, is the essence of beings long dead, whom we inwardly experience as a unity and a force in our evolution. If this has any truth in it, I believe our advancing science will discover these patterns in the matter of our planet, and see them as the basis of consciousness. In eating the minerals of our planet we take in the dead body of our God and transform it into consciousness.

Even if this is not the case, the symbol of the column, of Jacob's pillar, of the holy Ka'aba, has relevance to our own spirituality and cosmic life. Simply put, it is that out of matter and seeming unconsciousness our being arises and is shaped. The whole process is an evolutionary one. It is one of an emerging process, a maturing of consciousness itself. It is a process in which, first of all, the forces of nature themselves push toward and attain consciousness. Then it is an action wherein humanity itself must create its own being; must gradually unleash it from its past, its habits, its patterns, and unfold the potential of itself – or else fall back, for that is the pattern of nature. Wave follows wave. There is a rising and a falling. Consciousness rises to self awareness in the day, and falls back in sleep. It awakes in life and drops back at death. Like a seed it is planted in the womb of the mother and unfurls into identity, falling back into the womb or transcending the crest of the wave to a new dimension.

This is already the pattern of our race. Out of unconsciousness, of collective awareness, a wave of creatures leaped from the crest into self awareness. The story of Noah and the flood suggests that many fell back. In recent times a new wave crest was transcended, and a new dimension of human experience reached in the ability of reason. Now, forming like a baby in the body of humanity, dreams suggest a new transition is about to occur. It is a transition from rational individualism to individual creative cooperation. Through attaining healthy individuation, the personality no longer feels threatened by the forces of the unconscious, and through them develops a creative cooperation with the whole world process and society. It seems likely this emerging type of consciousness will dominate the activities of the world, just as the rational creative consciousness dominated the world when it arose.

Writing as long ago as 1901, Dr. Maurice Bucke, in his book, *Cosmic Consciousness*, tells of his own conviction that a new state of consciousness is becoming more prevalent. He sees the Christ as a symbol in subjective life, of this new consciousness, and our relationship to it. The main theme of his work is that this new level is evolutionary, and brings with it a sense of a living conscious relationship with the cosmos, and intuitive or internal insight into it.

There are no secret methods to reach greater maturity in this cosmic life. Every step of spiritual growth is a step in the growth of oneself as an individual. It comes about by the patient work on one's own being through dreams, or through meditation, one's work, or whatever is one's chosen spiritual tool. It is depicted beautifully by the Chinese Ox Herding pictures, which overall show the personality discovering the unconscious instinctive patterns and sexuality – the Ox in the thicket. These drives are then caught, confronted consciously and redirected – the Ox caught and led. Gradually the old patterns are left behind and a new direction is established. The inner life is transformed by bringing to consciousness what was unconscious – the Ox is led up into the mountains, turns from black to white, and becomes docile.

The wrestle with one's own dreams and one's own energies, and the attempt to live what is realised, encapsulates the whole spiritual discipline. The raw material of one's being is worked on, gradually changed, and the limitations we introvert are dropped. In doing so not only do we become a real individual, through creating our own inner life and being capable of self responsibility and making choices, but we also discover a new relationship with society and the cosmos. We find a work and a way of life which is an integration of ourself with the world. If we are still in conflict with the religion, art, science, society of our times, and with our own instincts, there is still work to be done. The integrated individual is not in conflict with society or his own unconscious. Nor does he necessarily accept them as they are, but change is brought about through transformation, not war. It arises from insight and awareness, not discontent.

The integration of our total experience, as already described, is also a vital process in the sculpting of the monument and experiencing cosmic awareness. By integrating our experience we arrive at insights into our personal life. When these many insights themselves are put together what arises is an awareness of our integral part in human society. The insights gained from that form into a still wider awareness. So, in this sense, our spiritual life arises out of gradually clarifying and ordering our concepts, but doing so in connection with a deep experience of our emotions, sexuality, and complete memory. So it is not simply an intellectual act, but a unified growth and organisation of our being.

CHRIST AND KRISHNA

Christ is as much a reality in the unconscious as our personal memories are. The Christ is a living force in the human unconscious and therefore in human society. If we are to venture beyond the boundaries of our own ego, we must be prepared to meet the Christ, just as if we venture beyond our garden fence or front door we must

201

THE INSTANT DREAM BOOK

be aware of passing cars. Not a great deal needs to be said about this, because so much has already been written by others in regard to their meeting with Christ.

It needs to be remembered, however, that the human unconscious objectifies and puts into a form its subtle sensations and contacts with personal or universal processes. As Christ or Krishna, perhaps under different names, appear in the spiritual life of so many individuals and so many nations, we can assume the Christ is a universal process or event in the human soul.

I believe the birth of the Christ in human experience can be understood by considering the forerunners. In early human groups as soon as the ability to pass on the experience of one human being to another through speech, drama or symbol came about, religions developed. Humans gained a sense of continuity with something bigger and older than themselves. For instance, the knowledge of how to hunt, how to plant grain, and of medicinal herbs, passed on from parents to children through many generations, and became a force in itself. It was not entirely the product of any one person or one generation, being shaped, refined, added to over many years. This knowledge was sacred. It was the essence of the whole family or tribe. In learning it, the individual actually took in the life and mind of their forebears. They felt a kinship with the spirit of their ancestors, they heard the collective wisdom of their own blood. They also had a sense of an eternal being which lived before them and which would take them into it and live on at their death.

This family or tribal history was often represented by a totem, a god figure, a drama or story. In a similar sense, human personality survives and preserves the essence of millions of cells living and dying in its lifetime. And perhaps those early gods were the 'personality' of a whole tribal group or race, which integrated its experience.

In the New Testament we are told that Christ was the son of God and the Son of Man. Also that Christ was a mystical body made up of the individual lives, or cells of those who's lives were integrated in a common direction. Could Christ by the forming 'personality' of the body of humanity?

In dreams, Christ is depicted as being the individual's sense of the whole essence of humanity. Christ is the deep bonds of integrating experience which humans have in common. Christ is the care and

202

love humans are capable of which preserves the health and unity of the human species. Whatever unifies the cells in our own body, and prevents cancer, Christ is that in the body of man/woman/kind.

Because in a certain way Christ is human society, there is usually a creative tension between the action of Christ in our unconscious, and the action of our personal biological drives for survival. This tension can be resolved through a marriage of the two in creative individual action – or the artistic/scientific creative process itself. In that way the urge to procreate also becomes an act of sharing oneself with society. That is why I have dealt with the search for 'right work' at length in the chapter on finding a happier you.

What is meant by this is that our own sexual drive, our personal drive toward gaining enough food, or a place to live, is often in conflict with the desires of the group we live within. An example will clarify this. A woman may be jealous of the relationship her husband has with another woman. Her own biological urge may be to hit or even kill the woman. But she feels the pressure of what the group she lives in would do to her if she allowed her feelings. Under that conflict she may break down.

However, the energetic stress of the situation could also be used by her to write a poem; sing a song about her love and pain; write a story from her experience; agitate to change the laws and social attitudes, and so on. These are acceptable to society and also reward her.

In meeting Christ there is a certain stage where it is no longer a separation between I and Christ. Then there is no Christ and Me. It is at this point directly appreciated that one is oneself the life process that penetrates all things – I am the way; I am the entire experience of life and death; I am the human condition with its misery and triumph.

Our meeting with Christ today is in our dreams and inner experience. Perhaps the meeting is like that in the already quoted dream of the Helper; or like this dream of my friend Tim.

'I dreamt Jesus came and talked to me. He looked me up and down and said, "You're a bit hairy (I have a beard) and rough, but you'll do." When I woke I felt great the whole day.'

Or like this dream of Lester's –

'I am a journalist reporting on the return of Christ. He is expected on a paddle steamer going upstream on a large river. I am very sceptical and watch disciples and followers gather on the rear deck.

'The guru arrives, dressed in simple white robes. He has long, beautiful auburn hair and beard, and a gentle wise face. He begins to tap a simple rhythm on a *tabla* or Indian drum. It develops into complete intermingling of orchestral rhythms as everyone joins in. I realise now this is Christ, and feel overwhelmed with awe as I try to play my part in the music. I'm tapping with a pen, and find myself fumbling. A bottle or can opener comes to me from the direction of Christ. I try to beat a complementary rhythm, a small part of a greater, universal music.'

Lester's dream is about meeting something in his experience which he first doubts. If we strip the images away, we see he contacts a sense of being invited to take a personal part in harmonious group actions. In fact, he is asked to blend his ability with others toward a common end. He senses in the Christ, a power which unites human lives and endeavour. When he tries to express himself in accord with what he senses, he then feels part of something larger than himself and universal.

This awareness of being a part of a universal and caring process is one of the fundamentals of the spiritual life. If we live without that awareness, to some degree we are incomplete, and feel it. If we shut the doors of our awareness to the living presence of the universal, depicted in many dreams as Christ, then we have a sense of denying something in us.

When we begin to take part consciously in this universal life, our dreams frequently express this as standing high on a mountain, or looking upon the world from a great height. In the Bible we find the same symbols where Moses climbs the mountain to hear God; and Christ standing upon a mount to teach. 'I will lift up my eyes to the hills', says the psalmist, 'from them comes help to me.'

I find again and again in people's dreams, and of course in their waking life, that the mountain is a reality, not a symbol. If the awareness of a relationship with the universal life is a fundamental of the spiritual life; standing upon the mountain is one of its transforming realities. It is because I do see here an attainable transformation, obvious in lives throughout history; because I do see an apparent psychological function here, that I am convinced of the reality of the spiritual force in human life.

The reality which lies behind the image of the Christ and the mountain is that the human unconscious can create *gestalts* – a united image and concept – out of the many separate impressions and experiences it receives. In this way, people have seen the whole cycle of the seasons instead of having awareness only of the autumn, the week, the moment they presently experience. They have seen the great sweep of human evolution and their part in it instead of being captured only by their personal life, their own misery, their own circumstance. Standing upon the mountains of awareness they can see the flow of history and human experience which led to and created their existence. They can see, as all can see on a mountain, the proportion human effort has in the great sweep of peaks, sky and distant sea. And on that mountain one sees not only with the eyes and mind, but one's very life senses its integral unity with the all.

The vision does not always bring peace, but it does transform.

THE VOID

It can perhaps now be seen that the unconscious is not simply one thing, but an area of our being in which many powerful processes are at work. If one drew a picture of the unconscious, one way of depicting it would be to draw an oval shape with the stone at the centre and a male and female figure each side of it. These figures are Radha and Krishna, or Felicity and Christ. At one end of the oval should be darkness and the serpent of evolution and the manifest. At the other end the Void, the light of the unmanifest. There should be no up or down, better or worse, higher or lower, for it is all part of our wholeness. To take any part away is to lose balance.

To explain what part of the whole the Void is I will quote a dream I had in 1982.

'I am with a congregation in a small church. There is such a feeling of accord and uplift, I feel close to everyone. I am reminded of the phrase, "they were all with one accord in one place", in praise and supplication. The power is so great I am lifted up in the air and float above the heads of the congregation as they continue to pray. Then a beautiful chant flows out from me spontaneously as I am moved by the Spirit. It is a Polynesian hymn. It is clear and lovely, and as I hear it, I understand intuitively that it signifies the Spirit, or wider awareness, is entering the assembly. We had been praying for this event.

'The room of the gathering now appeared different. It had been oblong like most churches, now it is ancient and square. On one wall is a large figure of a naked man made of metal. There is no cross, but it has arms out, Christ like. Suddenly I am lifted up beyond the building, beyond everything to an enormous height. It isn't into space, because there are no planets or stars to see. It is just empty, nothingness, and I lose all sense of being a person. Then a powerful descent occurs, rocket like. With tremendous power I re-enter the room and discharge a potent force at the figure of man on the wall. This descending energy imprints or etches a pattern on the abdomen of the figure.

'Previous to this the community was disciplining itself to receive a new impulse, a new life, now there is a feeling of having attained it. The disciplines are no longer necessary. Certainty replaces hope. A new activity within the community begins, as people go about tasks from a sense of working for a united goal.'

There are three main things in this dream. First, the united prayer or uplifted praise to God. Second, the influence of God in the activity of the Spirit, and the precipitation into the Void. Third, the descent and imprinting of the new pattern.

The dream shows a contact with God, and when I worked on the dream to find the reality underlying the symbol, I experienced direct awareness of God, and realised God has many aspects. Just as we have a body, sexuality, emotions, and thoughts, so has God or the cosmos. The physical universe is the body of God. The reproductive drive in life forms is God's sexuality. The feeling quality in every living thing is God's emotions. The God I met, the God one prays to, is only one aspect of the cosmic.

What I had a sense of experiencing was a buzzing, radiating consciousness of all creatures on Earth; the united consciousness of all people. Not simply an aggregate of social influence, but a living unity of consciousness real in itself. Because this God is not simply separate people doing things in the outer life which collectively have a unified effect, but is both the individual *and* the collective consciousness. It can both receive, be influenced by, and influence individuals and groups. Because it is the collective consciousness of all human beings and creatures, it is concerned, if that is the right word, with communal interest, with the whole, or with the individual in relationship with the collective. That is why most religions are so expressive of group morality, of communal care. It is this aspect of God they are meeting. Answered prayer appeared to me, as

I looked upon this, to arise from this collective living force, responding to certain requests which were unconsciously wanted by many people. If many people wish for something to occur, the certainty of it becoming manifest is almost absolute. This is almost like insurance statistics as a reliable guide to future events. The problem with humanity is that it is so divided in what it wants, that a confusion of creative action takes place.

But the Void is another aspect of God or the cosmos entirely. Really another aspect of ourself. It transcends opposites, it goes beyond truth or lies, or limitation of any sort. It is the opposite to habit, pattern, form, the already manifest, ego, definite, bound. To be able to have access to this aspect of ourself is of immense practical benefit, as in one way it is the wellspring of all fresh growth, of change, of creativity and liberation. In the dream itself it is shown as the force from which a new pattern is engraved upon the body of humanity or an individual. The group in the dream have a new impulse and goal. It is possible that the experience of the Void always precedes vital human change.

Some years ago in a dream workshop that Hyone and I were running, a woman told us she felt like a machine. She enlarged upon it by saying she felt like nothing more than a work machine, a mother machine and a love machine. She told us she had undergone a hysterectomy and afterwards felt she was no longer a person but a machine. She felt she had lost herself during her operation and work and lovemaking since then had become mechanical. As a group we practiced a meditation in which we imaginatively gathered our whole life and experience and brought it to light or the Void. During this, the woman, Barbara, cried out in joy. She told us she experienced a descent of light into her being, and suddenly realised that she wasn't her sexual organs. She was a person in her own right, and not just a machine.

We attain a sense of identity or self image with the help of many factors. As a child we depend upon our parents praise and recognition of us as a worthwhile person to build our own feeling of confidence. A confident feeling about ourself may also be bound up with what school we go to; what success we have at school; what social recognition our parents have; how they feel about themselves; what house we live in; what car we drive; what wage we earn; what we dress in; how many men or women admire us. If we lose our job or social standing it can be a severe, for some people a fatal, blow.

This is because our identity is actually, in its early stages anyway, made up of the things which form it. So that a person who has suffered a car accident and ends with a large facial scar may lose all confidence in themselves, since the body which gave them a sense of identity has changed. Similar breakdowns occur if our marriage partner leaves us, or our lover says we are inadequate in bed, or our work is criticised.

When we say that one of our children has grown up and become independent, what we mean is that their personality has learnt to liberate itself from some of the influences which helped form it. In a similar way, Barbara found liberation from her genitals.

At first sight that may not seem all that exciting or important. We may plan to hang on to our own genitals, avoid facial scars, and keep our identity intact. However, not only do each of us have areas of our being in which we feel inadequate, but the world is always in conflict because many billions of people gain identity under political, religious or national groups which are in conflict with each other to the point of war and bloodshed. Also death robs us of all our props. In that day we stand naked of body, people, work, sex, jewellery, cars and houses to maintain our former self image.

The whole process of human psychological, and perhaps even physical growth and maturity, is to do with gaining freedom from dependence. This begins with the gradual ability of being physically and emotionally independent of our mother and father. In the maturing process of an adult, however, it has no definite end, and as adults we achieve different levels of maturity in this area. We may remain tightly bound to one particular view of life, one type of work, or relationship, one religion, one political view, one social attitude, just like an infant bound to one person emotionally. Maturity in these areas is similar to that in childhood. It rests on the ability to be independent of any one person, one view, one religion, one image of ourself. The possibilities are immense.

Creativity also depends, to a large extent, on being able to stand outside old patterns, already formed ideas and views, and beyond what is already known.

In human relationships too, we can become so imprisoned within old hurts, habits of rejection, fear of continued failure and general overfamiliarity, the freshness of love and sharing may be lost or even die. How many relationships have foundered because one of the partners felt inadequate sexually and could not live a life independent of that feeling?

From the Void comes the chance to start afresh. It is the ability to find a new approach. It is the opportunity to create a new song or a new world.

As the dream suggests, not only do we need the experience of the Void to do this, but we also need to return to the world of opposites to create or live our freshness. It is in everyday life that we really find the liberation of our ego from its many dependencies. And through the ability to live and love from detachment instead of attachment, we find the ability to die also.

Seeing this, the spiritual life has only a simple basis. It rests upon a relationship with self which allows the process of growth to lead us from attachment and limitation to liberation. In that growing strength of our own ability to exist separately and independently, we forge deeper links with the cosmos and our fellows. While we may feel unsecure in ourselves, we cannot risk or give ourselves easily. When confident we plunge more often into the non-created like a joyful swimmer in the ocean. And we return to shore to share the wealth of our finds in creative action.

The liberating plunge can be physical, in that we find a new sensation. It can also be mental when we find rigid ideas and views melting and we move into a wider world of realisation. It can be personal in that images of ourself which bring pain and caution drop away in our joyful dance in the formless. For the waters of the Void wash them away.

So the simple facts of spiritual life are to work, love and learn with as much depth and richness as we are able. To work upon the rough material of our own being with craft and patience as a gift to ourself, the world – for each life penetrates the very earth – and God. To foster honesty in our dealings with each other; for in honesty I believe lies the future of a humanity without war and boundaries. By daring to emerge from whom we are into the renewing of the Void. And to stand upon the mount of awareness and be transformed.

'And it shall come to pass in the last days', saith God, 'I will pour out of my Spirit upon all flesh: and your sons and your daughters shall prophesy, and your young men shall see visions, and your old men shall dream dreams.'

Summary of Steps

FIRST STEP

1. *Am I Active or Passive in My Dream?*
   Page 23

Consider if the dream defines whether you are in a passive or active role. By passive is meant being only an observer; not taking the leading role; not attaining satisfaction; being directed by other people in the dream. If you are passive in the dream, consider whether a similar attitude is a part of your waking life. Define in which way.

SECOND STEP

2. *What Am I Feeling in the Dream?*
   Page 27

Define what is felt emotionally and physically. In the physical sense are you tired, cold, relaxed, hungry, etc? In the emotional sense are you feeling sad, angry, tender, frightened, etc? This clarifies what area of your life the dream is expressing. If you can become aware also of whether you allowed yourself freedom to fully express your dream feelings, it is a great aid toward dealing with the next question. For instance, if you felt sexual longings or anger and did not express it in the dream, it is important to seek ways of satisfying oneself in the next exercise.

3. *How Can I Alter the Dream to Find Greater Satisfaction?*
   Page 27

Imagine yourself in the dream and continue it as fantasy or a daydream toward satisfaction. Alter the dream in any way; experiment with it; play with it, until you find a way of full expression.

In doing this you must not ignore the feelings of resistance and spontaneous emotion and fantasy which may occur. Satisfaction comes only when we have found a way of integrating these into our conscious imagining.

210

THIRD STEP
4. *Is There Something I Need to Practice?*
   Page 37

In moving the dream images toward satisfaction you will notice that there are points of change. For instance, an anxious feeling may change into determination; a feeling of being withdrawn may change into one of self expression. Frequently we can recognise the first feeling as a habitual one, which is often a part of our conscious life. It is therefore helpful, using the image of the dream, to practice transforming the unsatisfying feeling into the satisfying one.

FOURTH STEP
5. *Am I Meeting the Things I Am Afraid of in My Dream?*
   Page 46

In this step we recognise that every part of our dream is an expression of some aspect of ourself, such as sexuality, creativity, ideas, and so on. So even the monsters of our dreams are part of ourself. If we run from them we are actually afraid of ourselves. So, in this step, we gradually meet and even imaginatively become the fearful image. In that way we transform our anxiety into available energy. We overcome our fear.

6. *What Have I Mistakenly Introverted?*
   Page 47

Our dreams are a unique area of self expression, and a safe area to experiment and experience in any way we wish. Often, however, we introvert, or take into our dream life rules and fears which have no place there. For example, we may fall into the sea and be terrified we will drown in a dream. But that is ridiculous because we can easily breathe under water in a dream, or fly, or die and be re-born. So this question is to make us aware of how we can remove such limitations from our inner life.

STEP FIVE
7. *Is Conflict or Co-operation Shown in the Dream?*
   Page 68

One of the aims of these steps is to bring greater harmony between our conscious personality and the emotions, drives and thoughts it deals with. Dreams objectify each part of us as a person, creature, object or scene. If we are in conflict with some part of our dream, we may be in conflict with our own energetic drives. Many people are in conflict, not with such obvious things as their sexuality or anger, but their creativity. So this step is concerned with recognising such internal struggles and consciously working them out.

8. *Do I Need to ask for Help?*
   Page 71

We can consciously stimulate our dreams to respond to questions we need

211

new ideas or fresh information on. By setting our dreams particular questions, we can more fully utilise our own potential. We need to define clearly our question. Avoid asking many questions in the one. Become involved in the area the question is dealing with, either emotionally or by thinking about the question and working at it consciously.

STEP SIX
9. *What is the Dream Telling Me?*
   Page 95
By looking at the descriptive or key words in a dream it becomes much easier to understand. Likewise, looking at the first scene and drama of the dream enables us to draw out of the dream images its underlying significance.

10. *Where Does the Feeling Arise From?*
   Page 99
By giving attention to what is felt in the dream, then looking to see where that feeling appears in our waking life. Strong connections can be made between the two.

It is helpful in understanding our dream to strip away the images and discover what feelings lie underneath. Also, by imagining ourselves as the dream figure, we can often uncover its feeling content.

This is important because it shows us out of which of our own attitudes and emotions the dream is formed. The drama of the dream then show us what we are doing with our inner life – whether constructive or self destructive – with a clarity we seldom otherwise have.

11. *Am I Limiting Myself?*
Page 99
The drama of our dreams often shows how we limit ourselves with negative self images or attitudes. We can remove these limitations by recognising them and altering them.

STEP SEVEN
12. *What is the Turning Point?*
   page 121
In many dreams there is a turning point which causes a problem to be resolved. These problems solving dreams are so important, especially in relationships, that it is helpful to define clearly just what brings about the change.

STEP EIGHT
13. *What's My State of Health?*
   Page 138

212

Regularly check your health by seeking a dream response.

14. *What Can I Helpfully Do?*
    Page 139

Some problems we can actively explore using coex, or asking a direct question of our dreams.

Notes

Chapter One
1 I witnessed this personally, and the child is now a young teenager. He still depends on drug use.
2 See *Self Watching*. Ray Hodgson and Peter Miller. Century Publishing Co. 1982.
3 Quoted from: *I'm OK You're OK*. Thomas A. Harris, M.D. Pan Books Ltd. 1974.
4 Quoted from: *Psycho Cybernetics*. Maxwell Maltz, M.D. Thorsons Publishers Ltd. 1960.
5 Quoted from: *Psycho Cybernetics*. Maxwell Maltz, M.D. Thorsons Publishers Ltd, 1960.
6 It is helpful for some people, to act out this scene of self incrimination, and so discover what one is negatively suggesting to oneself.

Chapter Two
1 'Identifying Factors Influencing Dream Recall' – 'A Diagnostic Inventory', by Henry Reed and Dick Kohr. *Sundance* Community 'Dream Journal', Vol. 11. No. 2.
2 *Creativity and The Dream*, by Joseph Adelson. Merrill Palmer Quarterly. As quoted in *Creative Dreaming*. Patricia Garfield.

Chapter Three
1. Described in: *Creative Dreaming*, by Patricia Garfield, Ballantine Books.
2 Quoted from: *L.S.D. Psychotherapy*, by W.V. Caldwell. Grove Press. 1969.

Chapter Four
1 Quoted from: *Anxiety and Neurosis*, by Charles Rycroft. Penguin Books. 1968.

2 Quoted from: *Anxiety and Neurosis.*
3 Quoted from: *The Practice of Zen*, by Chang Chen-Chi. Rider & Company. 1960.
4 Quoted from: *Lysergic Acid and Ritalin in the Treatment of Neurosis*, Dr. Thomas Ling and Dr. John Buckman. Lambarde Press. 1963.
5 This way of working with dreams was pioneered by Fritz Perls and used in *Gestalt* Therapy. Books such as *Gestalt* Therapy Now give more details on using the methods of *gestalt* with dreams.

Chapter Five
1 See later chapters for a fuller account of what abilities the dream process has access to.
2 Quoted from an article by Gayle Delaney, Phd, 'Mr. Sandman, Bring Me A Dream'. This appeared in the *Dream Network Bulletin*, Californian Edition Vol. 1. No. 11 January 1983. Gayle runs a daily radio show (KVI) on dreams. See her book, *Living Your Dreams*. Harper & Row. 1981.
3 Quoted from an article by Janice Baylis; 'Sleep On It – The Practical Side of Dreaming'. It appeared in *Sundance* magazine. Summer 1978. See Janice's book *Dream Decoding.*
4 For further information write: Ann Wiseman, 284 Huron Avenue, Cambridge, MA. 02138, U.S.A.

Chapter Six
1 Quoted from, *Powers of Mind*, by Adam Smith.

Chapter Seven
1 Quoted from: *The Human Race*, by Terence Dixon and Martin Lucas. Thames-Methuen. 1982.
2 Quoted from: *You Can Teach Your Child Intelligence*, by David Lewis. Souvenir Press. 1982.
3 Quoted from: *The Dream In Primitive Culture*, by J.S. Lincoln. Cresset Press. 1935.
4 Quoted from: *Myself And I*, by Constance Newland. Frederick Muller Ltd, 1963.
5 See – *Self Watching*, by Ray Hodgson and Peter Miller. Century Publishing Co. 1982.

Chapter Eight
1 Quoted from: *Dreams – Your Magic Mirror*, by Elsie Sechrist. Cowles Book Co. U.S.A. 1968.
2 Quoted from: *The Dream In Primitive Culture*, by J.S. Lincoln. Cresset Press. 1935.
3 This article, entitled 'A Surgeon's Experience With Dreams', appeared in *The Dream Network Bulletin*, Feb. 1963. Bernard Seigel, M.D., F.A.C.S.,

is a surgeon in private practice and assistant clinical professor of surgery, Yale University School of Medicine. He originated the 'Exceptional Cancer Patient' group therapy which works with patients' dreams and drawings. For further information, write to, 2 Church Street South, New Haven, C.T., 06519, U.S.A.

Chapter Nine
1 Quoted from: *Super Learning*, by Sheila Ostrander and Lynn Schroeder. Souvenir Press. 1979.
2 Quoted from: *The Listener*, 17 June, 1982.
3 See – *Explaining The Unexplained*, by Hans Eysenck and Carl Sargent. Published by Weidenfeld and Nicolson. *Super Learning* listed above, and *Into The Unknown*. *The Reader's Digest*.
4 See her books, *Everyman's Mission – Everyman's Search*. by Arthur James.
5 See – *The Magic of Findhorn*, Paul Hawken. Fontana. 1975.
6 Quoted from: *Dream Power*, by Ann Faraday. Hodder and Stoughton. 1972.
7 Quoted from: *Sundance*. Vol. 2. No. 2.
8 *The People Shapers*, Vance Packard. Futura Publications. 1978.
9 *Life After Life*, by Raymond A. Moody. M.D. Corgi Books, 1976.

Chapter Ten
1 Quoted from: an article in *Science Digest* – 'Bucky' Fuller – 'Synergistic Saviour', by Robert Auton Wilson. November 1981.
2 Quoted from: *Stress Without Distress*, by Hans Selye. Hodder and Stoughton. 1977.
3 Quoted from: *Dream Power*, by Ann Faraday. Hodder and Stoughton. 1972.
4 Quoted from: *Man And His Symbols*, by Carl G. Jung. Aldus Books. 1972.
5 I hope soon to write more fully about co-ex and how to use it. Meanwhile, Hyone and I are interested in helping any individuals or groups who need support and advice in developing and extending this skill.

Useful Addresses

ASSOCIATION FOR SELF HELP & COMMUNITY GROUPS.
7 Chesham Terrace, Ealing, London, W13 9HX. England.
Tel: 01-579 5589
Was started in Feb. 1977 to promote the idea of people doing things themselves, and to provide advice on finding the necessary skills and resources.
The association holds week-end workshops where people interested in self
help groups can discuss their aims and difficulties. Groups on dream work
are often organised.

THE INSTITUTE OF PSYCHOPHYSICAL RESEARCH.
118 Banbury Road, Oxford, England.
Tel: Oxford 58787
Set up to research into out-of-the-body experiences, lucid dreaming, and
related phenomena. The results are published in several books.

ASSOCIATION FOR RESEARCH and ENLIGHTENMENT, INC.
67th Street and Atlantic Avenue – P.O. Box 595, Virginia Beach – VA 23451
– U.S.A. (Edgar Cayce Foundation).
A.R.E: have more than twenty years' experience in running courses which
help people understand themselves and their lives in new ways. Courses
include Dreams, E.S.P., Expanded Consciousness, Healing, etc.

THE OPEN CENTRE
188 Old Street, London, E.C.1. England.
Organises workshops on dreams and related self-help subjects.

SUNDANCE – COMMUNITY DREAM JOURNAL.
P.O. Box 595, Virginia Beach, VA 23451, U.S.A.
Designed to serve a circle of cooperating dreamers personally interested in educational dream research guided by spiritual ideas. The variety of its articles and issues are wide and interesting.

THE DREAM NETWORK BULLETIN.
333 W.21st Street – Apt 2 FW – New York – N.Y.10011, U.S.A.
This bulletin is one of the most alive and exciting small magazines dealing with dreams and dreamers. It has good quality articles, plus link-ups between readers, researchers and resources.

THE DREAM RESEARCH CENTRE.
King Street, Combe Martin, Devon, EX34 OAG, England.
Organised by Tony and Hyone Crisp to collect dreams from all over the world. Also to support individuals and groups working with their dreams or co-ex. Please send any interesting or ordinary dreams to the Centre for help in further research, with your comments. The centre also runs a dream interpretation service.

Study courses in dream work and related subjects are run by:
The Skyros Centre, 1 Fawley Road, London NW6 1SL
Telephone: 01-431 0867

CENTRE FOR THE STUDY OF BIO-ENERGY
Kodatsuno 5-9-7, Kanazawa 920, Japan
Aims to teach a synthesis of Eastern and Western techniques bringing psychosomatic integration. Has ongoing groups in self regulation (coex).

Study courses in dream work and related subjects are run by:
Little Grove, Grove Lane, Chesham, Bucks.
Telephone: 0494 782720